D0174732

THE ART OF GETTING THINGS DONE

THE ART OF GETTING THINGS DONE

A Practical Guide to the Use of Power

Richard W. Brislin

Paul Pedersen
Advisory Editor

PRAEGER

New York
Westport, Connecticut
London

Library of Congress Cataloging-in-Publication Data

Brislin, Richard W., 1945–
    The art of getting things done : a practical guide to the
use of power / Richard W. Brislin.
        p. cm.
    Includes bibliographical references and index.
    ISBN 0-275-93761-5 (alk. paper)
    1. Power (Social sciences)   I. Title.
JC330.B72   1991
303.3'3—dc20   90-47542

British Library Cataloguing in Publication Data is available.

Library of Congress Catalog Card Number: 90-47542
ISBN: 0-275-93761-5

First published in 1991

Praeger Publishers, One Madison Avenue, New York, NY 10010
An imprint of Greenwood Publishing Group, Inc.

Printed in the United States of America

The paper used in this book complies with the
Permanent Paper Standard issued by the National
Information Standards Organization (Z39.48-1984).

CONTENTS

FOREWORD

Richard Brislin has accomplished a distillation of the theoretical and empirical literature about power relationships in a way that a popular audience will understand and will find useful. He has organized the chapters to focus on various aspects of power and power relationships, the understanding of those relationships, the acquisition of power, and the skills required to apply power usefully. He has documented each chapter using evidence from the research literature, as well as specific examples from his own life and the experiences of others, to clarify abstract principles.

The basic argument states that the reader can have access to power by learning certain basic skills. The absence of these skills will result in the absence of power. Those individuals or groups who lack power typically lack these prescribed skills as well. This book is an attempt to teach the reader how to obtain, cultivate, and become more sophisticated in the use of these "power skills."

There are many other books that describe power in a general sense, or that discuss power relationships more abstractly from within the perspective of psychology, political science, literature, philosophy, or any of the other relevant fields of study. Other literature has described power in its many different applications with examples, stories, illustrations, anecdotes, and a variety of other demonstrations; but I do not know of any other book that combines the macro and micro elements of power in a popular format aimed at a wider audience across fields and disciplines. I believe that this book is positioned to fill a niche that is not otherwise covered in the literature.

Brislin has personalized this book by drawing many entirely original examples from his own life and his direct experiences. The book reads like the conversation, late at night, of a small group of good friends puzzling and testing out one idea after another against their own experiences and observations. It is intimate in that regard, and the reader may feel privileged to be included.

Power, after all, has been defined in many different ways. It is usually described as the capacity or potential to influence others and, as such, is an important motive in human action or interaction. Power—or the lack of it—has been used to explain human behavior. From a motivational perspective, power is described as the need to have an impact and to influence others. To the extent that people are explained by their motives, power—as a motive has a very special relevance for understanding and predicting behavior. By itself, power is neither good nor bad, but, like fire, it has the capacity to be both useful and destructive.

Since this book crosses over several academic fields and disciplines, it acts as a link across these fields. In combining fields, this book brings together people whose primary emphases or perspectives might otherwise appear quite divergent. The basic perspective of Richard Brislin is, of course, psychological; as such it is written from a psychological base, but not in such a way that other fields are excluded. The book is written by an academic, but in its applications the book is not locked into any "ivory tower." It is written by a white, middle-class male, but it is especially relevant to the understanding and application of power in multicultural settings. Like the topic of power, this book crosses over many of the traditional boundaries which encapsulate us. It follows the topic of power, winding through disciplines, cultures, and perspectives, to seek out those skills, strategies, and tactics which become so urgently important in managing power appropriately.

Power relationships are becoming extremely important. The emphasis on equity, equal opportunity, racism, feminism, ageism, etc., in this book leads us to see relationships between persons and groups very much in terms of power. To a large extent, when we are trying to help people change what we are *really* trying to do is to help them become more powerful. This applies in the fields of counseling, communications, health, political science, law, business, etc., across a wide range of fields and disciplines.

I predict that the book will leave you, the reader, with questions about the role power plays in your own life. If so, that's good. Reading this book will be a conversation not only with the author but with yourself. Here are some of the questions that I discussed with myself while reading:

"How does one define power, both in the abstract and in one's own life?" The book presents power as a complex concept. The multiple definitions of power can easily lead to confusion and mis-communication, especially

when such a concept is applied to practical situations. The book challenges readers to become more concise in their understanding and articulation of power as a concept.

"Do different cultures define power differently?" Brislin's considerable expertise regarding multicultural and international applications of psychology provides a valuable perspective for the understanding of power as a culture-specific concept, even though the functions of power are universal. Separating the culture-specific from the culture-general understanding of power is identified as an important task.

"What is meant by the popular goal of "empowerment" as it is applied to gender and cultural differences?" The term "empowerment" has become a fashionable way to describe positive change through training or education, particularly when applied to minorities or persons perceived as powerless. While "empowerment" is not used frequently in this book, the skills needed to increase power are fundamental to its theme. The book goes beyond the popular jargon, and provides "point-at-able" examples.

"Does everyone want power, and if so, why or why not?" The book points out how everyone—even some who would deny it—can be said to want power. Wanting power has become an embarrassment for some and an illusion for others. Whether or not it is accurate to say that everyone wants power depends almost entirely on how power is defined.

"If power means something different to each of us, then how does one compare power across people?" This is one of the more difficult questions that the book raises. The reader will discover that power is an elusive concept, particularly as one grows to understand the complexity of power. Comparisons of power across people, populations, and cultures become an essential preliminary step to the accurate assessment of power.

"How does one lose power once attained?" Brislin describes power as an elusive goal that can both increase and decrease in life. Some of the skills and strategies described in the book apply both to the understanding and increasing of power as well as to the prevention of its loss.

"How does one decide when power is used ethically?" The ethical use of power is an important theme in political, social, and economic literature. This book addresses some of the key issues involved in the ethical management of power, although a complete treatment of this question would require a book in itself.

"Do the rules of power apply equally to individuals and to groups or societies of individuals?" The popular practice of holding countries responsible for the same ethical obligation we apply to individuals is a topic of some controversy. The question of where and when the strategies and rules of managing power generalize from individual behavior to the behavior of nation-states is addressed in this book as well.

"Does luck count?" Chance, accident, and luck are important factors in assessing the strategies, skills, and patterns of power. The extent to which

these chance factors are important as "wild cards" is addressed in this book, as is the tendency among those seeking power to overestimate the role of luck or chance.

"What are the down sides or negative consequences of having power?" Not all the consequences of power are positive. This book addresses some of the additional responsibilities, obligations, and difficulties that coincide with increased power. In some cases, at least, the negative consequences outweigh the positive rewards for people seeking increased power.

"How does one know the difference between the illusion of power and real power?" This very difficult question is also addressed. Given that perception is more important than reality in our day-to-day decisions, the "illusion" of power becomes as important as "real" power—at least in some circumstances. The book addresses both the differences and the consequences of this illusion.

"How does one take power away from someone?" While this question is distasteful and somewhat political, it is one of the real and important issues one must confront in considering strategies and tactics of power. The fear of using power to manipulate people assumes that manipulation always has negative consequences. The positive and negative consequences of power are addressed.

"How does one make someone else more powerful?" To the extent that one can give away power to people, they become more willing to support and to give power in return. The book describes people thrust into a position of power reluctantly who are more in a habit of helping others than helping themselves. The book also suggests that people who are overly enthusiastic to increase their own power are perhaps not the best guardians of power.

"Does the concept of power have any meaning outside a specific situation, circumstance, or role?" The concept of power as an abstraction is an almost religious question. Power is described as mysterious, elusive, and sometimes magical, that, like the wind, is more evident from its effects than from direct observation. Power is described as the energy or engine of life. The book describes how we seek to understand power and—in some cases—how we worship it as a deity.

The book describes power as a central concept to the understanding of many other fields and perspectives. The book points out that *every population* has some notion of power as a part of the essence of its culture. It would be impossible to understand the different populations without some understanding of what they mean by power. In describing the skills and strategies of power, the book demonstrates that *all skills* relate in one way or another to changes in power—either by increasing, decreasing, or redefining the concept. Being well-trained or well-educated has become almost synonymous with increased power. In applying power the book demonstrates that *all theories* are basically attempts to explain, understand, or predict power relationships. Nuclear physics even suggests that the stuff that holds things together in the appearance of solid objects is some sort of power. In describing the uses of power, the book suggests that *all authority* depends on power. In the ancient epic literature of Asia, for example, the polarity of the powerful and the weak is much more important than any distinction between the good or the bad in understanding a hero's behavior. In describing the attractiveness of power Brislin further suggests that *all needs* can be described in terms of the possession or the lack of power. Psychological, sociological, political, economic, and even theological realities are described in terms of power needs.

This book overcomes weaknesses typical of other books describing power in several specific ways. First of all, it contrasts a long-term perspective on power with a short-term one. Many of the problems regarding the management of power have resulted, as pointed out by this book, from trading off long-term (but more abstract) power goals for short-term (but more concrete) prizes. The book gives many examples of how delayed gratification of rewards and power are important to attain higher levels of development. Examples from literature and storytelling are given to demonstrate the dangers of trading off long-term abstract power goals for immediate and short-term ones.

A second weakness in the treatment of power that this book avoids is the tendency to treat power like property. Power is not easily defined, nor is it as tangible as property. In this sense power may be a religion of modern times. If Freud were developing his theories today he may well have substituted the analogy of power rather than the metaphor of sexuality to describe the relationships between the id, the ego, and the superego.

A third weakness addressed in this book is the tendency of people to fear power. Numerous examples are given in the book of people who were offered power but refused it for one reason or another. There is a great deal written about the dangers of powerlessness and failure, but not nearly as much about the dangers of powerfulness and success. The book describes leadership as the willingness to accept power as it is given. This may not mean forceful control over others, or even self-disciplined control over oneself, but rather becoming a participant rather than a spectator in one's destiny. This book attempts to help the reader understand power in his or her life at a very personal level.

Finally the book emphasizes that we do not live in a chaotic universe. There are patterns of power and rules that are obeyed by the individual, as well as by all other things. It is ironic that these basic questions—questions about power—are asked so infrequently in classes, businesses, assemblies, and communities. Most fields study the rational and ethical *applications* of power without regard for how this basic concept is understood differently by different people and under different circumstances.

This book's largest contribution is that it gets beyond the applications to deal with underlying assumptions about power. Brislin's examination of *power* forces the reader to reexamine assumptions and reconsider priorities about power in his or her own lives. This reexamination promises to make the reader uncomfortable and to make his or her life more complicated. However, it will also put the reader more closely in touch with reality on many levels.

Paul Pedersen

PREFACE

Some people are able to achieve the goals they set for themselves. They can "get things done." Other people, no less educated, hard working, or intelligent, can be far less productive. They set goals, but seem unable to develop plans to attain those goals. What is the difference between the two groups of people? One major difference, and the theme of this book, is that those in the first group have learned that power is not a "four-letter word." They have learned that a sophisticated view of power includes knowledge of various personality factors, skills, strategies, and tactics that people can combine so they can achieve their goals and get things done. For example, they know that some powerholders have a *need* to influence the behavior of others (Chapter 2). They know that they should develop a valued resource (Chapter 3) so they can share it among members of influential networks. They learn various long-term strategies (Chapter 4) for power acquisition and use, such as developing the image of oneself as a "winner," and integrating the skills and interests of various people so that many others can contribute their efforts to complex projects. Given a positive image and the support of others, people can then use various tactics (Chapters 5 and 6) to deal with the inevitable difficulties that arise as they work toward their goals. If they find themselves lacking in knowledge of various strategies and tactics, they learn to put themselves in various activities so they can learn to become more sophisticated about power's usefulness in getting things done (Chapter 7).

Whenever power is discussed, concerns about its ethical applications should be immediately integrated into people's thinking. Power can be intoxicating (Chapter 2), and people who become successful powerholders *over the long run* learn to deal effectively with the pleasure that it can bring. They learn to inhibit themselves and to refuse to use power in an abusive manner. They learn to integrate the contributions of many different types of people, thus increasing the chances of developing socially responsible projects whose benefits and potential difficulties have been carefully analyzed. They learn that if they develop a sophistication about power, then they have acquired a set of skills that can be used in the pursuit of many different goals. These goals can involve self-promotion, abusiveness, and graft; or they can involve a careful concern about a project's impact on others, social responsibility, and the quality of people's lives. If people give careful consideration to the ethical implications of pursuing their goals, they learn that power should become part of intelligent and compassionate leadership (Chapter 8). A sophisticated knowledge about power, then, helps people to become effective leaders. If people keep in mind that power is a tool in the service of leadership, they are far less likely to view power as an end in and of itself.

In addition to ethics, another concern involves exactly where the skills, strategies, and tactics associated with power can be used. I believe that the material presented in this book has the greatest application to societies in which democratic participation is desired. Democratic governments allow people to rise above the circumstances of their birth. In other forms of government, people have more chances of assuming leadership roles if they are born into royalty, or into a wealthy family, or into a family whose members have been active in the one accepted political party. In a democracy, people can speak their minds, can disagree with authority figures, and can assume leadership roles as long as they can persuade others to follow them. The skills, strategies, and tactics covered throughout this book can be used to help these potential leaders. Given the movement toward democratic governments today in many parts of the world, more and more people will be able to put their ideas forward and to pursue their goals without concern of reprisals from traditional authority figures. These ideas will not be put forward only by people concerned with their countries' formal political system. New ideas will also be introduced by people concerned with education, social welfare, religion, the status of women and minority groups, expansion of businesses, international relations, and so forth. But who will be successful in putting their ideas forward and who will be ignored? I believe that those people who are sophisticated and knowledgable regarding the role power plays in the service of compassionate and intelligent leadership will be those who assume prominent positions in countries currently moving toward a democratic form of government.

Just as democracy involves the participation of many people, this book benefitted from the contributions that others made at various stages of its preparation. One hundred and two sophisticated powerholders took time out from their busy schedules to share their ideas about power. A number of people read and commented on various drafts of chapters, gave me feedback after trying out the various strategies and tactics they learned during workshops that I organized, suggested ways of presenting some of the arguments about the use of power, and encouraged me when I was frustrated about my efforts. Some of these people are acknowledged in Chapter 7, where I discuss the content of the workshops that I organized. Other people to whom I am very grateful include Elaine Bailey, Milton and Janet Bennett, Robert Cialdini, Heidi Denecke, Tamara Echter, Sandra Garison, Elaine Hatfield, Diane Hutchinson, Meheroo Jussawalla, Diane Lindsey, Michael Macmillan, Richard Rapson, Larry Smith, Harry Triandis, Sheldon Varney, Geoffrey White, Edith Yashiki, and Philip Zimbardo. I hope I was able to benefit from their good advice.

THE ART OF GETTING THINGS DONE

1

INTRODUCTION: THINKING ABOUT POWER

Larry Speakes, the press secretary for the President of the United States, was confronted by an angry aide. Ignoring guidelines, Gary Schuster and Bill Plante, both of CBS News, and Sam Donaldson, of ABC News, had caught a ride in the press pool van on a day when they had no authority to do so. They wanted to beat their competitors to stories involving the public appearances of President Reagan that day. The aide was livid and wanted disciplinary action to be taken. Not wanting to anger the television reporters, but sensing the need to placate his aide, Speakes suggested that the matter be referred to the White House Correspondents Association. Unknown to the aide, the president of the organization was Gary Schuster, who turned the matter over to the vice president, Bill Plante. Sam Donaldson was appointed to a committee to study the matter. Several years after the incident, Donaldson reported that the "transgressors still have the matter under review."[1]

The aide lost the battle because she did not understand how knowledgeable people use power to their own benefit. She may have had a legitimate complaint. After all, if too many members of the press ignored guidelines and traveled to presidential appearances in any matter they wished, chaos would reign and the President's security would be threatened. But she did not follow through on her complaint in a sophisticated way. As a consequence, she was met with a classic power tactic: referral to an impressive-sounding committee the members of which will take no action.

Many people have found themselves in similar situations. They have had a legitimate point to make or an important policy matter to pursue, but they have been unsuccessful because they were outmaneuvered by opponents. In many cases a lack of success stems from naivete concerning the importance of power and how it is effectively used by experts. The purpose of this book is to explain what power is, to discuss its place in peoples' personalities and in their quests to achieve goals, and to suggest how people can become more sophisticated in its use.

POWER: HAVING AN IMPACT ON OTHERS

Power refers to the ability to have one's decisions accepted by others, to control the behavior of others, or more informally to "get one's way."[2] Further, power means the ability to direct the behavior of other people toward seeing that the individual's decisions are indeed implemented. The other people may *want* to engage in the behaviors necessary for the decision's implementation, and the decision may lead to demonstrably good results for the people and for their organization. In such cases, the powerholder is said to be engaging in intelligent leadership and to be helping others to achieve goals that are best for all concerned. If other people do not want to engage in the necessary behavior, the powerholder may have to coerce them through manipulation of rewards and punishments. As an example, assume that a company vice president proposes a new policy that affects the day-to-day working conditions of hundreds of employees. Are salary increases, public recognition, and promotions desired by the employees? If so, then people must do the bidding of the vice president. If the powerholder's decisions are not implemented, the punishment of a layoff, demotion, withdrawal of an expected salary increase, or removal of an organization's status symbols may follow.

Examples of powerful people can be found in all arenas of life:

- A U.S. congresswoman on Capitol Hill introduces a bill. Is it treated with respect by colleagues in the House and Senate, or is it treated with polite but nonserious referral to an obscure subcommittee?

- A faculty member at a prestigious university wants to teach a course not currently listed in the catalogue. The curriculum committee must decide whether or not to add the course. Does the proposal sail through, or do committee members feel that they can attack the proposal with impunity?

- A lawyer wants to represent two well-known defendants in a highly publicized trial. Do the defendants choose that lawyer, or do they select another lawyer who has a reputation for being more influential with juries and with the media?

- A newly-arrived couple joins a church in their community. They speak up about the old pump organ, arguing that its reeds are hopelessly corroded and that the church should purchase a new electric organ. Do members of the congregation take action to purchase a new organ, or do they dismiss the couple as upstarts trying to change the community in the first few months of their residence?

If the politician, professor, lawyer, and churchgoing couple have their desires implemented, since these desires involve the behavior of others, these people may be said to be powerful.

How do people acquire power? Are there strategies and tactics people can learn that increase the chances of their becoming more powerful in their work and in their community activities? I believe that the answer is yes, and the bulk of this book covers such strategies and tactics. I am making a number of assumptions.

1. When the strategies and tactics are used frequently, they become second nature to the people who are using them. They become skills, just as playing a musical instrument well enough for public performance is a skill. I will sometimes use the term "skills" when referring to strategies and tactics that are used by experienced and successful people.

2. The strategies and tactics I will describe deal with people's lives in their workplace and in their community. While some are applicable to the home and to wife/husband and parent/child relations, the domestic scene will not be an explicit focus of this book.

3. I will assume that the people involved expect to see each other, and to interact with each other, five and ten years from now. There may be times when a strident, caustic, and abrasive person can come into an organization and make major changes while angering coworkers during the entire process. But that person will usually leave a company within a short period of time, and so the tactics employed are of very limited usefulness. I may describe such enemy-producing tactics now and again just to prepare people in case they see them used by others, but I will not recommend the tactics, since I am assuming that long-term good will is a goal. The tactics and strategies I will describe should not interfere with positive relations with others, and often they will enhance such relations.

4. There are generic skills that are useful in all sorts of occupations, organizations, and community activities: politics, business, academia, churches, elementary schools, volunteer groups, and so forth. Certainly, the skills have to be modified and adapted as one moves, for instance, from academia to politics, but the underlying skills used by successful people are identifiable regardless of the arena in which they are used.

5. The generic skills discussed here are usable by people working within a current, well-established system. While many readers may want to change the system, there are more suggestions for using aspects of the current power structure than for changing it radically. Like many of these readers, I would like to see some changes. One of the facts to be discussed is that powerholders often make decisions based on an emotionally detached, sometimes callous calculation of the immediate advantages and disadvan-

tages that accrue to the person. Women have long been known to be more sensitive to the emotional needs of others and more concerned about *long-term* interpersonal relationships. The power structure would improve, I believe, if there were more attention being paid during the accrual of advantages and disadvantages, to people besides the powerholder and to the long-term consequences of decisions. Product quality is a problem in the United States. A slick-looking automobile may bring immediate sales and credit to the decision makers who design and market the product. But the automobile will not bring long-term credit to anyone if it constantly breaks down. Consumers will turn to the more reliable if less flashy products of other countries. As is well known, such a shift in consumer allegiance has occurred, with the reliable cars of Japan now commanding a large market share.

Female powerholders can add their interpersonal skills to their organizations and can improve the quality of decisions concerned with long-term impact. People disagree concerning whether change will occur slowly or rapidly. Even for those wanting rapid change of society's fundamental assumptions, the strategies discussed here may be helpful in their quest. After all, people wanting change have to begin with the status quo.

WHO IS INTERESTED IN POWER?

Who might be interested in the development of skills for the effective use of power? In general people might be interested if they want to become more influential in their workplace and their community, and if they want to "hold their own" and prevent the arbitrary use of power by others. Since the intelligent use of power is part of leadership, the strategies and tactics covered can be used by people who want to become better leaders, better managers, or better organizers of community activities. People also might be interested in developing the skills if they *do not* have the opportunities to acquire them naturally during their childhood and adolescence. This answer demands a treatment of the question, Who does learn them naturally?

My feeling is that members of the upper middle class and as I will discuss later, especially the male members, have a greater likelihood of developing power skills than other people in American society.[3] These males are likely to have parents who are themselves influential: bankers, lawyers, college professors, and business owners. They can learn how their parents handle power through discussions at the dinner table, by overhearing phone conversations about deals being worked out, listening to discussions at their parents' parties, and so forth. Further, since their parents have reached the upper middle class themselves, they have some knowledge of the skills their children will need to be influential, and they can guide the children into the activities necessary for acquiring these skills. Two such skills are writing well and speaking comfortably in public. The parents can encourage their children to take select courses in school, such as an elective course in creative writing or a *second* course (beyond that required for graduation) in public speaking or debate. The parents also have an explicit or implicit sense of other skills, which they may not be able to articulate well but which they know are important.

One important skill is the ability to work with people one does not like very much, but who may have to be integrated into a plan of action to achieve the goals of a proposed activity. This skill can be learned during school and during participation in community activities for children and adolescents such as scouting, church youth groups, student council, and team sports. The person playing shortstop on the baseball team may not care very much for the second baseman, but the two must work together smoothly to develop a good double play. Upper-middle-class parents are more likely to encourage their children to engage in these activities during their childhood and adolescence. I recently spoke with a mother with whom I had organized a three-mile footrace for our children's school. Our sons had also played on the same basketball team. She pointed out that her son's current baseball coach hollered at the kids a lot. She continued, "But that's okay, because he only hollers when there is a mistake that can be corrected. Plus, my son is developing a thick skin about it all. What's he going to do when his boss corrects him in a few years during his first job? Cry? The coach is helping out a lot." The mother spoke in a caring and concerned manner, obviously desirous of happiness for her son. Developing a thick skin, and developing the ability *not* to take criticism too personally, will be covered in greater detail in a later chapter.

To preview another skill, influential people are able to meet others quickly, put these others at ease, engage them in interesting conversation, and find a place in the others' memories so that later interactions will be profitable. This ability can be learned at an early age. Parents have dinner parties to which a variety of community leaders are invited. The 9-year-old son sits on the staircase, watching the people arriving, interacting, and circulating. This is a much more interesting event than any TV show that may happen to be on at the same time. His parents call him down from the staircase: "Paul, come say a few words to the people." Paul is *not* just expected to say a few words. He is expected to engage in intelligent conversation, involving give-and-receive over several rounds of speaker–listener rotation. As he grows older, Paul may participate in other activities, such as sitting at the dinner table and keeping up a conversation with a bank president. Or he may dance with the most successful ladies in the community. By the time he is 16, he has acquired most of the social graces that mark an ability to enter gatherings involving the "movers and shakers" in a society. Note also that he has developed a number of "contacts" he can call upon while looking for a job after completing his formal schooling.

One reason why social class standing, in addition to inherited wealth, is transmitted from generation to generation, is that skills[4] and contacts are passed on from parents to children.

People from social circumstances that limit their movement in the upper middle class are less likely to acquire power skills during their early years. These people include immigrants to a country, refugees, foreign students, women, and people from the middle and working classes. Of course, some of these generalizations will not hold up forever, because there are pressures for social change, especially among women. For instance, career women are becoming more aware of the need to acquire skills during adolescence and are encouraging their daughters to participate in more community activities. In the communities I know, there are far more soccer, softball, and track and field teams for females than there were 20 years ago. (There will be a longer discussion of what is learned from team sports in a subsequent chapter.) In addition to encouraging their daughters, many women with whom I have spoken recognize that they themselves have to play catch-up with men and have to develop the skills to which men have long had more access.

TWO EXAMPLES OF POWER SKILLS

At this point, it may be useful to discuss examples of power skills as they apply to different people who are seeking to achieve their goals. At the same time, the examples allow distinctions to be made between upper-middle-class males and other people who though equally intelligent, hard-working, and full of good ideas, have not had similar access to skill acquisition opportunities.

Example 1

David is a hard-working 30-year-old mechanic who lives in a mid-sized city on the East Coast. He did not have the opportunity to attend college because he had to obtain a job after high school to support his aging and disabled working-class parents. Wanting more for his two preschool children, David started a savings plan so that the children will have enough money for tuition, room, and board when they are ready to attend college. He started his savings plan in 1985, when taxes on the interest in the college accounts was paid by his children on *their income*. Since preschool children rarely have any income, taxes were nonexistent and all interest could accumulate for the eventual payment of college expenses. But under the "tax simplification" law passed by Congress and signed by the President, interest to accounts in the children's names has been applied to David's income since 1987. Because he is a well-paid mechanic, this added interest leads to a nontrivial increase in taxes paid. Far less money, then, is accruing for the children's eventual use.

David becomes convinced that the tax policy is penalizing parents who save and plan ahead. He watches the nightly news on television, and he frequently hears the economics reporter say that one reason for the lackluster economy in the United States is the relative absence of personal savings. Other countries, such as Japan, have a much higher rate of savings, leading to more money for business growth. David wants to talk to someone about changing the law so that certain types of savings are not taxed. What is his first step?

At this point, David will face a series of questions. Whom should he contact? Should it be someone in the banking community or in politics? If the latter, should it be someone at the local, state, or national level? What form should the contact take? Should it be a letter or a personal meeting? If David decides on a meeting, how should the meeting be set up? Can David make an appointment with the influential person directly, or is there a layer of people that has to be penetrated? If an appointment is made, how seriously will David be treated? He will certainly be treated in a polite manner by politicians since he represents a vote, but does he represent more than one vote? Does David know who is being well served by the current tax law and thus who is putting pressure on the politicians to maintain the status quo? As will be discussed throughout this book, this set of questions only scratches the surface of the questions David has to ask himself.

Example 2

A 30-year-old lawyer named Raymond lives in the same community and also has two preschool children. Raymond's mother is a surgeon and his father is a bank vice president. Raymond went to an elite private school during his college years and later attended a highly rated law school. He also is saving money for his children; he wants them to attend one of the expensive private schools. He realizes that if they can attend a school of the Harvard/Yale/Stanford/Princeton type, he will be buying both an education and a lifetime social network for his children.

Raymond is also struck by the 1987 changes that attach interest on children's accounts to his taxable income, and he wants to talk to some politicians about it. At this point, note the advantages Raymond has over David. Raymond can contact alumni of the schools he attended. From his parents, he can obtain suggestions concerning whom to petition. He has probably met the politicians he might approach, or their fathers, at social occasions over a number of years. From various members of his network, Raymond will learn whether it is best to approach certain politicians directly or whether it will be best to approach their legislative aides who are influential in tax matters. Prior to any appointment, Raymond knows that a good question to ask network members is, "Who will be for it and who will be against it?" This information gathering is part of the "homework" necessary to prepare a forceful proposal.

After making appointments with the key figures, Raymond uses his skills as a lawyer to make his case clearly and concisely. He is aware that before they support new legislation politicians want to know if there will be more benefits than damages. Raymond has learned who will be hurt by a change in the status quo (from the "who for and who against" question above) and can acknowledge this in his presentation. Of course he will emphasize the greater benefits stemming from his proposed changes, but by acknowledging the opposition, Raymond comes across as balanced, reasonable, and savvy. Politicians will treat Raymond politely, since he is a voter, but beyond that, not being stupid, they will treat him well, knowing the social circle in which he moves. As with the case of David, such considerations are only a fraction of those that arise when someone of Raymond's background decides to exert influence.

WHO DOESN'T HAVE POWER, AND WHY?

If upper-middle-class children and adults have access to power skills, why don't others? Basically, the reason is the lack of opportunities for direct experience with the skills. Just as teenagers cannot play a good game of baseball their first day or even their first year unless Little League experience was available to them at ages 7 through 12, adults are not going to possess complex power skills without having had the chance to practice them during some significant period in their lives. Two examples will help explain the need for direct experience.

Example 1

As mentioned, one power skill is the ability to work with others whom one does not like. These others may be abrasive, supercilious, or territorial, or may possess any of a host of other unpleasant qualities. But if they have influence over whether the person's proposal is acted upon or not, then they have to be involved in the decision making. One place to learn to interact with disliked others is through team sports. Another is club activities. Assume that a high school student wants to start a club that will deal with computers and programming languages. The club would meet after school. The student has to find a faculty adviser, has to obtain permission to use the school's computers, has to inform custodial service about after-hours use of school property, has to gain approval from the student council, and so forth. In maneuvering through this maze of regulations and procedures, the student is going to gain much valuable experience. After all, a high school is a complex organization with its share of unpleasant people who must be dealt with in the pursuit of important goals. This is also true of any of the organizations the student will encounter during adulthood.

Theoretically, any student could have an interest in computers and could propose the club's formation. But wealthier students will be more likely to pursue their plans.[5] Their working-class colleagues may have been less exposed to computers, since their parents are less likely to be able to afford one for the home. The working-class students may also have to work after school to bring in needed family income. Working-class children may have more responsibilities around their homes, since their parents can seldom afford domestic help. Even if the working-class student does pursue the plan, discouragement may set in when the inevitable mistake is made or roadblock encountered. The upper-middle-class student will also make mistakes and encounter roadblocks, but will be more likely to press forward. The wealthier students can obtain advice on strategy from their parents. The parents might occasionally intervene with a well-timed telephone call to the school principal. The student observes this procedure and learns a valuable lesson: Don't be a "lone wolf" during planning and approval gathering—involve others who have some clout.

Example 2

Another example may seem more exotic, but it also brings out general points. A foreign student from a developing country is pursuing graduate studies at a well-known American university.[6] All foreign students, like their American counterparts, have to choose a major adviser, and this has to be one of the professors on the graduate faculty. Ideally, the major adviser will have enough influence in the university department to guide the student over various hurdles and assist in the eventual search for a job after graduation. An unfortunate fact, however, is that in many universities a certain number of the tenured professors are no longer active. A term used for them is that they have "gone to sleep." The American students are better able to recognize such professors and avoid them. For instance, the American students can check the latest issues of the most prestigious journals and determine who is publishing regularly. They can also ask older graduate students, "Who's hot and who's not?" The students then approach the professors whose names come up positively during this information-gathering exercise.

A student from a developing country, however, may not know the names of the most prestigious journals. In many countries journals are scarce, and *any* academic publication may seem like a godsend. During their own socialization in their home countries, many of these students may have been encouraged to seek out the people with the greatest apparent status, according to their dress, bearing, or "old name" from textbook citations.

In actuality, the old name may be an inactive researcher without much current influence. Further, these students may not be members of a network that includes older graduate students who can give off-the-record advice. As a result of these limitations, this particular foreign student chooses an inactive adviser who is of no help. Since the professor does not know the current concerns of the academic discipline, the student is given little guidance in choosing a dissertation topic. Any final committee will consist of at least five professors, with the major adviser as the titular chair. An uninfluential adviser will be unable to help the student meet the demands of the other four committee members. The student may become caught in the crossfire between the inactive adviser and a currently productive professor who combines a move toward academic superstardom with ungraciousness toward those he or she perceives as hopelessly out of date. If the student does complete the dissertation, the adviser may then have little to contribute to the student's job search. Third-world students are not regularly known as the best and brightest at their universities, and their lack of power skills may be one reason. They may be influential in their home countries and may know the proper skills there, but they have not had enough direct experience with the American setting for the acquisition of the new skills they need in this situation.

DIRECT EXPERIENCE OVER TIME

Is there a substitute for direct experience, so that people can play "catch up" with those fortunate enough to have learned power skills during their adolescence? The word "direct" can also be applied to the answer, which is no. There is no substitute for direct experience. People can play catch up, but the major way of doing this is to seek out opportunities where power skills can be practiced. Further, the implementation of the newly learned skills should be done in settings where actual decisions are made and where their effects are monitored. There are a number of activities about which books and seminars can give guidance, and the development and use of power skills is one. But there has to be practice with the skills in real-world settings. Other activities besides power use that come immediately to mind include making love, losing weight, stopping the smoking habit, driving a car, and fixing a car. A complete novice cannot read a book on how to drive a car and then venture onto a city freeway. Similarly, no one can read a book on power skills (like this one) and think that the information can be put to immediate use in the pursuit of important goals.

Everybody wants a "quick fix," a simple solution to major problems that takes little time, money, and effort to introduce. When reading the academic journals concerned with research into seemingly intractable problems, such as homelessness, alcoholism, the quality of inner-city schools, the trade deficit, street crime in large cities, and recidivism among paroled prisoners, I find myself yearning for easy solutions. Every time a highly touted new administrator takes the reins of a troubled organization, its employees have a tendency to say, "Now things will improve!" But the new administrators will face the same problems that have long plagued the organization, and any improvements are likely to be modest at best. One power tactic for new administrators is to use this optimism, and their natural six-month honeymoon period, to strike quickly with imaginative innovations. If not, the employees will decide after six months that the new administrators are no more able to improve the organization than were their predecessors. Further, any innovations will be seen as old wine in new bottles. There will be disappointment, but chances are the employees will be able to console themselves that things are at least no worse than before.

There is reason to believe that a blind faith in the possibility of "quick fixes" is diminishing. People now recognize that some changes once thought to be relatively easy and straightforward take a great deal of time and effort. Weight loss is a good example.[7] Many people now realize that weight loss is not an easy matter. When people lose a significant amount of weight, such that it is noticeable to their friends, 90 percent gain it back. In fact, the physiology of the body's cells changes during the weight-loss period. The changed cells contribute to a craving for more food, and thus a weight *gain* over the level people carried prior to their weight-loss efforts. People now recognize that weight loss has to involve long-term attention and work aimed at maintaining the loss. Two years of constant attention to caloric intake and burnoff are necessary until new, lifelong eating and exercise habits are established. Even after the new habits are established, people must constantly keep in mind that their previous lifestyle is a source of temptations and that weight maintenance is a lifelong process. They must also realize that as they become older (for instance, over 40), their metabolism slows down and they have to give even greater attention to caloric intake and exercise. Dieters can learn a great deal from a book about food groups, nutrients, exercise, tasty low-calorie meals, life-span concerns, and so forth. They can go to weekend seminars or join support groups and be exposed to the same knowledge. But they also have to put the knowledge to use over a long period of time.

People who want to become more influential face a similar state of affairs. They can learn a great deal from books and seminars, but there is no "quick fix." They must put the knowledge to use in their everyday lives for a number of years. While more books might be sold if quick action was promised ("Become more powerful in a week!"), such claims would constitute hucksterism at its worst. Suggestions will be made for involvement in activities where direct experience can be gained. By putting their newly gained knowledge to use in these activities, people receive feedback on their efforts and can improve their use of a strategy the second time they try it. Only through such reiterations and conscious efforts to improve do they become more skillful.

MORE ON TIME, AND ASPECTS OF LIFE

Power takes a great deal of time to acquire, and it takes time to maintain. As I shall discuss later, one power strategy centers on the constant acquisition and maintenance of people in one's network. If a person drops out of a network, for instance by not showing up at testimonial dinners for stellar figures, then that person may fade from people's memories. "Where's Charlie? He used to be so involved. Has he lost interest in our work?" When such questions reach the tongues of too many people, Charlie may find himself on the fringes of influential groups rather than at their centers.[8]

The time and energy people devote to power acquisition and maintenance cannot be spent on other activities. People will not have as much time to bounce their children on their knees, help them with their homework, or go to their amateur-night performances. They will not have as much time to read books, exercise, stroke their spouses or spouse surrogates, or keep up their skills on musical instruments. If people want to become more powerful, they have to downplay other possible uses of their time.

Many people will not be willing to devote the necessary resources. Or if they do begin the quest, they will discover that the results are not worth the effort. These people are not demonstrating any shortcomings; power is only one aspect of life, and many people gain tremendous amounts of happiness in life without pursuing power. Their spouses, children, hobbies, outdoor sports, a steady job, church membership, and so forth are more important to them. People should pursue power and influence only if they would otherwise be unhappy. They should feel in their guts that they need the necessary power skills to achieve goals of importance to them. Those who choose to spend their time and energy on other pursuits should be respected for their decision, and perhaps thanked. Just as one key to the right of freedom of speech is that not everyone constantly presses the limits, or tests the gray areas of the law (such as shouting obscenities in crowded theatres), one reason for the relatively smooth functioning of society is that not everyone is constantly jockeying for more power. Some wags have pointed out that constant power seekers move to Washington, D.C., and amuse each other there, thus allowing people in the rest of the country to lead normal lives.

Just as there are many activities that people can pursue with greater or lesser vigor, there are aspects of people's personal makeup that can be given greater or lesser emphasis. People are bundles of potential: the same person may be altruistic, callous, loving, demanding, hard driving, and supportive of others during the same day. Pressures coming from the job, family, friends, and enemies strongly influence the exact behaviors in which people engage. Psychologists put it another way. They point out that behavior is determined by people's personalities together with situational pressures.[9] Even the most boisterous, gregarious person will act in a solemn way at funeral services that take place in a huge cathedral. The fact that such a person is being quiet does not mean that he or she has suddenly lost that extroverted personality. Rather, the pressures of the situation overwhelm any tendency to behave in a humorous manner.

Other situations allow different personalities to express themselves. At an informal after-hours office party, extroverted people may be loud and entertaining while introverted people may be quiet and demure. The situational pressures associated with after-hours office parties allow both sorts of behaviors. But to add complexity, it is reasonable to expect that some people who work quietly, effectively, and productively during office hours may be quite raucous at the party. These people have a number of potentials, or aspects of their personalities, that are brought out by different social situations.

People commonly call upon different potentials at different times. It is not hard to imagine a school principal engaging in the following behaviors on the same day:

1. Meeting with teachers and setting up an English-language program sensitive to the needs of refugees from Southeast Asia in her school district. One of her potentials, brought out by the situation, is empathy for the plight of others.

2. Meeting with the school superintendent or the city council on budget matters. Here, all sorts of power strategies and tactics are useful in her lobbying efforts.

3. Becoming very angry at a driver who cuts in front of her on the freeway while she is driving home.

4. Coming home and sharing the day's experiences with her husband and children, giving and receiving emotional support.

5. In the firmest and most assertive manner, calling the complaints section of the department store where she bought a refrigerator. Only a year old, the refrigerator has broken down three times.

6. Playing bridge with close friends.

The power skills useful to the second activity, lobbying for the school's budget, constitute only one of her potentials. In fact, it would be unwise and damaging if she used certain of her power skills during the emotionally supportive time with her family or during her activities with close friends. Power is one aspect of life, no more and probably less important than many others. Some people will be interested in acquiring power, while others will be far more interested in other aspects of life, such as enjoying close relationships with family members and friends. For those interested in acquiring power, and also for those more interested in other aspects of life who have an intellectual interest in how people make and implement complex decisions, this book may be useful.

MY INTEREST IN POWER

My own interest in power developed out of my work experiences. After completing my formal schooling (in 1969), I had a series of jobs over a ten-year period. Since I was under 26 and was leaving school during the Vietnam War, I had a military obligation. After considering various options, I went to work for a research organization associated with the Department of Defense in Washington, D.C. Soon thereafter I became an assistant professor at a small university in the state of Washington. Later, a visiting and then a permanent appointment opened up at the East–West Center in Honolulu, Hawaii. The East–West Center is an international research and educational institution that provides scholarly exchange programs among people from the United States, Asia, and the Pacific Island nations. While holding these jobs, I had quite a bit of experience consulting in business and industry; participating in professional membership organizations; following the progress of legislation related to my work during a sabbatical year in Washington, D.C.; writing books for publication; and editing the books of others.

Slowly, over time, I became aware of a number of disparities. First and foremost, I came to realize that the most intelligent and creative people do not necessarily become the best-paid administrators or most influential power holders in their organizations. In some cases, I saw very unproductive people being advanced to positions of administrative responsibility or taking over the role of power broker if a weak administrator refused to make decisions. For instance, in the research and educational organizations I encountered, the most respected and best-published scholars did not necessarily become the deans, vice presidents, or behind-the-scenes power brokers. Far less professionally visible and unproductive faculty members were becoming the formal or informal heads of various units within their organizations. And in my opinion, these heads were by no means the most hard-working people. What struck home the most, of course, was that these people were getting their proposals accepted by higher-ups while mine were being given far less attention.

These observations caused me to think back on what my father told me as I went off to graduate school. "Richard, work hard and develop good ideas and you'll have a successful career." This comparison of my father's advice with observed reality had quite an emotional impact. My father, the most influential person in my life, may have overlooked something during his discussions with me. At long last, I came to realize that what the deans and vice presidents knew, and what my father missed in his advice, was a set of political strategies. Upon figuring this out, I shared my insight with a colleague whom I consider both hard-working and savvy. She said, "So you just figured that out? How old are you? Better late than never, I guess."

Early Experiences

My colleague's mention of age then led me to examine the development of skills over the entire life span, and it was at this point that I became interested in the greater access to power skills of upper-middle-class adolescents. I did not grow up in the heady heights of the comfortably wealthy—instead, "lower within the middle class" would be a more accurate description. My father was the son of a railroad conductor and a full-time homemaker. In 1928 he went to college, the first of his extended Irish-American family in central Vermont to do so. That is, he began college in 1928, but when he returned in the fall of 1929 for his sophomore year, the stock market crashed, the Great Depression began, and he withdrew from school for lack of funds and to bring in needed family income.

Over the years, he had a number of jobs in various aspects of public service and recreation: The Catholic Youth Organization, the Red Cross, summer camps, and the United Service Organizations (USO). These allowed him to provide a pleasant though not luxurious living for his family.

Four children were born over a period of 13 years. We lived in a collection of middle-class, single-family homes in Rutland, Vermont. My brother's wife, who is Chinese-American and grew up in Hawaii, maintains that in our family pictures from the 1950s we look like cast members of the "Leave it to Beaver" TV show, and I suppose she is right. Although my mother had extensive work experience as a teacher of secretarial skills prior to her marriage, she stayed home full time when the four children were young. It was the first marriage for both of my parents, who had been together 43 years when my father passed away in 1981. We were protected from such troubles of life as divorce, child abuse, intense family arguments, extramarital affairs, gambling, drugs, and alcohol.

I don't think I grew up believing that life is a Garden of Eden, but the darker side of humanity was compartmentalized. One of my father's jobs was as head of the fairgrounds, where in addition to the fair, carnivals came during the spring, summer, and fall. Between the ages of 6 and 12 I would walk down the rows of booths and tents with him, as he closed down sleazy strip joints and pitch-till-you-win games that had big-money gambling operations off to the side. I learned certain interesting economic lessons from this. People paid 50¢ to have their weight guessed. If the pitchman guessed wrong, the person won a doll. But the dolls cost the carnival owner far less than 50¢, since they were bought in bulk. So the pitchman won whether he guessed the person's weight correctly or not.

But these lessons did not seem to have anything to do with my everyday life of school, friends and neighbors, boy scouts, church, part-time jobs, and so forth.

Some of the lessons I learned from the carnival era *should* have become better integrated into my long-term thinking. When the Rutland Fair was on, one of my father's responsibilities was to supervise the grandstand shows, and my first job was to serve as an usher. One show was quarter-midget auto racing, in which a traveling company of race car drivers would compete against each other and supposedly vie for prize money. The cars were one-fourth the size of Indianapolis race cars. The announcer, who traveled with the drivers, described the race over the loudspeaker system in a tone of voice suitable for reporting the earth's demise. "And Jack Edwards passes on the inside, just avoiding a collision with the leader! Dick Ferris hovers in third place, doing nicely! Is he playing possum?" My father observed to me, "I've never liked the auto races very much. Without the announcer, it would be mind-numbingly dull." And he was right. If I covered my ears to block out the announcer, the excitement was gone. The cars were only going about 40 miles an hour, slower than we would travel to home. The cars left a little rubber on the track and released some black exhaust smoke now and again, but these theatrics became very old very quickly. The grandstand show was carried by the announcer's enthusiasm.

I should have recognized the importance of enthusiasm far earlier than I did. Enthusiasm is a major component of the Dale Carnegie method of influencing people [10] and is covered in every good university-level communication course. My speech teacher in college used to say, "That talk was duller than dishwater. You sound bored to tears. Are you?" Such feedback, blunt as it was, led to a number of realizations. Enthusiasm is contagious; people like to listen to exciting speakers; there is nothing so frustrating as listening to potentially interesting ideas presented in a dry, dull manner. If they are not naturally blessed with a dynamic speaking style, powerful people take pains to acquire one. If they happen to be ill or tired, they deliberately work to "get themselves up" for their audience. They realize that if they are to be successful, they must communicate enthusiasm and cannot afford to appeal to their illness or fatigue.

I may have internalized one lesson sooner than others, and that is the value of keeping the goodwill of others. Besides holding the fair and hosting the carnivals, my father brought in circuses[11] that set up at the fairgrounds. While many people think of circuses and carnivals as similar, there are important differences. One is that circuses far less often have "games of skill" associated with them and thus have far fewer opportunities for gambling operations. Another is that circuses are often sponsored by local civic groups. Service organizations such as the Shriners or the Lions Club book a circus, take care of many of the local arrangements, sell tickets, and split the pro-

ceeds with the circus owners. The "Shrine Circus" that many people pa-
tronize is actually an intact unit sponsored in a community by the Shriners.
The next week, that same circus may be sponsored by the Rotary Club in
another town and appear under its own organization's name, such as the
Pollack Brothers Circus. If a service organization sponsored a dishonest
show, this would reflect poorly on the organization and the community. In
addition, word would get around and no club would ever sponsor the circus
again. The circuses I knew, then, depended on their good reputation and on
repeat business in the same communities year after year. While there were and
are less reputable outfits, the well-run circuses sponsored regularly by service
clubs are known as "sunday-school shows."

Therein is the lesson about the value of goodwill. The most powerful people will insure that others want to be associated with them well into the future. While some people will use "hit-and-run" tactics and will "burn up the
territory," these are not the individuals who need the continued goodwill of
others to maintain themselves in powerful positions. As will be discussed in
various parts of this book, especially Chapter 4, a concern with the long
term and ethical use of power leads to specific strategies and tactics. Power
is often dependent upon the building of coalitions to support a given proposal, and these coalitions change as different proposals are developed. Therefore, powerful people make as few enemies as possible. People who are on the
other side of today's proposal should be treated with respect, not contempt,
since they may be allies on tomorrow's proposal.

The concept that people should make as few enemies as possible so that
there will be more potential allies in the future has been expressed by many
powerful people. Hubert Humphrey, for instance, said that this was a lesson
his father passed on to him. This lesson seems to be a permanent part of
certain people's makeup. It becomes part of their thinking about a wide
variety of decisions, actions, and negotiations.

Allowing Active Thoughts

Personal childhood experiences and informal discussions with successful
adults led me to consider the role of active thinking in people's lives. It
occurred to me that more-powerful people think differently than less-
powerful people. In addition to learning helpful lessons such as "don't
make enemies," powerful people allow more thoughts into their minds.
They are less likely to automatically exclude a course of action if it does
not seem immediately possible. They have knowledge that allows the con-
tinual processing of new thoughts.

For instance, consider again the two people who have the same idea
about tax reform. David, who does not know a large number of influential
people and does not have extensive knowledge about how to lobby for
reform, may terminate his efforts to change the tax law. With few contacts

and little knowledge about procedures, he may not have much confidence in his ability to be effective. Raymond, on the other hand, is part of influential community networks and is savvy about political maneuverings. He will be more likely to continue his quest for tax reform because he will be less likely to say to himself, "I can't get anything done." One way to explain this distinction is to say that David and Raymond differ in their thinking. David is less likely to think he will be effective. Raymond has important political resources and so is *allowed to think* about continuing his efforts.

This concern with people's thinking is an emphasis in recent psychological research,[12] and so I was able to benefit from progress at the same time that I was analyzing power. Some of the clearest findings have emanated from research on psychological disorders. A major difference between severely depressed and psychologically untroubled people is that the former often overinterpret events in their lives and become upset *due to their thoughts*. For instance, consider people who interview for a job but are not offered the position. An applicant who overinterprets the event in certain ways may become depressed. The overinterpretation may consist of having thoughts on the wrong side of the following three dimensions:

—global-specific: Is everything in life affected, or just one specific aspect?
—stable-unstable: Is the problem permanent, or can there be change?
—internal-external: Is this failure the applicant's fault, or is it caused by something about the world outside the individual?[13]

The wrong side is the left, or beginning side of the questions in this list. If a person's response to the lack of a job offer is global, the self-directed thinking might include, "I'm not a good candidate for the job market. I'm worthless." If the responses are stable, they might include, "And I'll always be inadequate and worthless." If the responses are internal, they might include, "It's all my fault—I'm totally to blame." This pattern of responses, or self-directed thinking, can lead to depression.

There are significant differences if the person thinks according to the good, or right-hand side of the questions. A specific response would be, "I didn't get the job, but this doesn't mean that I won't get another." An unstable response would be, "Things will get better if I keep trying." An external response might be, "The job turndown may have been due to some quirk of the interviewer." These appeals to self-directed thinking are obviously healthier and more productive than the pattern leading to depression.

With this focus on thinking, stimulated by informal discussions with successful people and by the psychological research literature, I went back again to childhood experiences. It struck me that the presence or absence of certain thoughts had had major impacts at different points in my life.

I focused again on upper-middle-class children, compared with the rest of society. One of my colleagues at the East-West Center had attended one of the most prestigious private schools, Phillips Exeter Academy in New Hampshire, during his high school years, and he later went on to Princeton. Rutland, Vt., is close enough to allow a few students to attend and still spend weekends with their families. Let us assume, just for the sake of argument, that I could have qualified for admission to Exeter. The point for the purpose of power analysis is that the thought never crossed my mind. My parents did not think about it, nor did any of my friends, relatives, or neighbors. The idea of going to Exeter was so remote that it never came close to entering our consciousness. And so, since the thought did not exist, no action could be taken.[14] Upper-middle-class experiences allow upper-middle-class adolescents to think in terms of possibilities denied to the rest of society. They can think in terms of "Harvard" or "Wall Street lawyer" or "life-long influential contacts" in ways that do not enter the minds of people from more modest backgrounds.

Powerful people also purposely learn a style that includes an aura of confidence, social smoothness, and a "can do" attitude.[15] They learn the importance of this style and then put it to daily use. I remember the year I spent in Washington, D.C., observing the comings and goings of business-people vying for government contracts. One of my colleagues advised. "Watch the successful ones. They present their proposals in an extremely confident manner. If they can't answer a question, they will never admit that they don't know. They won't lie, but they'll answer the inquiry as if the knowledge is available to them."

My father accepted a job with the United Services Organization in Anchorage, Alaska, during my high school years. While we were there my mother worked as secretary to the psychologist who served the Anchorage school district, James Coats. Mr. Coats was very generous with his time and answered questions when I came into the office to see my mother. These experiences allowed the concept "psychologist" to enter the minds of family members. I often wonder if I would have studied psychology if my mother had accepted another job in Anchorage.

My conclusion from the combination of informal discussions, psychological research, and analysis of childhood experiences described in this section of the chapter is not that "knowledge is power," but that powerful people have thoughts that permit action to follow. Other people are less likely to have these thoughts and consequently do not engage in power-generating behaviors. Further, the thinking of powerful people is based on specific sets of knowledge, possible courses of action, and a conscious awareness of style that are not available to everyone. Style is especially important. The thinking of powerful people and their accompanying behavior focus on "I can do it" rather than "Here are all the reasons it can't be done." Powerful people focus on specific steps that can be accomplished and do not become bogged down with global aspects of a problem that have no point at which intervention can begin. Their confidence is contagious, and others want to become associated with them. Powerful people combine this style with specific knowledge, such as contacts to approach and procedures to be followed, that permit progress to be made.

As my friend who asked "How old are you?" was pointing out, others had probably figured out such things a long time ago and integrated the knowledge into their own lives. To play catch-up in my own analysis of power skills, I decided to move from informal to more formal attempts to document what powerful people do. My way of making this move would include talking with a large number of successful people and determining whether strategies and tactics could be identified that differentiated more and less powerful people.

INTERVIEWS

I asked a large number of people (102 in all) to talk with me about power, and these talks were scheduled over a three-year period. I was interested in generic skills, that is, skills that would be useful in large numbers of settings. Ideally, they should be such skills that would be worth the attention of the large numbers of people who desire to become more influential. Some generic skills have already been discussed. One set of these skills consists of ways of meeting people quickly, putting them at ease, and forming a place in *their* memories so that profitable interactions can take place as long as six months into the future. On the other hand, an example of a much more specific skill, of interest here only as it gives insights into a more generic skill, is the ability of campaign managers to report the contributions of Political Action Committees (PACs) in compliance with legal guidelines and in such a way that the candidate does not come across as the pawn of special interests.

Because of the search for generic skills, I spoke with people from many occupations: politicians, agency heads, church officials, ambassadors, lawyers, labor negotiators, businesspeople, fund raisers, university administrators, and so forth. The exact occupations, and numbers associated with each, are listed in Table 1.

Two of the occupations may seem odd. Entertainers and filmmakers were included because so few people hoping for careers in these fields are successful at making a full-time living in their desired specialties. Those who are successful become quite visible and influential, and they are often asked for advice on career success by aspiring entertainers and filmmakers. The successful few also become powerful in the sense that they can influence the advancement of these aspiring professionals by sharing contacts, offering jobs, and so forth. I play in a semiprofessional music group and have collaborated with colleagues who work with the Performing Arts Series at the East-West Center, and I have met many entertainers because

Table 1
Occupations of the People Interviewed

Occupation	Number
Administrative officers, large organizations	4
Agency heads, state level	4
Agency heads, Washington, D.C. (national level)	3
Campaign managers, political	2
Chief executive officers, businesses	3
Church officials, pastors, bishops	4
Deans, colleges and universities	4
Diplomats, rank of ambassador	2
Directors, international research projects	4
Editors, newspapers	4
Entertainers (who make living as actors, musicians)	4
Filmmakers (make living at occupation)	2
Fund raisers (full time occupation: at least million dollars per year raised)	3
Heads, citizen action groups	3
Heads, training units within large businesses	5
Lawyers, partners in firms	3
Lobbyists, political, national level	1
Lobbyists, political, state level	3
Negotiators, dispute resolution	3
Negotiators, labor	3
Negotiators, multinational ventures, representing one of the parties about to enter into joint ventures	1
Officials, labor unions	3
Officers, military (rank of Navy Captain, or equivalent in other services, or above)	5
Owners, small businesses	3
Politicians, elected, national level	2
Politicians, elected, state level	4
Presidents, professional membership organizations	4
Presidents, volunteer organizations in communities	3
Principals, high school	3
Professors, university (achieved full professor rank before age 40)	4
Program heads, international organizations	4
Vice-presidents, executive, large organizations	2
Total:	102

of these activities. Various professional entertainers are brought in to give public performances under the auspices of this series. I have met filmmakers through the Hawaii International Film Festival, also sponsored by the East-West Center. I carried out interviews with these people at the same time that I was talking with others who are more frequently viewed as powerful, such as politicians and businesspeople. The skills and strategies reported by all of these individuals were similar.

During some very informal interviews, prior to the more serious effort with the 102 respondents, I found that the following form of inquiry yielded good responses. It became the question that provided the major focus for the 102 interviews. "Imagine two people, A and B, in your field or in your organization. Both are attractive, hard working, intelligent, and have good ideas. Person A gets those ideas integrated into the organization, but B never seems to get anywhere with his or her ideas. What's the difference between A and B?" Another question that worked well was, "In terms of getting things done or having your decisions implemented, what do you know now, because of your firsthand experience, that you wish you knew when you first started out?" If people could give answers to these, the rest of the interview centered on elaborations and more answers to the same questions. What resulted from each interview was (1) a collection of behaviors that people like Person A do that people like Person B do not do, (2) a set of lessons or pieces of advice for being more influential in decision making and decision implementation, or (3) both.

When initially responding to the questions, some of the 102 respondents gave general advice that was rather tame. They would relate the sorts of advice that a high school principal might give to a graduating class: "Do your homework before going into an important meeting." "Don't wait for opportunities to come your way—take the initiative." "Strive to be the most capable person possible in your specialty." While these are true and are sometimes the reasons for success in power acquisition, I was also looking for strategies that are not well known and not widely discussed. One reason these strategies are not more widely known is that they are effective, and powerholders feel that they will not be so effective if everyone knows about them. Certain tactics also have a dark side, which people are uncomfortable discussing. But it is these controversial, manipulative, and cunning tactics that are *encountered* in organizations. People should know about them and should be prepared to be the target of their use, even if they decide not to employ manipulative tactics themselves.

If the people being interviewed gave only frequently-heard, placid answers, I attempted to move the discussion to more controversial tactics by describing a strategy discussed by Niccolo Machiavelli in his treatise *The Prince*.[16] In my opinion, the following is the most explicit long-term strategy Machiavelli recommended for a problem facing a leader. I have made a few adaptations, but the key elements are from Machiavelli.

A chief executive officer (CEO) of a large company wants to make major changes, including a large-scale reorganization and the removal of certain people. He brings in a vice president in charge of operations. The vice president, over a six-month period, introduces the reorganization, encourages some people to leave, and fires two popular employees. A number of department heads make an appointment with the CEO, and he says, "I understand that there are concerns, but after all, we have to give this vice president a year to get his bearings around here and to learn the organizational culture." The vice president continues his activities. At the end of a year, the remaining employees are in an uproar. At this point, the CEO fires the detested vice president. The CEO is considered a hero by the employees for getting rid of the miserable bastard who has been plaguing their lives. But note that the company reorganization and removal of undesired employees, all planned by the CEO, have already been implemented. I also noted in my discussions that I have seen this tactic used twice in organizations with which I have been associated.

I used this description of a strategy in the hope that the interviewees would match it with descriptions of other manipulative tactics. They did, and the tactics they came up with will be covered in different parts of the book, especially Chapters 5 and 6.

I took extensive notes during the interviews. The later analysis took the form of extracting usable pieces of advice for power acquisition, generic skills, and background information useful in understanding how power skills work in an imperfect society. The rest of the book draws from the interviews and combines the insights of the 102 respondents with those of other analysts, as well as with my own observations. The work of the other analysts is available in the published literature and includes contributions by psychologists, political scientists, sociologists, journalists, and biographers of powerful individuals.[17]

ORGANIZATION OF THE BOOK

Chapter 2 introduces key concepts, such as power as a personality variable, the corrupting possibilities of power, success in leadership, the dangers of power abuse, and the use of power in an imperfect world, where decisions have to be made concerning the competition for resources. I believe that this background information is necessary to understand how skills, tactics, and strategies can lead to desirable or undesirable ends. Chapter 3 covers the abilities and skills necessary to become influential. Special attention will be given to those playing catch-up in relation to their more advantaged peers. When abilities and skills are practiced and called upon frequently, they become part of the permanent makeup of people. These well-practiced skills allow people to use certain strategies and tactics much more effectively than those who never had opportunities to acquire them. Chapters 4, 5 and 6 are concerned with these strategies and tactics, or combinations of behaviors, that are important in the acquisition and maintenance of power. The specific tactics involved are divided into two types: those useful for gaining support (Chapter 5) and those useful for dealing with an opposition (Chapter 6).

Chapter 7 presents ideas about how these abilities, strategies and tactics can be acquired. Suggestions are made for choosing activities that will encourage an understanding of what power is and how it is most effectively used. Chapter 8 summarizes the key themes of the book, suggests a set of thoughts that differentiate sophisticated from naive users of power, and makes recommendations for viewing power as *one* component of intelligent, informed, and compassionate leadership.

NOTES

1. S. Donaldson, *Hold On, Mr. President* (New York: Random House, 1987). Direct quote is from pp. 150–51.

2. These views of power are strongly influenced by the writings of David McClelland. See "The Two Faces of Power," *Journal of International Affairs* 24 (1970) no. 1, pp. 29–47; and *Power: The Inner Experience* (New York: Irvington, 1975).

3. Insightful treatments concerning the effects of social class membership can be found in D. Gilbert and J. Kahl, *The American Class Structure: A New Synthesis* (Homewood, Ill.: Dorsey, 1982); and M. L. Kohn, *Class and Conformity*, 2nd ed. (Chicago: University of Chicago Press, 1977).

4. M. Argyle, "Interaction Skills and Social Competence," in *Psychological Problems: The Social Context*, edited by M. P. Feldman and J. Orford (New York: Wiley, 1980), pp. 123–50.

5. H. C. Lindgren and W. N. Suter, *Educational Psychology in the Classroom*, 7th ed. (Monterey, Calif.: Brooks/Cole, 1985).

6. Many of the problems facing foreign students are analyzed by O. Klineberg and F. Hull, *At a Foreign University* (New York: Praeger, 1979).

7. K. D. Brownell, "Obesity: Understanding and Treating a Serious, Prevalent, and Refractory Disorder," *Journal of Consulting and Clinical Psychology* 50 (1982): 820–40; and J. Rodin, "Current Status of the Internal–External Hypothesis for Obesity: What Went Wrong?" *American Psychologist* 36 (1981): 361–72.

8. Mayor John Lindsay of New York City wrote about the necessity for constant participation in key events in "The Rites of Power," in *The Power Game*, edited by C. Felker (New York: Simon & Schuster, 1969).

9. A good introduction to the importance of looking at both personalities and situational pressures can be found in N. Endler and D. Magnusson, *Interactional Psychology and Personality* (Washington, D.C.: Hemisphere, 1976).

10. A good overview of Dale Carnegie courses can be found in an article by R. Conniff, "The So-So Salesman Who Told Millions How to Make It Big," *Smithsonian* 18, No. 9 (October 1987), pp. 82–93.

11. I summarized my experiences with the circus in R. Brislin, "Psychology in circus life," *The White Tops* 53, no. 5 (1980), pp. 5–8.

12. Basic ideas about the role of active thinking, and how experiences allow the development of categories, can be found in H. Gardner, *The Mind's New Science: The History of the Cognitive Revolution* (New York: Basic Books, 1985); and S. Fiske and S. Taylor, *Social Cognition* (New York: Random House, 1984).

13. L. Abramson, M. Seligman, and J. Teasdale, "Learned Helplessness in Humans: Critique and Reformation," *Journal of Abnormal Psychology* 87 (1978):49–74. Other treatments of the importance of positive thinking can be found in P. McWilliams and J. Roger, *You Can't Afford the Luxury of a Negative Thought* (Los Angeles: Prelude, 1989); and D. Gershon and G. Straub, *Empowerment: The Art of Creating Your Life as You Want It* (New York: Delta, 1989).

14. It is intriguing to fantasize what might have happened had I attended Exeter. Would a group of future Wall Street lawyers and investment bankers have gone en masse to carnivals in the area? Would these people have analyzed the relative risks of Guess Your Weight versus Picking Up Plastic Ducks in a Pond, Throwing Balls at Kewpie Dolls, or Dumping Bozo in the Drink? Would the lessons they learned there have prevented the 500-point drop in the Dow-Jones average on October 19, 1987?

15. There is an analysis of this confident style in E. Chaika, *Language: The Social Mirror* (New York: Newbury House, 1989).

16. N. Machiavelli, *The Prince. The Discourses* (New York: Modern Library, 1940).

17. Some important additional sources are S. H. Ng, *The Social Psychology of Power* (London: Academic Press, 1980); D. Kipnis, *The Powerholders* (Chicago, Ill.: University of Chicago Press, 1976); C. W. Mills, *The Power Elite* (New York: Oxford University Press, 1956); F. G. Bailey, *Strategems and Spoils: A Social Anthropology of Politics* (Oxford, England: Basil Blackwell, 1970); B. Crick, *In Defence of Politics*, 2nd ed. (Middlesex, England, and New York: Penguin, 1982); R. A. Caro, *The Power Broker: Robert Moses and the Fall of New York* (New York: Random House, 1974); W. Slack, *The Grim Science: The Struggle for Power* (Port Washington, N.Y.: Kennikat, 1981); H. Smith, *The Power Game: How Washington Works* (New York: Random House, 1988); R. Cialdini, *Influence: Science and Practice*, 2nd ed. (Glenview, Ill.: Scott, Foresman, 1988); N. Bartley, "Politics and Ideology," in *Encyclopedia of Southern Culture* edited by C. R. Wilson and W. Ferris (Chapel Hill: University of North Carolina Press, 1989), pp. 1151–58.

2

THE BACKGROUND OF POWER ACQUISITION: POLITICS, PEOPLE, AND RESOURCES

When there are limited resources in a democratic society, but many people who desire them, there has to be a method of distribution that allows as many people as possible to be satisfied. Politics is a major part of the system of distribution.[1] Many people want resources, but there are not enough to go around; who succeeds in the competition? People said to be powerful compete well for those limited resources.

EXCHANGES IN HUMAN RELATIONSHIPS

The competition for resources is part of a broader picture of human behavior that is well understood by successful power brokers. As best they can, people behave so as to maximize rewards and avoid punishments. Although a few masochists search for pain, most people seek activities, jobs, friends, and lifetime partners that will maximize their happiness. People behave in certain ways, such as holding down a job and remaining in a relationship, as long as the benefits outweigh the costs. People seek equity in their lives, which means that they want benefits to accrue to them in a fair exchange for their contributions. When the relationship between contributions and benefits becomes unbalanced, then inequity results.[2] People decide whether or not they are in an inequitable situation by comparing their contributions and benefits with those of others.

The comparison process is an important step.[3] People determine what is possible in a relationship or activity given their past experience and the experience of visible others. They develop an idea of what is realistic, given a combination of the past and present as they know it. As discussed in Chapter 1, I did not feel inequitably treated in my schooling since the possibility of going to an elite school like Phillips Exeter did not exist in my mind. I would have felt badly only if the actual choice of school differed from a more prestigious possibility that I felt was attainable. Similarly, people develop a rough idea of their contributions to their jobs, combining such aspects as their education, work hours, tangible outcomes, and the efforts of others at the same job level. Feelings of equitable treatment occur when there is a correspondence between self-determined contributions and outcomes, the latter heavily influenced by the question, "What are others getting?"

The most common form of inequity occurs when people feel underpaid or underappreciated given their self-perceived contributions. A sales representative might be writing $2 million worth of insurance policies a year, but another sales representative selling far less is promoted. The first would feel inequitably treated, and this feeling would be augmented if other factors were added into the personal analysis. For instance, if the one selling more also worked in a more difficult sales territory, his or her feelings of inequity would be even larger.

Sports figures often claim to be poorly treated. I assume that there will be recent examples from the sports pages no matter when this material is read, given that the principles involved are so basic to people's thinking about themselves. For instance, a football player has rushed for 2,000 yards or more during each of the last six seasons, and is considered one of the top three running backs by sportswriters. But he is paid $300,000 a year less than another running back rated no higher than tenth best. The elite running back experiences severe dissatisfaction, demands contract renegotiations, and asks to be traded. During the time of his dissatisfaction, his performance on the football field deteriorates, as if one way to reduce inequity is to produce at the same low level as his perceived benefits. At times the athlete will use such phrases as, "I don't feel appreciated." Using the slightly more technical language of this chapter, the athlete could say, "I don't feel equitably treated."

The need for equitable treatment, or perceived balance between contributions and benefits, occurs even in the most seemingly altruistic behaviors.[4] Assume that there are three senior citizens in a small community who do volunteer work at the library. Because of their efforts, the library can stay open two extra evenings a week. Citizens exclaim, "What unselfishness!" There *is* this aspect, but there are also benefits accruing to the senior citizens. They have an interesting activity they can look forward to. They meet large numbers of interesting people. Out of such meetings, other social activities are likely to develop. They receive the respect of others and are given a good deal of status. If the library head is a good administrator, the volunteers receive an occasional luncheon or ceremony.

Good administrators realize that there are other volunteer agencies that are happy to have senior citizen involvement: blood banks, museums, hospitals, orphanages, and so forth. Given visible appreciation for their efforts, the senior citizens experience a balance between their contributions and the benefits they receive.

All readers have experienced inequity. Most people can recall an activity in which they eagerly participated, but later cut down their involvement and perhaps ceased the activity entirely. When they explain why, one set of reasons boils down to the fact that there were not enough pleasurable outcomes to match their time, effort, and other contributions. Friendships sometimes cease to exist when an imbalance in benefits occurs. If one person always expects the other to be a shoulder to cry on, but is never around when the *other* has a problem, then inequity exists. The relationship is not likely to continue at the same level of intensity.

To preview a piece of advice for power acquisition and maintenance (see Chapter 5), people should make sure that they are behaving equitably in their relationships with others. If a person is constantly receiving benefits from others, then that person must make a point of assisting the others to achieve *their* goals. If powerful people are constantly on the giving end of relationships, they begin to feel "used" and place limits on their interactions with those who do not reciprocate.

There are many ways to benefit others. People have access to resources they can use to make sure that equity is being maintained in their relationships. Problems begin to emerge, however, when the resources are limited and when decisions have to be made about resource allocation. The many activities summarized by the label "politics" have a great deal to do with allocation of scarce resources.

TYPES OF RESOURCES

While money may come first to mind when scarce resources are discussed, there are five other broad types: status, information, services, love/ sex, and goods.[5] There often are not enough of these resources for all people wanting them. People must therefore decide how to compete for what they desire, realizing that if they win, others lose or at least do not do as well. In many societies around the world, and too often in our own, the competition takes the form of armed conflict and the planned elimination of the others. In some societies the competition is eliminated when a powerful and wealthy few monopolize key resources and let the poor fend for themselves. In democracies, people have decided that a better system involves fair and nonviolent competition according to a set of well-known rules. Although far from perfect in its actual use, the political process is the system that has evolved for such competition.[6]

Competition for *money* in the form of tax dollars is the clearest example.

Socially conscious and community-minded people would like to see various programs introduced or improved that would help the needy. The handicapped deserve better access to public buildings; the elderly deserve better health care; students from a background where English is infrequently spoken need special attention in the schools; the poor would benefit from public housing projects; and underpaid schoolteachers should receive salary increases. And don't forget current public programs, such as maintenance of roads, mass transportation, school buildings and support of the arts. The list could go on and on, and there is little doubt that in a perfect world all these projects deserve funding. But as Hamlet said, "There's the rub!" The world is imperfect, and there are limited tax dollars to pay for these programs. Citizens are unwilling to see large increases in their tax burdens; politicians are not elected if they call for large tax increases. So various spokespeople for the programs compete for the limited resource—money— in the political arena. They write proposals, form coalitions, lobby elected officials at the city and state levels, court contacts who work at the city's newspaper and television stations, communicate their messages to voters in readily understandable terms, and so forth. The various spokespeople play according to a set of rules. While not as clearly defined as in sporting events (and herein lies a problem that favors the wealthy and well-connected), the rules guide the competition for public funds.

The political process also applies to the distribution of the other five resources—status, information, service, love/sex, and goods. Many people want *status* and its accompanying perks: deference from others, attention, florid speeches in their honor, easy access to others with high status, a greater chance of obtaining a serious review of their proposals, and so forth. But high status is possible only where there are others of lower status to be deferential, to be attentive, to give the speeches, and to lose the competition for the limited time of people who might seriously review proposals.

The acceptance of status distinctions may actually be wired into our genes. People may have grouped together in our distant ancestral past to increase their chances of survival in a hostile environment. Isolated individuals could perish due to predators, foul weather, or unsuccessful attempts to find food. Faced with inevitable internal conflicts, those groups may have disbanded unless there were leaders to whom members deferred concerning such issues as the distribution of food. Individuals sensitive to status distinctions may have had a greater chance of survival and thus to pass on their genes to future generations.

Many readers may have experienced small-scale attempts to eliminate status distinctions. For instance, elementary schools sometimes encourage children to participate in a series of games and then give medals to everyone, winners and losers. Does this work? My experience is that the children lose interest and do not treat the resulting trophies or ribbons with respect.

Information is a resource, especially in today's extraordinarily complex world where no one person has sufficient information about all aspects of even one policy issue. Information becomes a resource that is exchanged, and access to information becomes part of the political process. Assume that one political action group wants to flouridate the city's water supply and that another group does not. One way to increase the chance of winning in the political arena is to have more information than the opponent on such issues as tooth decay, costs of dental care, and long-term health risks.

Services, another resource, involves the willingness of elected politicians and appointed officials to do their jobs on behalf of one side versus another. Only legislators can introduce bills: do they provide this service for the pro- or for the anti-flouridation group? Officials in the Department of Health can compile and release key information. Do they do this readily, or do the officials throw roadblocks in the way of one group? If the latter, that group may have to use other resources (especially money) to petition the courts for the information.

Love and sex are also resources that can be used in relationships involving the exchange of benefits. Historically, and in some cultures to this day, arranged marriages have been used to further political goals, to acquire access to land, and to increase the social status of an extended family system. Only naive people are unwilling to admit that sexual favors are exchanged for other resources such as money, goods, or the status brought on by easy access to powerful figures. Extremely attractive people may be courted by a number of suitors who have serious proposals of marriage. The suitors may engage in strategies similar to those of professional politicians. For instance, a suitor may enlist the help of the desired person's aunt or grandparents, having learned that the target person has long sought their advice concerning important matters.

Scarce *goods* become a resource that can be used in various deals. Land is a good example. Person A might sell land to Person B rather than Person C, even though both can pay the fair market price in cash. Person A might feel that B is more active in the business world and will be able to pass on opportunities at a later date. Automobile dealers who handle prestige cars usually have a limited number of such items as Rolls-Royces to sell. The people wanting them are competing for a scarce resource, and this may bring in considerations other than the direct exchange of money for goods. For instance, a sale to a well-known celebrity can bring status and accompanying publicity to the dealership.

Some of the benefits for which people compete are best looked on as involving combinations of the more basic resources. When unemployment is high, jobs can be considered as scarce goods. In large cities political machines have been built through the control of a significant number of patronage jobs. Jobs involve the acquisition of money, and some jobs immediately put people into high-status positions. In an "old boy network" the control of high-paying, prestigious jobs becomes a bargaining chip in long-term business and political arrangements. If Person A hires the protégé of Person B for a job desired by many, then B has to remember that fact when A's son or daughter graduates from college five years from now.

A number of resources have been grouped under services by other analysts, but in the development of power strategies it is best to give them their due and consider them separately. These include the time that people can devote to various activities and the energy that they are willing to invest.[7] The intelligent use of time and energy will be discussed in a number of places in different chapters, since the wise versus foolish use of these two resources distinguishes more from less influential people. All people have these resources, which they can invest in various ways. People may not have money or goods that can be used in exchanges, but they can decide how to spend their time and energy.

RESOURCES IN ACTION

The importance of competition for resources can be seen more clearly if the examples from the early part of Chapter 1 are reexamined. Four individuals or small groups want their decisions to be implemented, but they have to compete with others who want different decisions to be made.

1. The member of the U.S. House of Representatives introduces a bill.
2. A faculty member wants a new course introduced into the university curriculum.
3. A lawyer wants to represent two well-known defendants in a highly publicized case.
4. A couple, newly arrived in a community, wants to replace the organ in their church.

Example 1

The congresswoman is able to introduce a bill, but so are 434 of her colleagues. There are too many bills introduced during a session for serious consideration of even a fraction of them. Some bills are introduced solely to pay off campaign debts. The congresswoman can tell her constituents, "I introduced the bill and it received a first reading. So this is the first step—more attention is needed during the upcoming session." The fact that all bills receive a first reading is not mentioned. This progress report will likely be followed by a request for contributions to the upcoming reelection campaign.

If the congresswoman is serious about the bill, then she has to compete for scarce resources: the time and attention of her colleagues. She might approach the chairperson of the committee or subcommittee to which the bill will most likely be referred. At this point, the chairperson is likely to ask (a) whether the bill has merit, addresses an important issue, and should receive attention and (b) whether the congresswoman is worthy of support. Assume that the answer to the first set of questions is yes. This is no small matter, since there are far too many meritorious bills addressing important issues to be considered during a session. Attention then shifts to the second question (b). The chairperson will ask whether the congresswoman has helped others get their bills passed, whether she has been of service to the party, whether she has formed a coalition of powerful colleagues, whether there might be a future reciprocal action that might help the chairperson, and so forth. The longer the congresswoman has held her seat, the more time she will have had to distribute her resources and accrue the gratitude of others. At some point she can try to call upon this gratitude so that her bill will receive serious consideration.

Example 2

The faculty member is competing with the problem of numbers. Many professors would like to introduce new courses, since such action allows them to teach material in which they have a special interest. But a university can only list so many courses in its catalogue. If there are too many courses there will be too few students for each and the entire system will become financially unfeasible. Untenured professors like to introduce potentially popular courses, such as human sexuality, since they attract large enrollments. Data on enrollments, and corresponding ratings of course popularity, can be used in their negotiations for tenure. Given the widespread desire to offer new courses, the question becomes, "Which of many possibilities will be approved?" Certainly merit plays a part. Other considerations are whether or not the new offering overlaps too much with courses already listed in the catalogue. Is there overlap with courses offered by influential professors who have staked out certain study areas as their "territory?" Is the professor who proposes the course one whom the university wants to keep, or would the administrators be happy if the person went elsewhere? Does the professor have other resources besides teaching skills? At many universities, the most powerful professors are those who can bring in external funds in the form of contracts and grants.[8] Money brought in from outside the university includes an amount called "overhead," and universities have some discretion over how this money can be used. Universities always complain of skimpy budgets, and so professors who bring in money to the school are of great use. The professors exchange this usefulness for favorable consideration of their proposals.

Example 3

The well-known defendants, who face charges of murdering a man on behalf of an abused female relative, are looking for an aggressive lawyer who can examine all aspects of a case so as to be better prepared than the prosecuting attorney. The lawyer should also be able to swing jury members with arguments and tactics that reach both their minds and their hearts. For these services, the defendants are willing to pay a great deal to the lawyer.

The defendants might also look for a lawyer who is skillful in working with the media. But media space, especially television time and front-page newspaper coverage, is a scarce commodity, and many people want it for their causes. If the defense lawyer can work effectively with the media, the defendants will be portrayed in a favorable light prior to the trial. This might have an impact on those who will eventually be selected for the jury.

The lawyer for the defendants will also be interested in the media because the publicity generated by the trial will create or improve name recognition. Given the frequent use of the lawyer's name in the media and in people's conversations, new business for the future is likely to be generated. The defense lawyer will also benefit from portraying the defendants in as sympathetic a manner as possible, as the champions of an abused woman rather than as murderers. The lawyer's name will become associated with humane causes, and this fact will also contribute to the acquisition of future cases.

The media also benefit from distribution of resources purposely made scarce by the skilled lawyers, such as exclusive interviews, interesting angles not considered by reporters, and especially, intriguing "leaks" given to one TV show or newspaper but not to their competition.

Example 4

A common expectation older and established church members have of a newly arrived couple is that the new arrivals will contribute to *ongoing* activities for a significant period of time. Only then do they have the right to propose changes. The unstated rule, then, is that significant amounts of service can be exchanged for serious consideration of a new idea.

Another scarce resource comes into play when the new couple wants to replace the old pump organ. The status of certain well-established members may be threatened. Who donated the old organ in the first place? How will they respond to their contribution being replaced? The organists who are able to play the old organ, using tricks learned over a period of years that allow the coaxing of near-acceptable sounds, may be threatened if the new organ can be played easily by large numbers of people.

In addition, any proposal from newcomers can be an implied insult to the old order. The insult is that the established church board is not sensitive or intelligent enough to see the need for a new organ.

Finally, the new couple may be threatening symbolic aspects of the church. People become accustomed to the sound of a certain organ played over a long period of time, even though outside experts might diagnose major problems with its reeds. The church hymns played on the old organ become *the* way the tunes should be heard, just as the King James version of the Bible sounds more "Biblical" than the modern translations.[9] Further, the old organ may bring back memories of seemingly happier days, when the elders were children and attended church with their parents.

Good advice for newcomers is to be quiet for at least a year, to give service to the church, and to figure out the written and unwritten guidelines for introducing new proposals. They may find, for instance, that it is better to plant the idea in the heads of two or three respected elders and let them introduce the change to the entire congregation.

POWER AS PART OF PERSONALITY

In all four examples, people wanting to become more influential need to identify who is powerful. Power involves relationships among a number of people, and is not the prerogative of one individual to ride roughshod over others without regard for consequences. The questions to be asked include:

Who can make decisions and make them stick?

Who can say "Yes, it will be done," with assurances that the decision will be implemented by others?

Will the others rebel, given that the powerholder has not taken their needs into account?

In identifying and interacting with powerful people, it is important to understand as much as possible about their psychological make-up.

The need for power is greater in some people than in others. For the former, power is an internal drive state that directs action. That is, the people have a deep-seated drive to be powerful ("fire in their belly," as politicians say), and this drive strongly influences their behavior. If the power need is not satisfied, then they are unhappy, frustrated, and often angry. Powerful people, then, seek out opportunities to exercise a major aspect of their personalities.

For example, a colleague of mine in academia, retired and comfortable with a handsome pension, once accepted the presidency of a small college faced with major budgetary problems. He had previously been vice president of a large university. I asked one of the people interviewed for this book about our mutual acquaintance. "Why would this person want the headaches of that financially troubled outfit?" The response was, "I guess he wanted to run something." That short phrase speaks volumes about the power need of some people.

The concept of drive is best explained by examining other, more everyday examples. Hunger and thirst are drives. They are internal states that direct behavior, in this case the acquisition of food or water. If those needs are not quickly satisfied, the people are unhappy, uncomfortable, and frustrated. Sex is another drive. People want to satisfy their internal needs through certain behaviors, and they are uncomfortable if they cannot engage in those behaviors. After satisfying their needs through food, water, or sexual release, people no longer feel the drive state for a certain period of time. People who crave satisfaction of their drive states within a short period of time, for instance dieters keeping their caloric intake down or runners participating in a race on a hot day, are said to have strong needs.

The three drives considered here—hunger, thirst, and sex—are physiological in origin, since they involve specific and known parts of the body (e.g., stomach, gonads). Power is psychological, since it involves behavior guided by the brain without cravings signaled by other parts of the body. In addition to power, the other psychological needs to be considered here are the desire to affiliate with others and the desire to achieve goals set by oneself. While the role of biological factors in psychological needs is currently an ardently debated topic, for the present a safe conclusion is that experiences during childhood, adolescence, and early adulthood play an important role in the need for power, affiliation, and achievement. While we cannot do much about any biological influence, we can have an impact on the experiences that affect these needs. The term "motives" is sometimes used to distinguish psychological drives from the basic physiological needs. [10] The similarity is that both physiological needs and psychological motives direct behavior. The need for power leads to behaviors that involve control over others. The need for achievement leads to behaviors that involve work toward challenging goals. The need for affiliation leads to behaviors that involve warm interactions with others and the desire to be liked by others. Different people have varying patterns of high and low motives for power, affiliation, and achievement, and they are frustrated when a strong motive is not satisfied.

Reading Others

Power, achievement, and affiliation combine in important ways, and so each will be discussed in more detail. As they are described, you will probably recognize people you know who have one or more of the motives. While a detailed treatment of the measurement of motives[11] is beyond the scope of this book, a few guidelines useful in everyday life can be presented. Motives are most clearly seen when people have no pressure to respond (or not to respond) in a certain way. Recall the example of the solemn funeral from Chapter 1. If a person is affiliative, this fact would be hard to determine at the funeral. The affiliation motive is most clearly seen when the person has a choice of how to behave and chooses affiliative behaviors over others. Similarly, at final exam time, almost all students appear achievement oriented and hard working. The college's libraries suddenly become full of would-be scholars. But given the obvious external pressure to behave in a certain way, conclusions about the achievement motive would be unwise. A better time to see the achievement motive in action would be early in the semester, when students behave in a variety of ways because there are no immediate pressures brought on by important tests.

When people are said to be able to "read" others, I believe that they are sensitive to the presence or absence of situational pressures. Good readers of personalities pick up clues to "how the others tick" by observing what they say and do (and how they seem to think) when there are limited constraints on them. Making inferences about others two days before a budget deadline may be unwise, because last-minute pressures direct certain behaviors. A better time to infer motives is during calm periods, when people have a good deal of choice concerning what they say and how they behave. To make this discussion more complex, good readers of personality become aware of the other person's behavior during calm periods and later observe how it changes during crisis periods. Changes from the calm-period baseline brought on by crisis are also diagnostic of people's personalities.

Indicators of the Power Motive

A number of behaviors and verbal expressions should be looked for when making inferences about another person's power motive.[12] Power includes the need to be in charge, to direct others, and to be the boss. Power is associated with a fondness for clear, forceful, dominant actions that impress others. Power also includes the desire to be looked up to by others; to be given the respect, status, and deference associated with rank; and to be in the company of high-status people. Powerful people want to be in control and to have other people implement their desires. They also think of the world in terms of power and power relations (recall the discussion in the section on allowing active thoughts in Chapter 1), and want to take a high-status place within the power structure. They surround themselves with the trappings of status and prestige, such as the most sought-after version of the American Express credit card, handsome offices with expensive furnishings and a nice view, and the currently fashionable style of dress.

Interestingly, not all commonsense predictions about power are accurate. For instance, while owning the most prestigious and expensive car possible might be consistent with the ideas presented so far, David Winter found that powerful people preferred a different type of automobile.[13] People with a high need for power preferred the cars that were the most maneuverable and handled the most responsively, that is, they preferred to emphasize the control aspect of power. Winter also found that college-age people with a high power motive tended to choose friends who were not the most popular or best known on campus. Again, control seems to be the key. The powerful people wanted to associate with others who would do their bidding and who would not compete for status or prestige.

Consideration must be given to the way motives fit into people's relationships to their organizations. Again, motives are most clearly seen when people have free choice among activities. In an accounting firm, for instance, people with a high power need would be more likely to attend a reception for the board of directors than to listen to a friend's problems (affiliation) or attend a lecture so that they might master the new tax laws (achievement).

Indicators of the Achievement Motive

People with a strong achievement motive set goals for themselves and work hard toward attaining the goals.[14] They are able to keep the final goals in mind while structuring various tasks along the way to final goal attainment. The visible signs of goal attainment, such as wealth after starting a successful business, are valued more for their message of "I've succeeded" than as the vehicle for obtaining life's luxuries. The goals are realistic and moderate in difficulty, involving risk. If people set their sights too low and take no risks by working only toward easy goals, then they will have a trivial success and are not demonstrating an achievement orientation. If they set goals for themselves that are impossibly difficult, they will surely fail and again are not demonstrating a motive to achieve. In fact, setting impossible goals provides an excuse for people who are not motivated to achieve. They can say, "I tried, but after all everyone knows that the goal was impossible to attain." Such people may be responding to societal expectations that they work hard and achieve. But reacting to the expectations of others is not reflective of achievement orientation.

Motivation refers to an internal drive, deeply felt by people who want to satisfy the motive and who become displeased when their efforts fail. Achievement-oriented people have been exposed to societal expectations, but they have *internalized* the expectations and are not just responding to societal pressures. The way they satisfy their motives, in their judgment of themselves, is to obtain the goals they set out to accomplish.

The satisfaction, however, can be short-lived, and achievement-oriented people have to keep setting new goals and working toward them. One interesting fact about achievement motivation helps answer a frequently heard question. "Why do some entrepreneurs keep working after they have obtained millionaire status? They have plenty of money to live comfortably." The key, again, is inner drive. The motive of achievement is not satisfied by a comfortable life. It is only satisfied by the combination of goal setting and attainment. People with a need to achieve do not sit on their laurels. They keep working, using visible trappings of success such as money and the admiration of others as signs that they are accomplishing their goals.

Goals, of course, are different according to the social settings and occupations in which people find themselves. Achievement-oriented students work for good grades not so much for their social recognition function (the honor roll) but rather as a sign that they are progressing well in their studies. Businessmen establish new companies; politicians work their bills through committees, through the full legislature, and through the executive branch; scientists and inventors discover new facts and obtain patents; writers spend time and energy on their manuscripts and then see to it that their works are published; salespeople set goals for their yearly volume and work toward meeting them.

Culture plays a part in the way the achievement motive is expressed. In societies that stress individualism, such as the United States, the achievement motive is seen in the actions of a single person working toward self-selected goals. In societies stressing collectivism, people feel deeply attached to a group.[15] Their sense of personal identity is much more closely linked to others (e.g., family, community) than it is in individualist societies. In collective societies, people can satisfy their achievement motives by accepting the goals that a group sets and by working with others toward successful attainment. Harry Triandis believes that one reason for Japan's stunning economic success since World War II is that group loyalties have shifted from the extended family or the community to work groups in organizations.[16] The need of Japanese people for loyalty, respect, and acceptance by others, all of which used to be satisfied through membership in an extended family, are now satisfied through work-group membership. The organization takes advantage of these, plus other values that have long been part of Japanese culture: hard work, thrift, and obligation. Combining all of these cultural values, the path to respect and acceptance has become achievement within a work group. When a Japanese group succeeds, all its members glow in the satisfaction of achievement and respect that has been brought on by their hard work.

Understanding cultural differences can lead to insights into why borrowings from other cultures sometimes fail. The Japanese management style,[17] involving such elements as the use of quality circles, has been tried in the United States. But the United States does not have as strong a tradition of group loyalty in the organization or a tradition of advancement by working toward task accomplishment with others. In the United States people frequently leave one organization to obtain better opportunities in another. Promotions are based on an individual's contributions; yearly fitness ratings are filled out with individuals as targets, not work groups. In fact, when groups are successful in producing products, executives complain that they cannot decide how much each individual contributed. Consequently, some of the individuals may be undercredited with accomplishments when the executives fill out yearly evaluations. Individuals are often confused when they have a suggestion that might help a coworker. Suggestions are as likely to be received with a verbal or nonverbal response of "mind your own business" as with gratitude. Other motives and abilities must be added to any analysis of group productivity in individualist societies, and the need for affiliation is one.

Indicators of the Affiliation Motive

People with a high need for affiliation enjoy the company of others.[18] They have close relations with large numbers of people; they spend large amounts of time in the company of others; they want to be liked by many others; and they are able to point out good points in seemingly abrasive and socially unskilled acquaintances. Affiliative people are willing to listen to others' problems and to help out in times of need. Some affiliative people actively seek out opportunities to help, and they would be insulted if friends did not call upon them during times of difficulty. They enjoy going to parties and interacting with others whom they have just met. If the party has attracted many high-status people, affiliation-oriented individuals enjoy interacting with the less lofty as much as they do with the elite. They are sensitive to the needs of others and try to take the feelings of their friends, colleagues, and acquaintances into account during interactions with them. If negative feedback has to be given, they try to soften their message by surrounding it with as much positive content as possible.

Impulse Control

A fourth aspect of personality has to be added to the analysis of power, achievement, and affiliation. Impulse control[19] refers to the ability to keep one's needs from rising to overt, visible behavior. In everyday language, impulse control refers to the ability to say no to oneself. If power-oriented bosses want to shout at their secretaries, they may purposely control themselves and soften their message. They behave in this way because they have learned that, in the long run, shouting at secretaries yields far fewer benefits than working cooperatively with them. But they *wanted* to shout! They didn't because of their impulse control. Another common way of referring to the bosses is that they are "in control" or have a great deal of "self-control." Many power-oriented people realize that they can be perceived as tyrants unless they keep their motive "under wraps" and call upon it selectively.

As another example, consider politicians who desire to be reelected. They might enjoy the power that their office gives: directing a large staff, keeping company with other high-status pecple, and receiving deference from others. To win reelection, they may decide that they should demonstrate some solid accomplishments. They may downplay or control their power need at such a time, to emphasize the more achievement-oriented aspects of themselves or their staffs. If the goal is an important policy decision, such as funding significant and noticeable improvements in public transportation, the achievement motivation has to be brought into the total set of needs, skills, and behaviors necessary for success.

In addition to power-oriented people who can control their motive so as to better interact with people so that positive long-term relationships are maintained, at times people with the other needs will also find impulse control useful. Highly achievement-oriented people may want to "talk shop" at parties with like-minded others who are starting businesses or doing scientific research. This may irritate guests who look upon the party as more of a social activity. To maintain good relations with these others, the achievement-oriented people may control their motives and make a point of engaging in pleasant small talk. People with a high need for affiliation must also control their motive if they are to hold down a job. If they express their needs all day by interacting pleasantly with people, they are likely to accomplish little and may consequently find themselves unemployed. Many college students would prefer to be in the company of others during much of the day. But there are times when they must sequester themselves in a room to study for tests, write term papers, or complete their individual study projects.

DIFFERENTIATING PEOPLE

Another way you can analyze the four aspects of personality is to think about people with whom you are familiar. Consider the following four questions. In answering each of them, write down the names of three people who come to mind. The same people can be listed as responses to more than one of the questions.

1. You are planning a party that is meant to be a pleasant social occasion. Whom would you invite?

2. You want to see a major shift in priorities within your organization. You want to propose the shift, but the formal proposal will take the efforts of several people over a long period of time. They will have to gather information, formulate precise plans, and present the plans in written form. Whom would you ask to assist you in these efforts?

3. Given the completed write-up of the same proposal, who would you talk to about actually accepting the proposal and implementing the plans?

4. You have a controversial proposal concerned with rezoning residential land (single-family homes) so that commercial high-rise buildings can be erected. There is to be a meeting where community members will surely criticize the proposal in a loud, intense manner. Whom would you ask to present the proposal to the interested citizens?

Chances are you have listed different names in response to the four questions, even though the instructions included the possibility of duplications. The people named in response to Question 1 are likely to be pleasant, socially skillful individuals who are fun to be with. Question 2 elicits the names of hard-working people who are willing to put in long hours to complete their tasks. The people listed in response to Question 3 are likely to be authority figures who can say "yes" to a proposal—or they will know the best ways to approach and persuade the relevant authorities. Question 4 elicits the names of people able to hold their emotions in check. Any proposal to build high-rise buildings in a residential area is sure to attract bitter attacks on the speaker who defends the plans. People able to control their desire to respond in a similarly abrasive manner will increase the chances of the proposal's eventual adoption. (There will be a longer discussion of imperturbable responses to bitter attacks in Chapter 3.)

Different people have different motives, abilities, and skills, and the others with whom the people interact frequently are aware of this. As I am sure you will surmise, the four questions are aimed at identifying people with the needs for affiliation, achievement, and power, and the skill of impulse control, respectively.

The Four Factors in Combination

Few people are extremely high on one of the four factors and very low on the others. If they were, many opportunities would be denied to them that *could* be offered by friends and colleagues. People very high in power-need but low on the other factors are ruthless tyrants who want to be in charge, or to be the boss. But with no achievement drive, they have no goal that a power need might serve. Mercifully, I have known only one such individual. He wanted to be the boss, the chair of every committee, and the person who could say "no" to every proposal. It did not matter what the content under consideration dealt with; he just wanted to control everything that happened in the organization. Since he had no affiliation motive, he did not care how many people disliked him. Eventually, he created so much resentment that he was asked to leave the organization without a good set of recommendation letters to accompany him.

Achievement-oriented individuals without any of the other factors can be single-minded drones with few friends. A more subtle problem is that since they have no power drive, they will not have the connections, resources, or communication skills to follow up on their completed goals. For instance, they might develop a superb plan for a new business. Other factors besides an achievement drive would be necessary to attract investors, hire staff, and delegate responsibilities. Single-minded achievers clearly need others to fill in for their inabilities. One reason for industrial and scientific progress in the United States, I believe, is the tolerance U.S. society has for individuals who are driven toward a self-selected goal but who are nonconforming, neurotic, temperamental, and socially unskilled. Other individuals are willing to work with the achievers to see that their needs are met.

A moderate affiliation need can take the edge off the negative consequences associated with a very high achievement orientation or a very high power drive. High achievers become more interesting people, since they learn that they must have more than one topic of conversation to interact well with others. People with a high power need become more aware that their actions can have negative impacts on others, and they learn to care about this. Ruthlessness can be decreased when people are concerned about their impact on the targets of their power.

Leadership in Large Organizations

A unique combination of the four factors under consideration has been identified as contributing to the success of leaders in senior management positions.[20] Some of these ideas may be useful in the analysis of other types of leadership (e.g., a senior scientist working in a laboratory with younger colleagues), but the main focus here is management in large organizations. The leadership pattern consists of average-to-high power need, and this need should be stronger than the affiliation motive. There should be *some* affiliation motive, however, so that the leaders do not become tyrants who are intoxicated with their power. The leaders' impulse control should also be high, so that emotions are kept in check. The achievement drive should be high enough so that the leaders will have reasonable goals, but not so high that it dominates their lives. Senior managers do not work by themselves to achieve individually set goals. Rather, they work with others to see that (a) the individual goals of their achievement-oriented subordinates are met and (b) these individual goals combine well to meet the overall policy direction of the organization. The overall policy usually includes growth.[21]

Another way of describing successful leaders in large organizations is that they are interested in directing and influencing others. Further, the direction is set by the leaders (high power need). This need has to be higher than their affiliation desire, since they will often have to make decisions that cause them to be disliked for a period of time. However, they must have a good deal of impulse control so they do not abuse their power or make poor decisions during times of stress. They must be able to control their emotions, either putting them aside or waiting for a calmer future during which more rational deliberations can take place. They cannot be overconcerned with their individual achievement drive. The job of successful leaders in senior management positions is not to satisfy their individual needs to achieve. Rather, their job is to control, influence, and work with others so that broad organizational goals are attained. One way to influence others is to assist subordinates in achieving their more individually oriented goals. The senior manager's achievement, then, is of a different kind than those discussed earlier in this chapter in the section on achievement motive indicators. Instead of setting one's own goals and working toward their attainment, the successful leader sets broader goals (some of them dictated by even higher levels of management) and sees to it that many people work toward their realization.

High achievers often must change or adapt if they are to be successful leaders. One reason for the phenomenon described by the well-known Peter Principle[22] is that the skills that bring recognition and promotion to a person are often not the skills necessary for success in a higher-level job. A person may have been led by his or her achievement drive to earn four patents. This person may then be put in charge of a large organization's research and development department, where the achievement need plays less of a part in success. For the new position a power need and corresponding skills of influencing and directing *others* to discover new facts and obtain patents are more important.

WAS LORD ACTON CORRECT?

While a greater concern with power is necessary if people are to assume senior management positions, there is also a dark side to power acquisition. Like fire, power can be used for beneficial or evil purposes.[23] Fire can be used constructively (heat, cooking, energy) and it can be used destructively (arson, death). Similarly, power can be used to benefit individuals if leaders use their influence justly and wisely, and if they assist others in meeting their goals. Or it can be used for evil purposes when powerful people become more interested in benefiting themselves than benefiting others.

One of the most frequently cited quotations dealing with power is from Lord Acton: "Power tends to corrupt, and absolute power corrupts absolutely." Many writers have observed with grave concern that people with power become so fascinated with its use and effects that they desire even more. Further, powerful people become defective in judgment and use power unwisely and in ways that purposely harm others. Edmund Burke wrote in 1791 that "Those who have been once intoxicated with power, and have derived any kind of emolument from it, even though but for one year, can never willingly abandon it."[24]

Recent research in the behavioral sciences has indicated that Acton and Burke were extraordinarily insightful. David Kipnis has carried out studies in which people were brought together, one given power, and the others given the roles of subordinates or followers.[25] The purpose of the research was to discover if people given power changed their attitudes and behaviors compared to the subordinates. As when analyzing many research studies into human behavior, you may want to think about people you have known who have been thrust into powerful positions.

The findings of Kipnis's research focus on the ways in which power has metamorphic effects. While not everybody who was given power behaved in the same way, the changes were frequent enough to be considered dangerous possibilities of power acquisition. People become fascinated with power and want more. In everyday language, power goes to their heads. The word "intoxication" has been used by many analysts other than Burke. The use of power becomes pleasurable, and people seek out opportunities to obtain even more power and pleasure. I am sure that physiologists will one day discover areas of the brain, and corresponding brain chemicals, that are stimulated by the wielding of power so that intense pleasure is felt. The acquisition of power and the pleasure it gives become ends in themselves, unattached to such worthwhile goals as improved policy, a more humane workplace, or a more efficiently run organization. Great amounts of time and energy are then invested in power acquisition so that the person has more and more control, influence, and corresponding pleasure. The same time and energy become unavailable for other activities in life, such as love, achievement, ethical concerns, or education.

From the intoxication due to power, and from the fact that other activities become less important, people's judgments become cloudy. They become tempted to use power for their own benefit, and the resulting actions are often illegal or enter very gray areas of the law or of the commonly accepted ethical standards. The self-benefit is not necessarily monetary; powerholders do not always line their pockets. A common use of power is to hurt one's enemies. For example, tax laws or accounting standards are sometimes used as bludgeons by powerholders. Tax laws are so obscure and complex that anyone making over $100,000 a year has to make decisions about income taxes that may be challenged. Powerholders can use their influence to direct the attention of a city or state department of taxation to a certain person. Similarly, the accounting standards for what can and cannot be reimbursed after a trip for one's organization are not crystal clear. High-level managers can make life very difficult for subordinates by directing the accounting office to examine a certain person's claims. Even if these challenges are unsound, the targets have to use their resources in mounting a defense and may encounter a good deal of stress. The power wielders do not think of themselves as unfair or corrupt when they direct the tax officials or the accountants to their enemies. Either they do not think very much about their actions because of the cloudy judgment caused by power, or they justify their actions as necessary steps in the quest toward a greater good.

Given their ability to punish others, powerholders do not receive good feedback from others concerning how their leadership might be more effective or how their organization might have a greater chance of prospering. There is often no shortage of followers who cater to the powerholders through flattery and through the provision of only positive feedback. Speaking about the people surrounding his brother, Billy Carter commented about the way many subordinates are willing to kiss up to a powerholder. (Billy Carter's way of expressing this insight was somewhat more earthy than the version presented here.) Followers learn that there are more punishments than rewards for bringing negative information to the attention of powerful people and that it is frequently best to keep constructive criticism to themselves. Powerholders do not enjoy receiving negative information, since suggestions for improvement can interfere with their pleasurable intoxication. Since they receive no negative information, they come to believe that there are no problems within themselves or within their organizations. This leads to an unrealistic view of themselves and of their work, and it makes them susceptible to mistakes, such as inadequate attention to important departments within an organization.

A number of organizations produce and market similar products, such as television sets or automobiles. The unrealistic view powerholders develop can lead to shortsightedness on the part of the heads of these organizations, which benefits the organization's competition. These powerholders do not receive the constructive criticism that would enable them to maintain competitiveness in key areas, such as analysis of changing consumer tastes, quality control, and marketing.

On a personal level, the lack of negative feedback has the additional effect of creating an exalted sense of self-worth. Since there is nothing in their immediate environment to suggest otherwise, these powerholders come to believe that they deserve their absence of negative information. Because of their exalted view of themselves, and the lack of constructive feedback, the powerholders begin to think of themselves as better than others. Combined with the fact that they have power over their subordinates, this exaggerated self-esteem begins to lead the powerholders to think less of their followers. They avoid social contacts with subordinates, preferring to keep company with those who have similar amounts of power, status, or prestige.

Their subordinates are faced with a paradox. They are apt to cater to the wishes and preferences of the powerholders so as to be well liked, to keep their jobs, and to avoid wrath from above. But in doing so they lose the powerholders' respect.

The problematic dynamics of the powerholder-subordinate relationship extends to work generated within an organization. Powerholders begin to take credit for the accomplishments of their followers. They conclude that it is their policy decisions, rather than the work of their subordinates, that has led to success. For instance, if the sales figures in a manufacturing organization are high, the powerholder gives less credit to the salespeople than they deserve, because the powerholders have come to believe that it is their efforts in motivating the salespeople, or making final decisions about the division of sales territories, that yielded the profits.

At times such credit-taking becomes part of accepted public displays of power. Many workers must put in tremendous efforts to insure that a forthcoming joint venture involving two large companies is successful. When the venture is announced, the company executives are likely to step in to receive accolades from the media and the public. Given the cloudy judgment caused by power, the executives are likely to take more credit than they deserve and to devalue the efforts of the many workers who made the venture possible.

Kipnis's research findings can be summarized as the eight potential cumulative metamorphic effects on a holder of power:

1. The use of power is pleasurable and intoxicating.
2. The powerholder puts efforts into achieving more power.
3. The judgment of the powerful person becomes cloudy due to a preoccupation with gaining influence and control.
4. The powerholder uses the resources for self-benefit.
5. Negative feedback is no longer available from subordinates and instead the powerholder is the beneficiary of flattery.
6. The powerholder develops a lofty view of his or her own self-worth.
7. The worth of subordinates is devalued by the powerholder.
8. The powerholder takes too much credit for the accomplishments of subordinates.

The word "potential" is important, and it introduces a distinction between powerholders and leaders. Good leaders realize these potential drawbacks of power and make efforts to keep them in check. For instance, a frequently recommended step in procedures for making important decisions is to assign people to bring negative information into the deliberations.[26] This can be done by asking people to role-play opponents with opposing viewpoints, to develop worst-case scenarios of proposed policies, to make a point of disagreeing with every suggestion, or to play the role of devil's advocate. The purpose of all of these techniques is to bring out information that might be overlooked, given the tendency of subordinates to flatter powerholders rather than to give them constructive criticism. More will be said about dealing effectively with these potential ill effects of power in Chapters 3 and 5.

Organizations sometimes deal with these metamorphic effects by bringing people up through the executive ranks carefully and slowly. Over a number of years, the future executives are given a variety of responsibilities, each involving a little more power than the last. Under this policy, they learn to deal with the intoxicating effects of power by becoming accustomed to it in slow steps. They learn to deal with their power intelligently and humanely rather than in a headstrong or ruthless manner. One of the many explanations for the excesses of the Nixon administration, such as the Watergate Scandal and the creation of an enemies list, is that the key figures in the White House were thrust far too quickly into extremely powerful positions. None of the now-familiar litany of people involved—Haldeman, Erlichman, Magruder, Colson, and Dean—had held a position of power prior to their assignments in the White House. They had not learned to deal with the consequences of power well enough to work effectively according to a rational view of themselves and their country.

DEALING WITH DISTASTEFULNESS

People who feel that they are at a disadvantage because of ignorance concerning power and power skills often take steps to sophisticate themselves. They may join a political party, make a point of meeting high-level executives, or do volunteer work for agencies known to attract the attention of powerful people. In fact, many of the 102 successful individuals with whom I spoke recommended that such steps be taken. But after spending time where it is wielded, people often find that the use of power is distasteful to them. They observe the exalted sense of self-worth powerholders have, as well as the other metamorphic effects, and conclude that the powerful are repugnant. They observe the constant exchange of resources and conclude that the ongoing emphasis on "What's in it for me?" is irritating. They observe people expressing their power needs at the expense of others who would rather put their time and energy into achievement or affiliation. They see the others making compromises, and they take this as a sign that integrity and commitment are watered down when power is involved.

All of these observations are accurate in some settings and with some powerholders. The key to understanding the use of power is that it takes place in an imperfect world. The ego of powerholders plays a part; people must make compromises if any progress is to be made in solving problems; if there are winners, then there are also losers. All of these observations cause emotional reactions, and many people conclude that they would be better off avoiding the acquisition of power and decide to seek happiness in other ways.

The reason for this distaste may be clearest in the case of state and national politics, although similar analyses could be made for other arenas where power is prominent. In their book *All About Politics*, Paul Theis and William Steponkus present a great deal of information about how the U.S. government works in this real rather than ideal world. In discussing politics as "the art of the possible," they write that:

the term means compromising not on what must be done but on what can be done. . . . Basically, the practical politician is a realist rather than a pure idealist, who works towards an objective, accepting conditions as they exist and people for what they are rather than for what he thinks they ought to be. He is prepared to take half a loaf when he knows that a whole loaf is unattainable. That is the essence of politics.[27]

Idealists have visions about what *must* be, such as their view of what their organizations should do. They find it distasteful to compromise with *other* idealists who have equally intense but different views. Part of the quotation refers to "accepting conditions as they exist." Again, this is not an easy matter for people with high ideals, who feel that a far better world would exist if everyone behaved as the idealists feel they should.

Theis and Steponkus also discuss the issue of favoritism in national politics. While arguing that favoritism plays less of a role than it did in the past, they identify a recurrent problem when giving an example of presidential appointments: "The newly appointed ambassador not only must have adequate credentials for the job, he must be able to pass close Senate scrutiny prior to confirmation."[28] Note that they did not indicate excellent credentials. Adequate credentials seem acceptable, given that the ambassador may have been chosen because of past service to a political party. Again, this is unsavory to many observers, but it is part of the use of power as it exists in the real world.

Successful powerholders, I believe, have accepted the realities under discussion here. When faced with political reality, they do not become emotionally upset but instead go about their work. They do the best they can in an imperfect world filled with munificent egos, deals cut in private that affect many not present, and political payoffs for past favors rendered. Perhaps an analogy will help describe the role that emotional reactions play in the use of power. All of us have taken tests in school that made us highly anxious, and other tests that did not cause an intense reaction.[29] The differing reactions can be depicted on a graph. (See Figure 1.) Moving left to right, consider points A, B, and C. At Point A people have absolutely no anxiety, but there is the danger that they will not take the test seriously and will not score highly (low performance). At Point C, they are so anxious

Figure 1
People's Anxiety and Their Performance on Tests

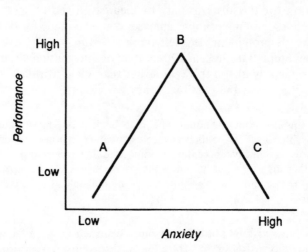

that they can hardly think, also leading to poor performance. At Point B, however, people are aroused enough to take the test seriously and to prepare for it, but not so anxious as to be debilitated.

The amount of participation in decision making where there are components can be analyzed in a similar way. Keep in mind that as discussed in the section on types of resources earlier in this chapter, politics comes into play when there is to be distribution of scarce resources, and so political aspects can be found in the decisions made by people in all sorts of organizations. In this case, the axes of the graph are involvement in decision making and people's perception of the number of political considerations in the decision-making process. (See Figure 2.) At Point A people see no political consideration, but one reason may be that they are apathetic. If this is true, they will be happy to have others make their decisions for them and to be told what to do. At Point C, people may perceive so much political involvement that they feel the substance and merit of their own proposals is downplayed. They find the politics distasteful and withdraw from further involvement. At Point B, people perceive moderate political content, but because they have a power need, political skills, and an interest in the decision to be made, they remain in the negotiations and become highly involved. Further, since they have the appropriate needs and skills, they will ask questions like, "How can I take advantage of the obvious political nature of this decision so that my side wins?" An important point is that in an *objective* analysis of the political content, all the people would discover the same amount. But because of their individual differences, at Point A people are apathetic, at Point C they are disgusted, and at Point B they are eager to proceed.

Figure 2
People's Involvement in Politically Loaded Decisions

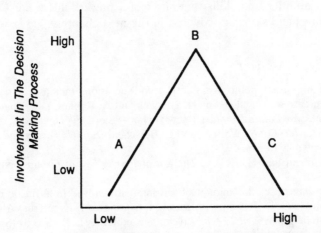

Percieved Political Considerations In Decisions

The differing reactions of people to the political aspects of decisions can be compared to the work of lawyers. Because both commercial and public television have presented information about what lawyers actually do, people have become more aware of the work of lawyers and have been able to gauge their own emotional reactions toward that work. If Person A is suing Person B, lawyers must be able to argue for both sides. If they only take cases for the sides with which they strongly agree, they may not be able to stay in business. Lawyers must defend clients they know to be guilty. If they do not give as vigorous a defense as possible, they can be chastised by the judge. Lawyers must engage in very unpleasant, sometimes bitter cross-examinations to bring out facts that witnesses would prefer not to make public. Their abrasive behaviors in the courtroom would be unacceptable in any other part of polite society. But they learn not to take vigorous exchanges with opposing counsel personally. They can engage in the most brittle exchanges with another lawyer between 9 A.M. and 5 P.M. and then have a pleasant social encounter with that same lawyer in the evening. Many observers find these behaviors loathsome. Some of my best undergraduate students have been accepted by good law schools and then dropped out because they could not accept the fact that they would be expected to engage in these behaviors. Lawyers learn to look upon themselves as playing a part in a complex system in which the goals are to uphold the law and to protect people's rights. But not all people can play such roles.

Similarly, many people will not want to play a role when decisions that might affect them have a political component that involves the power needs of others. Those who find use of power and involvement in political considerations acceptable, challenging, interesting, or exciting should be aware of certain abilities and skills that successful powerholders must possess. Such abilities and skills are covered in the next chapter.

NOTES

1. The important point that political considerations increase as desired resources decrease was discussed by H. Lasswell and A. Kaplan, *Power and Society: a Framework for Political Inquiry* (New Haven: Yale University Press, 1950).

2. E. Walster, G. W. Walster, and E. Berscheid, *Equity: Theory and Research* (Boston: Allyn & Bacon, 1978).

3. J. Thibaut and H. Kelley, *The Social Psychology of Groups* (New York: Wiley, 1959).

4. A discussion of the amount of self-interest involved in altruistic behaviors can be found in C. D. Batson, "Prosocial Motivation: Is It Ever Truly Altruistic?" in *Advances in Experimental Social Psychology*, edited by L. Berkowitz (San Diego, CA: Academic Press, 1987), vol. 20, pp. 65–122.

5. U. Foa, "Interpersonal and Economic Resources," *Science* 171 (1971): 345–51.

6. B. Crick, *In Defence of Politics*, 2nd ed. (Middlesex, England, and New York: Penguin, 1982).

7. The necessity of considering people's time and energy is frequently mentioned by H. Mintzberg in *Power in and around Organizations* (Englewood Cliffs, N.J.: Prentice-Hall, 1983).

8. G. Salancik and J. Pfeffer, "The Bases for Use of Power in Organizational Decision Making: The Case of a University," *Administrative Science Quarterly* 19 (1974): 453–73.

9. E. Nida and C. Taber, *The Theory and Practice of Translation* (Leiden: Brill, 1969).

10. J. Atkinson, ed. *Motives in Fantasy, Action, and Society* (Princeton, N.J.: Van Nostrand, 1958).

11. A good introduction to the measurement of motives can be found in D. McClelland, "Motive Dispositions: the Merits of Operant and Respondent Measures," in *Review of Personality and Social Psychology*, edited by L. Wheeler (Beverly Hills, Calif. Sage, 1980), pp. 10–40.

12. D McClelland, *Power: The Inner Experience* (New York: Irvington, 1975).

13. D. Winter, *The Power Motive* (New York: Macmillan, 1973).

14. D. McClelland and D. Winter, *Motivating Economic Achievement* (New York: Macmillan, 1969).

15. C. H. Hui and H. Triandis, "Individualism-Collectivism: A Study of Cross-Cultural Researchers," *Journal of Cross-Cultural Psychology* 17 (1986): 225–48.

16. H. Triandis, R. Brislin, and C. H. Hui, "Cross-Cultural Training across the Individualism-Collectivism Divide," *International Journal of Intercultural Relations*, 12 (1988): 269–89.

17. W. G. Ouchi, *Theory Z: How American Business Can Meet the Japanese Challenge* (Reading, Mass. Addison-Wesley, 1981).

18. A. Mehrabian and S. Ksionzky, *A Theory of Affiliation* (Lexington, Mass.: Heath, 1974).

19. McClelland, *Power: The Inner Experience*.

20. D. McClelland and D. Burnham, "Power Is the Great Motivator," *Harvard Business Review* 25 (March-April 1967): 159–66

21. H. Mintzberg suggests that the achievement motive must change to a general desire for company growth when successful individual achievers are promoted to executive positions. Mintzburg, *Power in and around Organizations*.

22. L. J. Peter and R. Hull, *The Peter Principle*. New York: William Morrow, 1969. The Peter Principle states that people are promoted until they reach a position in which they function poorly, making them both incompetent and professionally static.

23. Winter, *The Power Motive*.

24. Both quotations can be found in J. M. Cohen and M. J. Cohen, eds., *The Penguin Dictionary of Quotations* (Middlesex, England, and New York: Penguin, 1960).

25. D. Kipnis, *The Powerholders* (Chicago: University of Chicago Press, 1976).

26. I. Janis and L. Mann, *Decision Making* (New York: Free Press, 1977).

27. P. Theis and W. Steponkus, *All about Politics* (New York: R. R. Bowker, 1972). Quote is from p. 9.

28. Ibid.

29. There is a treatment of fear and anxiety in E. Ferguson, "Motivation," in *Encyclopedia of Psychology*, vol. 2, edited by R. Corsini (New York: Wiley, 1984): pp. 395–98. This encyclopedia entry also reviews some general theoretical ideas about motivation that may be helpful in understanding power as one of the major specific motives.

3

ABILITIES AND SKILLS FOR POWER ACQUISITION

When asked "Who is successful at getting ideas accepted?" many respondents discussed specific individuals and said that they were "politically astute," "good at office politics," or "effective in the political arena." But unless the follow-up questions were very precise, these people had a difficult time explaining exactly what made these individuals politically sophisticated. This chapter identifies various skills and abilities that astute people possess. In contrast with strategies and tactics (Chapters 4 and 5), abilities and skills are called upon over long periods of time and are part of power acquisition in a wide variety of settings. Further, as the abilities and skills are used frequently over a period of years, they become habitual and part of a person's permanent makeup, as summarized by the word "personality." Strategies and tactics, on the other hand, refer to behaviors useful in certain situations, such as in negotiations with an opponent concerning an outdated policy or in testing the waters to find the points of opposition to a new policy idea. Certainly there are linkages between abilities, strategies, and tactics. For instance, people with the ability to form a network of influential acquaintances can then use specific tactics to encourage certain of those acquaintances to coalesce so that an innovative proposal gains supporters.

The abilities and skills will be grouped around a number of general headings: resource development, personality traits, and sensitivity to the context in which power is to be used. These categories are meant to be helpful for the presentation of a great deal of specific information, rather than hard and fast concepts. Again, there are overlaps across the content of these categories and they often should be considered in combination. For instance, people with pleasant personalities and resources to exchange are invited into more social settings, where they can learn to diagnose contextual information.

As discussed in Chapter 2, power and politics come to the forefront when there are limited resources and when many people want those resources. Resources are exchanged to benefit the most active and successful participants in this competition. An important fact about powerful people is that they have a resource that they can exchange in the political process. Developing such a resource is of central importance.

RESOURCE DEVELOPMENT

In my discussions with them, the respondents frequently mentioned that people should develop an ability that will make them useful to powerful people. This ability then becomes their entry point, and they exchange their skills for other benefits. For instance, I asked a diplomat to distinguish young foreign service officers (FSOs) who were successful on their first assignments from those who were not. The response was that the successful FSOs could write in a way that was useful to the ambassador. This skill is to be distinguished from a general ability to write well. The more specific skill refers to writing in such a manner that the ambassador can use the material immediately and without revision. Ambassadors are extraordinarily busy and do not have time to write all their own letters, speeches, and reports to the Secretary of State. Young foreign service officers who can draft all these documents, in the appropriate style, have a tremendous advantage over their peers. What is the return to these FSOs? There will be invitations to important meetings with high-level officials so that notes can be taken for later drafting. These will give the young FSOs visibility among senior officials. In addition, the FSOs may be able to lobby for their own ideas, perhaps by putting them in one paragraph of a speech or report. The ambassador may cross out such a paragraph, but this does not imply a rejection of the rest of the draft, and, as the diplomat respondent pointed out, "the FSO's idea is planted in the head of the ambassador. Even if the idea is rejected in the short run, it may become part of later policy as the seed takes root and blossoms."

The types of resources reviewed in Chapter 2 provide a good introduction to the ways people engage in exchanges with others. The first way is the dispersal of *money*, and here I have a confession to make: if people are independently wealthy or have direct access to large amounts of money, this is the only paragraph in this book that they need read to enter the ranks of the powerful. The only thing wealthy people have to do is identify promising politicians and let it be known that they are willing to make campaign contributions. Ideally, the first few politicians so favored will be talkative and loyal to their party, both features leading to much word-of-mouth communication with their colleagues. The wealthy will then be courted by large numbers of powerful people who want to be supported in upcoming elections or to assist the candidates they favor. Later, as word spreads about the willingness of these wealthy people to contribute, powerful representatives of such organizations as symphony orchestras, universities, and charities will pay visits. As the money continues to spread, the wealthy contributors will receive invitations to dinners, with status-giving seats at the heads of tables. If they are at all clever, the wealthy people will thereby hear of investment opportunities in the community and use them to make their own financial picture even more favorable.

People who are themselves not very wealthy can become powerful through access to money. Some people with extensive networks, good interpersonal skills,[1] and willingness to ask others for help become fundraisers for charitable organizations or for institutions that supplement their budgets by soliciting of contributions. Professors able to bring in money to a university through their ability to write grant proposals become influential and are much more "marketable" if they decide to seek a position elsewhere. They trade this grant-acquisition skill for other resources, such as direct access to the president of the university. People who can maneuver themselves onto the budget committee automatically gain power in virtually any organization, whether it is the local elementary school or the U.S. Senate. When Bob Woodward and Carl Bernstein were investigating the Watergate scandals, the character or composite of characters called "Deep Throat advised them to "follow the money."[2] This is a good way of identifying the powerful in any organization.

The use of *status* as a resource is often associated with money. Colleges without huge endowments give prominent businesspeople the status of "trustees." In exchange, although it is never stated so crassly, the businesspeople are expected to attract money to the college. The money can take the form of direct contributions that the businesspeople arrange through their networks, or advice on investments. Individuals skilled in massaging the egos of high-status people can trade this unique talent for other resources. As part of the development of many nonprofit organizations, potential funders or contributors pay visits to decide how far to extend their financial involvement. Members of review committees also visit and later write reports recommending the continuance or withdrawal of funds. The organizations that receive these visitors often assign select employees to accompany the visitors and to arrange dinners, receptions, and introductions to community leaders. These select employees have a great deal of charm and graciousness, and they are very skilled at making the visitors seem important. The visitors put so much of their time and energy into receiving these ego massages that they overlook faults in the organization. My colleagues who have gone to work for such government funding agencies as the National Science Foundation tell me that preparation for this treatment is part of their training. They are told, "Representatives of the organization who accompany you on the site visit are not being attentive to you. They are being attentive to the big bag of money you represent."

The problems that stem from the status accorded to visitors can be seen in issues of national importance. The first set of visitors to mainland China in the early 1970s came back and wrote incredibly positive reports, overlooking problems that now seem obvious. The reasons for this include the fact that they had the status of being among the first and that they were reacting to the attentive hospitality they received from carefully selected hosts. After catching on to the way they were being treated, journalists reporting on the Vietnam War in the late 1960s began to complain about the "lollipop tour." This term referred to a tour of facilities in and around Saigon that the military provided for journalists, complete with receptions, lunches, and gracious escorts. The journalists were being shown exactly what the generals wanted them to see and were not being allowed free access to information about the war's progress.

The specific resources classified under the general heading of *love and sex* refer to people's emotional relationships with others. Policies have been made, and careers have been advanced, because certain people had genuinely warm ties with one another. Even though the political arena has the reputation of attracting the cold, calculating, and callous, it is important to remember that most of the people involved have emotional needs that can be satisfied only through genuine friendships. Robert Caro points out that when Lyndon Johnson was a young congressman from Texas in the 1930s, he attached himself to Rep. Sam Rayburn.[3] Although influential on Capitol Hill, Rayburn was a lonely person who had nothing but an empty room to look at after his workday. Lyndon Johnson frequently invited Rayburn to his home, where he and Lady Bird Johnson offered warmth, hospitality, and a family-like atmosphere. Since he and Rayburn both enjoyed talking about politics, Johnson received more insider information than most of his peers. Also, other Capitol Hill people began to realize that if they tangled with Johnson, they also tangled with Rayburn. Rayburn eventually became Speaker of the House, and as his fortunes rose, so did Johnson's.

Warm ties with people are important in all organizations. Most employees want cordial and pleasant relationships with their coworkers. Some people leave organizations if they do not find such relationships, taking a salary cut to join a company where relations are known to be pleasant. Success in "office politics" requires an ability to have others *care* whether or not one remains with an organization. One way to generate such caring, in addition to general everyday cordiality, is to participate in office social occasions. Contributions to baby showers, attendance at Christmas parties, and participation in luncheons during Secretaries Week are very important. I have known tremendously hard-working, productive individuals who did not participate in such activities. They argued that they were hired for their ability to work, not to participate in social activities. While this is true in the narrow sense, this attitude made them less influential. When they were faced with a difficult problem or an upcoming deadline, they had trouble enlisting the support of others. Personnel in the computer center had other priorities; the person in charge of supplies was not willing to ignore red tape to bring in a piece of equipment quickly; and the secretaries were unable to put aside what they were currently doing. If the people who had ignored social obligations made a major mistake and were threatened with dismissal from the organization, they were not as likely to receive supportive outcries from coworkers.

Sex has long been used as a resource that is exchanged for others. Even when a sexual relationship starts for the purpose of purely physical release, an emotional attachment frequently follows. One way that physically attractive people from the less favored social classes raise their status is to marry into the upper strata. The member of the upper class obtains a physically attractive spouse; the other obtains social status and access to money. Relationships often falter, however, when sexual favors are the only resource a person possesses. From my interviews, the general advice was, "Don't use sex as a resource in the power arena." Or if you are unwise enough not to follow this good advice, don't think that a sexual relationship can be kept secret. In the long run there is usually more danger than benefit from the use of sexual favors as a resource.

People who have access to scarce *goods* can use them as a resource. Jobs are best thought of as goods, and they become an important resource when unemployment is high. Jobs that are linked to loyalty to political parties have long been used as tools in the acquisition of power. If someone works hard for a successful political candidate, the unwritten expectation is that the candidate will use his or her influence if the supporter wants a job, either in the politician's office or in the organization of someone from the party's extensive network. One respondent told me that he advises unemployed people to become involved in a political campaign. Even if the candidate loses there are many benefits. It is more impressive to list "working on the Senatorial campaign of Peter Jones" than to list "unemployed" on one's resume. Even if Jones can't help with a job, the person involved in the campaign will meet a large number of influential people, and some of these new contacts may lead to job interviews.

People who have access to wholesale-priced goods can use them as a resource. For instance, they may supply food or liquor "at cost" to office parties or to charity fund-raisers, thereby trading goods for contacts and/ or a reputation for generosity. One of my friends advised me, "When you give workshops for organizations, don't charge $300 for the tuition and

$50 for the books. Charge $350 and give the books to the participants 'for free.' People feel that they are being treated well and are more likely to recommend you to others."

Information is one of the two most useful resources to develop if one is not independently wealthy. The saying "knowledge is power" has many possible connotations; here, it is a helpful reminder that people can use specialized knowledge to enter arenas where the powerful work and to stay there through the exchange of resources. Not just any information will do, however—the information must be useful to people at the executive level. I have studied American and Irish folk music for many years, but I can not trade this knowledge for power because few CEOs feel the need for it. Individuals who do not have much power should consider spending time acquiring a useful and specialized knowledge base that can later be their resource in exchange relationships.

A good example of a useful knowledge area is tax law, which is so complex that not everyone can understand it, but is something everyone has to deal with yearly, if not more frequently. This knowledge can be used in a wide variety of settings: charities, business and industry, universities, political campaigns, and so forth. Other useful knowledge areas are accounting, investment strategies, fund-raising methods, computer technology, public relations, methods of preparing environmental impact statements, writing in a particular style (e.g., journalistic, eulogistic), and communicating with different audiences.

Sometimes the knowledge consists of the arcana of an organization's decision-making system, such as the rules for introducing bills, as well as the rules of debate in the state or national legislature. Some people enter the arena of power because of their knowledge of Robert's Rules of Order. They are asked to sit next to the CEO and other executives so they can rule on procedures when people speak from the floor.

Another knowledge base consists of people in one's network. If an individual knows many people who have different areas of expertise but who are not widely known, then the individual can become a gatekeeper who permits access to the others. I have a manuscript, who knows a publisher? Who can cut through this red tape? Who can I see about this lemon of a car I'm stuck with? I need open heart surgery; who's really the best surgeon? I need an entertainer at my fund-raiser; who will work cheap? If someone can answer these questions with names of specific people, together with their private phone numbers, the one with the answers can call in debts at a later time.

Services, the other of the two most useful resources for those who are not wealthy, consist of the performance of various behaviors to assist others to meet their goals. One person may look and sound good on television and so become the spokesperson for a certain cause. Others may write well and may start an informal company newspaper (on their own time) that is meant to build the morale of company employees. If the newspaper is successful, many people will lobby the editors so that their stories or successes are included. If a newspaper is unfeasible, people may turn their attention to the company's annual report. Especially in companies too small to have their own public relations offices, someone who takes over duties such as preparation of the annual report will free up an executive for other duties and earn a great deal of gratitude. There are other places where writing skills become a valued service. Executives rarely have time to write their own speeches. If people are skillful at writing in the executive's style they can earn a great deal of credit, which they may cash in when negotiations for promotion are underway. Some people are very good at working with volunteers. Since many nonprofit organizations depend upon the services of volunteers, the person who can keep the volunteers motivated and committed becomes an influential figure. Other services include provision of entertainment at fund-raisers, volunteer work for political candidates, lobbying the powerful on behalf of an organization, and cutting through the red tape associated with delivery of goods or services. People who want to serve Person X but not Person Y can put aside the rest of their work so they can work for X, but appeal to the size of the stack in their in basket when Y makes a request.

Information and services are clearly linked, since the services a person does or does not provide to others often involve a knowledge base. In research organizations, only a few people are likely to know the most advanced statistical procedures; yet many must use the procedures if their work is to be read and respected by others. The knowledgeable individuals are sometimes willing to serve a select few by agreeing to requests for help on statistical matters. In my experience, the knowledgeable ones are so busy that they have to pick and choose among requesters or they would spread themselves too thin and accomplish nothing. In making their choices, they often become powerful figures because of their specialized knowledge and potential for service.

Qualities of the Resource to Be Developed

The resource you choose to develop should have as many useful features as possible. The following descriptors of the most beneficial resources may be helpful in making a choice.[4] The most useful resources are those that are familiar to powerholders, essential to the success and smooth functioning of the organization, concentrated in only a few people, irreplaceable, and serving to reduce the uncertainty that organizations face. Ideally, the resource should also be useful when immediacy is needed. These six features are important enough to warrant an expanded treatment.

Familiarity may seem commonsensical, but many power seekers fail on this point. If the CEOs are not familiar with a potential resource, the first necessity is to acquaint them with its benefits. For instance, a number of people have attempted to introduce cross-cultural orientation programs (a service) into large corporations that have international branches. These programs cover such issues as the adjustment problems that are faced when managers accept overseas assignments, methods of successfully negotiating joint ventures in other countries, and the rudiments of the local language. But the necessity of programs to prepare managers for overseas assignments is still not a familiar concept to many CEOs. Consequently, the attention of these busy people becomes concentrated on other issues.

A resource is *essential* if the organization cannot exist without it. For instance, since all organizations have to deal with the Internal Revenue Service, tax specialists have an essential resource.

A *concentrated* resource is one that only a few people have. Many people can type, and so this is a resource that is hard to turn into an important bargaining chip in exchange relationships. Far fewer people can successfully lobby philanthropists for large donations to nonprofit organizations.

Sometimes resources are deliberately concentrated to increase a group's power. Lots of people can change light bulbs, but if a contract says that only members of the electrician's union can change bulbs, then the resource becomes concentrated. Extensive job training programs in prisons are often opposed by unions, since the more workers there are with a special skill, the less the concentration of resources.

Being *irreplaceable* is similar to being essential, but there is an additional connotation: irreplaceable means that one resource cannot be substituted for another. In a statewide or national political campaign there is no substitute for the effective use of television. People skillful in communicating through television have an essential and irreplaceable resource. At times the entire set of contributions people make can be analyzed in a similar manner. It is essential that a company have a competent CEO, but there are many people who might fill this need. The person who creates the image of being irreplaceable is certain to have great influence.

An important insight into the nature of power is that if people can *reduce uncertainty*, they increase their chances of being influential. Organizations are faced with many uncertainties: the amount of their future growth, the effects of the competition's efforts, the impact of newly proposed legislation, the effects of turnover of key personnel, the outcome of upcoming litigation, and so forth. People who have a resource that can reduce uncertainty are of great use. Lawyers use the threat of uncertainty to settle cases out of court. Assume that a corporation is being sued for a faulty product that caused an injury. The defense lawyer might tell the client, "I think we have a good case, but no one can ever predict which way a jury will go. It may be better to accept this out-of-court settlement to make sure we don't lose big." As another example, consider successful grant writers on university campuses. Universities are always concerned about their future budgets. If a professor can reduce the uncertainty of budget worries, that professor becomes very influential on campuses.

Immediacy refers to a resource that can be marshaled at a moment's notice. Companies are constantly faced with "brush fires"—problems that demand immediate attention. People who can write a 500-word explanation for a controversial company policy by 2:00 P.M., having received the assignment at 1:00 P.M., are demonstrating that their resource has immediacy.

Some people gain a reputation as good troubleshooters. They can enter a problem-filled branch office and bring events back to normal. Often CEOs are so preoccupied by emergencies that they have little time to think ahead and engage in long-term planning. A person who can handle everyday brush fires, permitting the CEO to spend time on long-range goals, becomes a valued employee. The CEO is likely to appreciate this service and be willing to grant the person's request.

Exchanges of Resources

Once people have a resource that is useful to the powerful, they can attempt to enter into reciprocal relationships. They can seek out opportunities to be of use to powerholders, and in return they will be admitted to meetings that the powerful attend, thus improving their networks. Once admitted, if they continue being useful, these people can begin to exchange favors: Person A does something useful for Person B, and Person B later reciprocates by doing something for Person A. It is pleasant, of course, to receive favors, but it is sometimes difficult to return them. If people do not return favors, however, they will be dropped from the exchange process and will no longer find themselves in powerful circles.

A congressional staffer told me of a recently elected senator who had taken his seat as a relative unknown compared with the other senator from his state, who was a powerful national figure. The new senator made himself useful to his colleagues by doing all sorts of favors and helping them to achieve their goals. He did this in a pleasant manner, never complaining about the "ditchdigging" tasks he accepted. When he had acquired enough visibility and gratitude for these favors, he felt that he could introduce an important piece of legislation. It was passed with the help of several powerful senators, who acted as cosponsors. The staffer continued, "No one was particularly interested in the bill, but senators felt that he deserved one piece of legislation because of his usefulness." Because the legislation had a certain amount of public appeal, this senator became much better known.

Service without complaint is important. A colleague with some influence over hiring decisions told me about a recent recipient of a master's degree who had approached my colleague and said, "Please let me work with you. I'll do anything—typing, photocopying, filing." Her goal was to make herself known as a hard worker so that decision makers would later be able to attach a favorable impression to her formal application for a position. The executive accepted the offer and put her to work typing a long report to the stockholders. Two weeks later she complained that typing was beneath her abilities. By complaining she broke her promise that she would "do anything" and made a nuisance of herself instead of being a useful addition to the office.

The initial exchange for favors rendered is continued access to powerholders. Over time, the powerholders are likely to grant more favors, since they will intuitively sense that the time has come for more resource allocation on their part. Later, they may call in these favors with requests of their own. Ideally, the target of the requests will be comfortable granting them and will do so cheerfully. If for some reason the favors are difficult to grant, a turning point has been reached in the quest for power. Assume that the powerholder has granted several favors and now wants the beneficiary to take on the son of a friend as an apprentice, or wants a certain task to be undertaken. If the beneficiary finds the new person unprepared or the task questionable, then a choice among behaviors must be made. The person can (a) refuse the request, (b) explain why the request is objectionable, or (c) grin and grant the request. At times alternative (c) has to be the choice. All influential people have to go along with requests that, in their view, have objectionable components. Recall the discussion in the section of Chapter 2 on dealing with distastefulness. Part of participation in power arenas is compromise. Alternative (b) is possible, but powerholders are only willing to listen to so many excuses before they label the person as "whining," "difficult," or worse. If people choose alternative (a), they risk being eliminated from the arenas of power. No one says very much; no recriminations are handed down; there is no public display of hostility; and the people remain pleasant with one another. But the person who chooses alternative (a) is often simply dropped from the list of people invited to meetings with the powerful. They are privately labeled as unable to keep the exchange process going and as ungrateful for favors rendered.

An understanding of exchange relationships is sometimes helpful when analyzing national events. I doubt that Richard Nixon made an explicit deal with Gerald Ford regarding Nixon's pardon (1974). He did not have to, because he drew on his knowledge of unstated rules regarding the exchange of resources. Nixon realized that Ford had been successful in the House of Representatives because Ford was a good giver and receiver of resources. He played the game by the rules. Nixon made Ford his vice president, and Ford was expected to return the favor in some form at a later date. The expectation of a return did not have to be stated because people who are successful in the system over a long period of time know the rules and do not need reminders. When Ford had a chance to return the favor after Nixon's resignation, he did so.

PERSONALITY TRAITS

As part of the exchange process, people should give their favors in a cheerful and uncomplaining manner. This is just one personality component of people who successfully acquire power. Many of the 102 respondents talked about the personality features of powerholders, and the following discussion provides a compilation of their views.

Energy

Powerful people have a great deal of energy. They can put in a normal, hard-working day from 8 A.M. to 5 P.M. and have plenty of energy left over for various sorts of evening meetings. Whereas by 4 P.M. many people are dragging their feet and looking forward to an evening in front of their television sets, high-energy people are looking forward to an evening fund-raiser, political meeting, or cocktail party at which influential people will be present. Because of their energy, they can take on additional tasks at work, above and beyond their formal job descriptions. Or they can take on tasks for various service and professional groups that have visibility in the community. While carrying out these tasks, they can use their resources, building up credit in the exchange process. People with a great deal of energy are useful to organizations, since they communicate the positive attitude that "things can get done." This enthusiasm and energy, however, is to be distinguished from a manic, out-of-control state of elation. Powerful people are energetic but are always able to keep their emotions in check.

Balance

Several respondents used the term "a balanced personality." This refers to a comfortable mid-range between dull and strident, as in Figure 3. Balance has many benefits. It allows interaction with many different types of people. It leads to favorable attributions from others. Balanced people earn the reputation of being reliable, pleasant individuals who should be sought out for future interactions. Balance also allows for the occasional foray into emotional appeals or disinterest, again shown in the diagram. People occasionally want to show an extreme emotion, whether it be enthusiasm for a policy or disgust at a severe transgression. If they are usually balanced, then the extremes are easy to read. And powerholders *want* to be read when it suits their goals. They want to communicate their feelings to colleagues and subordinates. For instance, they want to communicate

Figure 3
Moving from a Balanced Personality

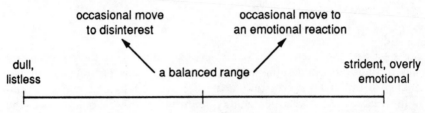

interest in a certain proposal and want to communicate a lack of enthusiasm regarding another possibility if they feel there are too many shortcomings. The problem with the constantly strident is that intense interest in a topic cannot be distinguished from their normal emotional output. Eventually a constant stridency becomes tiresome and the strident people are either not included in gatherings of the powerful or purposely avoided. People who constantly show extreme emotion may earn a headline now and then because of their colorfulness, or they may be allowed to win a small victory just so the powerholders can be free of their presence. But they rarely have a long-term influence on important policy matters. People who are constantly dull are also difficult to read and, of course, instill little fervor in their potential followers.

Congeniality

The combination of a balanced personality and willingness to engage in the cheerful exchange of favors allows people to work effectively with others. Cooperative interaction with others is a key to understanding power. While one image of "power" is of a deranged monarch in a bad Hollywood epic that brings Machiavelli to the silver screen, power far more often involves quiet work with others. If people are pleasant, cheerful, and balanced, then others enjoy their company and are willing to work with them on tasks of mutual interest. Consequently, people are able to meet many others whom they can eventually call upon for various favors or for the purpose of forming coalitions.

In addition to the image of the powerful tyrant that has to be downplayed, there is a problem with the more realistic image of the congenial person who works well with others. There is the connotation that a pleasant person who seeks influence in powerful circles has no substance. In actuality, powerful people combine a substantive area of expertise (or some other resource) that they use in exchanges, together with a congenial personality. There will always be exceptions: some people are so expert in an important area of knowledge or have so many influential contacts that others tolerate

their abrasive nature. Some people are so socially skilled that their congeniality becomes their resource and they are useful to others as hosts and
hostesses at important gatherings of the powerful. But more often, successful people combine a resource and a desirable personality. They take
advantage of their congeniality to develop a wide network of acquaintances,
and they take advantage of their substance to be useful to members of
their network. A favorite debate topic for junior high school students is
whether success in life is based on what people know or who people know.
In most cases, people combine the "what" and the "who." People should
have an area of expertise or some other resource, but they can demonstrate
their knowledge only if they have a network of people with whom they
interact frequently. There are very bright people who have the potential
to become influential because they have a great deal to offer to others.
But if they have no network, they can not demonstrate the availability of
their resource.

The world is not a stable place, and the rules and guidelines for success
in life change over time. Individuals also change over the course of their
lives. Many readers will disagree with this analysis of the "what-who"
combination, and they will be able to point to unpleasant people who are
so wealthy, well connected, or knowledgeable about an important topic
that others flock to them. Three replies can be given:

1. The person may have been congenial while *acquiring* an influential
reputation and may have become abrasive as a result of obtaining power.
(See Chapter 2.)

2. No matter how powerful they are, these people may have cut themselves off from even more influence because their personalities repelled
others who had opportunities for them.

3. Many of the resources these powerful but unpleasant people had are
now more widely available. Because of the increasing number of people
who go to college and then on to postgraduate studies, more individuals
have areas of expertise that once were monopolized by one or a few powerholders in a community. Further, advances in computer technology have
made once-restricted information available to anyone having the skills
needed to use the appropriate hardware and software. Working with difficult people is not so necessary as it may have been in the past. In addition,
given the greater knowledge that people now have about preventive measures they can take to protect their own health, unpleasant others have
become even more unwelcome. People realize that working with a caustic
individual can be stressful for them, leading to such problems as increased
blood pressure, headaches, and ulcers.[5]

All these factors lead to a common experience that I, together with many
of the respondents, have had. A person writes a favorable letter of recommendation for another. The letter stresses the technical aspects of the
job for which the other is applying. The letter writer receives a phone call

from the prospective employer. The caller says, "I see that you feel the person is an expert with respect to the job demands, and there is no question about his formal educational credentials. But is he a pleasant person who will be a good colleague in the workplace?"

A Thick Skin

Power often involves a seemingly odd combination of factors. In addition to congeniality, which allows interaction with many different others, powerful people have to have a thick skin when those others disagree on important issues or criticize perceived character flaws. Good criticism is potentially beneficial and centers on the quality of ideas, proposals, or suggested plans of action. Such criticism can lead to improvements. But far too often, people are unable to disassociate themselves from their ideas.[6] When they present the products of their thinking and analysis and find that others disagree, these people interpret the disagreements as attacks upon themselves. Or, if they are in favor of a proposed policy change, they feel that any preference for the status quo is directed at them.

In reality there are so many reasons for accepting the status quo, such as comfort with present policies and the uncertainty of change, that considering a lack of enthusiasm for a new proposal as criticism of themselves as human beings is an overinterpretation. One of the respondents and I had long discussions on policy changes that I was suggesting for an organization we both knew well. Admittedly, the proposals would have involved a major shift in the goals and priorities of the organization. I am sure that I expressed frustration and disappointment when I reported the difficulties I was having in implementing the changes. She replied, "You're not taking this personally, are you?"

The importance of a thick skin becomes even greater when the attacks are against people's character rather than their ideas. Responding to criticism of one's ideas is hard enough; responding to accusations of dishonesty, insensitivity, incompetence, sleaziness, or laziness is even harder. At times the attacks are genuine and not just products of careless tongues. Those individuals on the attack are convinced that their targets have character flaws, and they are willing to be public with their criticism. In doing so, they move beyond the gentlemanly and ladylike etiquette they should have learned as children, choosing to ignore the dangers of ad hominem (which means "to or at the person" attacks) rather than attacks on ideas. Attacks of this kind are not considered proper in sophisticated debate or in a collegial environment. The attackers risk communicating a lack of etiquette, sophistication, and desirable qualities in their own character when they criticize in this manner. Nevertheless, such attacks are a constant possibility when people enter powerful circles.

Unwillingness to deal with public criticism is one reason why some people avoid seeking greater power. Public figures who are urged to run for high political office sometimes admit that they are too thin-skinned to enter the rough and tumble of the competition for elected office. When they do not refer metaphorically to the depth of their outer epidermal layer measured in millimeters, they refer to similar feelings with expressions such as "putting myself and my family under the microscope of public scrutiny." In politics especially, but also in other public arenas such as the business world, long-term participants in the quest for power realize that they cannot be overly sensitive to criticism. "Only amateurs take it personally" and "If you can't stand the heat, get out of the kitchen" are two pieces of advice that are often given to newcomers.

There are a number of ways to deal with intense criticism. At times, ad hominem attacks become part of a carefully arranged drama, played out for the public and especially the media, in which both the attacker and the target benefit. When liberal politicians criticize conservatives, and vice versa, they all benefit from the media coverage aimed at their own constituencies. In the early 1960s, certain Southern senators actually enjoyed the criticism they received from Northern liberals because it "played well" to their constituents. Thomas "Tip" O'Neill and Ronald Reagan both received favorable coverage from key media outlets when they exchanged charges of "insensitivity to the poor" and "demagoguery" during the mid–1980s.

At other times the criticism is meant to have a damaging impact. For instance, up-and-coming young people are sometimes attacked by elders who feel that their long-held power is being threatened. If the young targets can focus on other reasons for these attacks besides their own character traits, then they are less likely to become the trophies of their opponents. For instance, if the targets can attribute the criticism to "the rough and tumble of politics," "threats to the status quo," or "the expected response during competition for scarce resources," they are less likely to be the victims of their attackers. Put another way, undamaged targets are able, in their own minds, to attach the criticism to external factors. In so doing, they are able to keep the criticism from "getting under their skin" and damaging their sense of self-worth. The ability to attach criticism to external factors,[7] such as the tensions resulting from changes in the status quo, is one of the skills that separates those who remain in and those who leave activities that have a strong political component.

Imperturbability

If people can attribute personal attacks to external factors, they are less likely to become visibly angry. People able to respond to intense disagreements and attacks with a cool, calm manner have a very important skill. If they can communicate to others that they are too dignified to enter the fray of petty personal attacks, they have a powerful style that is attractive to potential followers. By responding to attacks in a calm, even friendly manner, people often earn the admiration of others who wish that *they* could be so calm in the face of hostility. Further, if these people can maintain their unruffled demeanor over a long period of time, observers begin to feel that the attackers are unreasonable people who have no substance behind their jibes. One of the reasons for Ronald Reagan's personal popularity, apart from certain policy decisions, is that he has always had such a calm, imperturbable manner in the face of extremely probing questions from the press and virulent attacks from his critics. During his presidency, many people grew to dislike the White House press corps, feeling that they were constantly sniping at a dignified man who was doing his best for the nation. Ronald Reagan was looked upon favorably as a man of reason who had to deal with a collection of jackals.

Besides a favorable image in the minds of observers there are other benefits to imperturbability. Some people are able to mask their tensions and anger behind a carefully rehearsed positive facade, while others genuinely do not become aroused when attacked. The thinking and analytical skills of the latter group do not diminish when they are challenged. When people experience stress or feel genuinely angry, their thinking becomes rigid and they are able to focus only on the most obvious, familiar, and easily considered aspects of the issue at hand. At times the most obvious and familiar aspects will be those that these people have experienced since childhood, such as "getting even" or "not giving in to bullies." One reason for an angry response to attackers, then, is that people's thinking narrows and they respond in ways reminiscent of children. Observers often comment on such responses as being "childish" and "immature." The person who is blessed with a natural ability to not become angry, or who has learned this skill, keeps his or her analytical skills intact and can constantly focus on the substantive aspects of the issue. They are seen by observers as mature, dignified people with potential for leadership.

The effects of imperturbability at work can be seen in the efforts of good public speakers who give presentations on extremely controversial topics. I remember attending a meeting of psychologists some years ago during which researchers discussed the abilities of people from various racial groups. The details are unimportant here, but the basic conclusion of one speaker was that members of one racial group had less innate intelligence than members of other groups. As might be expected, the speaker attracted great hostility, in the form of shouted insults from some audience members, an organized picket line, and challenges to take over the speaker's microphone. During the entire proceedings the speaker remained unruffled, and during those periods when the chairperson was able to assume control of the microphone, the speaker spoke calmly and confidently. Over time, people in the audience whispered remarks like, "You've got to admire the guy for remaining calm through all this." As the session proceeded, audience members became tired of the attackers and began to shout comments such as, "Let him have his say!"

One finding from the research of psychologists is that a minority group without much power can sometimes persuade a majority to go along with its recommended positions if its members behave according to certain guidelines.[8] The minority should (1) give its recommendations in a concise, easily understood form; (2) deliver them in a calm, unthreatening, and consistent manner; and (3) continue to advance them over a long period of time. By maintaining an imperturbable manner the members of the minority group will keep the members of the majority group from dismissing them as hotheads, whiners, or radicals. If the majority members hear the recommendations consistently put forth by reasonable people, they may find themselves beginning to incorporate the minority's views into their own thinking.

Sense of Humor

When people feel that they should practice an imperturbable manner, one quality they can emphasize is a sense of humor. There are many advantages.[9] A sense of humor is attractive to others and contributes to a reputation for congeniality. It is a buffer against stress. When maneuvering through the ranks of the powerful there will always be difficulties, roadblocks, and tensions. A sense of humor, especially an ability to make light of difficulties and avoid internalizing them, helps us to continue to say, "I can keep trying." Humor can also be used to soften the barbs of critics, and it can assist in the formation of powerful coalitions.

I once gave a talk on the psychology of humor to a group of screenwriters, filmmakers, and critics. I suggested that humor can be directed at people from different groups so as to reinforce an ingroup identity between the speaker and valued others. When this is done, humor is being used as a tactic in the political process, since one group is gaining resources (esteem, status) while another is having them denied. For instance, proponents of abortion rights have jokes about antiabortion groups, and vice versa. Republicans have jokes about Democrats; people in urban areas have jokes about their country cousins; and Blacks have jokes about Whites. Of course, in all these examples humor also travels in the other direction. One result is that people maintain their identity as members of one specific group, part of that identity involving the fact that they are *not* members of the other.

An interesting aspect is that the ingroup identity can be splintered into very fine distinctions, depending on the purpose of the moment.[10] For instance, there can be jokes by liberal Republicans about conservative

Republicans and, even more specifically, jokes by conservative Southern Republicans about conservative Northern Republicans. Consequently, humor helps form precise ingroups that coalesce for specific purposes in the political process.

The writer and actor Harry Shearer, best known for his work on "Saturday Night Live" and in the film *Spinal Tap* asked me to comment on humor as a political weapon when a high-ranking official is facing critics. I did not handle the question particularly well and instead mumbled some generalities and moved on to another question. Speakers usually remember the questions they handled least skillfully, and so I later gave the matter a good deal of thought.

I made a point of observing a large number of televised press conferences. It became clear that, in skillful hands, humor can be used as a tool to deflate criticism, to take attention away from a policy being challenged, to put down political opponents, and to contribute to the speaker's image as a decent human being. This is quite a combination. Mild, self-directed humor is best, since there is less risk of unintentionally offending someone. The politician campaigning in California who tried to link himself to voters there by expressing thanks that he wasn't campaigning that weekend in New Jersey offended people in the latter state.

My favorite example of effective self-directed humor was presidential candidate Alexander Haig's response to a question about a controversial policy matter. The reporter asked about the policy, summarizing it in precise, simple terms. Haig responded, "I couldn't have said that—it's far too clear." He earned a big laugh and the press conference moved on to a policy matter that Haig was more comfortable addressing. Given the pleasant mood that the joke created, the reporter could not follow up his question with impunity, because if there had been a firm follow-up question, *he* would have come across as the unpleasant heavy attacking this pleasant presidential candidate.

I found this tactic at faculty meetings on university campuses, in the boardrooms of large corporations, churches, and even at an organizational meeting of parents who wanted to support Little League baseball. When they do not want to address an issue, skillful speakers can turn challenges into occasions for humor. If the person continuing the challenge keeps pressing the issue, he or she comes across as an unhelpful, even hostile complainer.

Occasionally the challenger can move along well with the humor, maintaining it with other jokes while keeping up the questions. This approach, however, takes great skill and can backfire when the humorous ripostes begin to involve others who might take offense. Often, a better tactic when faced with humor is to take the approach of the influential minority, as already reviewed. When people do this they make their points in a clear, precise, and congenial manner so that their ideas enter the heads of decision makers; then they retreat from the encounter, at the same time planning to make their points again (consistency over time) at a later date.

Loyalty

Maintenance of and identification with an ingroup were mentioned as two functions of humor. Broadly speaking, ingroups consist of people with whom an individual is comfortable. People in an ingroup spend time together, look forward to each other's company, have positive feelings about each other, and look after each other in times of difficulty. On the other hand, outgroups consist of people who are kept at a distance. Members of outgroups are avoided, disliked, and often viewed as inferior in such critical areas as intelligence, abilities, and social background.

People in ingroups also feel that they can share their innermost feelings with each other and that their thoughts will not be broadcast outside the group. People in an ingroup also expect loyalty.[11] There may be disagreements about issues within a group, but this fact should not be communicated to the outside. A few of the people may have misgivings about an action that the entire group wants to take, but to be loyal they support the action if at all possible through commitment of their resources. If those people show disloyalty, they will be excluded from group activities and, if their reputation for disloyalty precedes them, may have a difficult time joining another ingroup.

If people so channel their drive, resources, and social skills that they are invited to join a powerful ingroup, expectations of loyalty accompany the invitation. In the course of my survey, "loyal to friends" was a frequently used phrase in respondents' descriptions of powerful people. This quality has advantages when people reap the benefits of members' loyalty. It can have stressful effects, however, when loyal support of others' problematic proposals is expected. People cannot shift their loyalties and still be trusted. If someone supports Candidate A one year and then shifts his or her support to Candidate B the next year, Candidate B may distrust the support, saying "This support is wafer thin and could go to someone else later." An appeal to loyalty is one way powerful people maintain positive relations with large numbers of people. They might say to Person X "We think that your proposal has a lot of merit, but we already promised Person Y our support." Person X may be disappointed but will not be hostile, since the value placed on loyalty is well known among sophisticated users of power.

Analyzing loyalty, trust, and benefits of a small ingroup is sometimes useful in understanding the behavior of extremely powerful people. Some powerful individuals seem ruthless in their pursuit of advantage to themselves, hostile and arrogant with the press, and scathing in their response to criticism. They seem to see the world as full of enemies. In their interactions with most people, this may be an accurate description of their perceptions and behavior. There would seem to be risks in maintaining such an outlook: lack of support from others when coalitions are needed, damage to their physical and mental health, and a constant escalation of hostilities as attacks invite retaliations. These difficulties are lessened if they balance this view of the world with the expectations that members of a small ingroup will be trustworthy, loyal, and supportive. The ingroup can consist of family members and a few long-term business and political associates. Within their ingroup, these powerful people can be cordial and pleasant. As long as they have the support of a small ingroup within which they give and receive loyalty, they have a buffer against the consequences of their hostile view of the world at large.

At times, one resource that can be offered by a would-be ingroup member consists of effective representation to the outside world. The representative can be of service to the powerholder by communicating to the press and critics such positive comments as, "This person is misunderstood. He may have a gruff exterior, but it masks a heart of gold. He prefers to remain anonymous when it comes to his charitable activities."

Self-Insight

Robert Burns expressed a wish concerning his relationships with others:

> O wad some Pow'r the giftie gie us
> To see oursels as others see us!
> It wad frae mony a blunder free us
> And foolish notion.[12]

Self-insight is the quality to which Burns is referring. With this quality, people can examine their drives, resources, and skills to determine whether they lack an essential skill or are using one incorrectly. With this information, derived from accurate self-examination, they can make intelligent decisions about future steps.[13] For instance, someone might decide to acquire a skill, such as a more confident public speaking style. Another might decide that he or she will never be good at some essential skill and instead will give attention to team building and coalition formation, making sure that at least one person on the team possesses the key resource or skill.

One way to gain self-insight is to interpret the subtle cues that others send during interpersonal encounters. Does a new proposal elicit a polite but unenthusiastic response, coupled with occasional glances out the window by one's colleagues? Then it may be best to revise the proposal. Once people become powerful, they do not often receive constructive feedback. As discussed in Chapter 2, the followers attracted by powerholders are more likely to cater to their whims than to offer serious analyses of proposals. The powerholders come to believe that their current skills are responsible for success within their organizations and see little need to improve themselves. Consequently, self-insight is frequently not found among powerful people. It may be useful in acquiring power, but one of the metaphoric effects of this attainment is that self-insight diminishes. Realizing this, some effective leaders make a point of assigning subordinates to play the devil's advocate for new proposals, so that as much criticism as possible is generated, together with suggested improvements.[14] Similar steps can be taken by people who, during their early career development, discover that they do not have a great deal of self-insight. They can ask others what skills they should work on to be more successful in their organizations. Although not pleasant at the moment of reception, though easier for thick-skinned people to take, information of this sort can be very helpful in career development.

Charisma

Many powerful people have the mystical quality called charisma.[15] There is no widely accepted explanation of the concept, and a few analysts feel that ambitious people cannot attain charisma even with prolonged effort. According to these analysts, some people are born with the qualities that lead to charisma and others are not. Many respondents to the survey, however, felt that while gifts are given to some at birth, many aspects of personality and resources can be emphasized to increase people's chances of gaining a reputation as charismatic.

A charismatic leader attracts followers who feel that a current problem will be solved if they hitch their wagon to the leader's star. The problem should be one that engages people's emotions. One reason why wars encourage the acceptance of charismatic leaders is that the public wants solutions to clear and pressing problems. Other issues do not seem to attract such leaders. The budget deficit does not seem to attract the emotional involvement of the public, and consequently no leader with potential solutions is widely admired.

Given the presence of an emotionally arousing problem, certain qualities are likely to be found in the leaders that come forth from the crowd. If a potential leader is personally attractive, confident, and imperturbable and clearly has an area of expertise that can be applied to the problem, then the chances of that leader's gaining a reputation for charisma are increased. The leader must be capable of generating trust that the problem will be eliminated. A charismatic leader, then, is popular because people relieve themselves of worry by the confidence they place in the other person. Charismatic leaders seem much "better" than the average person in a society, given their expertise and "can-do" attitude.

An important point about charisma is that it is situationally based. If leaders are seen as generating confidence that a certain problem will be solved, they can lose their followers once the problem is effectively addressed. Winston Churchill lost his position as Britain's prime minister after World War II despite his untiring and inspirational wartime efforts. George Patton ("Old Blood and Guts") was a charismatic leader on the battlefield during World War II, but he became an embarrassment to General Eisenhower upon becoming an administrator after the war. As a teenager, I heard John Glenn speak shortly after his heroic efforts as the first American to orbit the earth (1962). I remember the sense of awe I experienced just being in his presence. However, he was not able to generate such enthusiasm in audiences during his quest for the Democratic presidential nomination in 1984.

These examples of charismatic people who did not transcend a problem or era bring up a more general point about the use of power. In addition to people's drives, resources, and skills, the use of power takes place in a social setting and in a specific context. The ability to understand the context in which people find themselves is a very important aspect of power, and it is the topic to which we now turn.

SENSITIVITY TO THE CONTEXT IN WHICH POWER IS TO BE USED

Psychologists frequently begin their analyses by stating that human behavior is due to a combination of personality factors and the situations in which people find themselves.[16] For example, certain people might be naturally gregarious, but this allows us to predict little about their behavior unless we know the nature of the social gathering they are attending. If the gathering allows them to roam about freely, as at a cocktail party, we can predict that these gregarious people will have a large number of pleasant conversations with others. If the gathering is for the purpose of listening attentively to a well-known speaker, however, we can predict little about gregarious people that might distinguish them from shy people.

Combinations of personal and situational factors can be complex. For example, shy people might show up at very few of the social gatherings to which they are invited. The *choice*, then, to be in a situation can be influenced by personality factors.[17] Or, if people find themselves in similar social settings again and again, they may begin to enjoy themselves; these feelings, in turn, can affect their personalities. Good teachers try to arrange the educational tasks they offer so that students feel the pleasure of success. Given encouragement in school over many days, underachievers can begin to enjoy schoolwork and may internalize a view of themselves as hard workers.

Social situations are combinations of factors, external to individuals, with which individuals must deal to accomplish their goals. Many complex behaviors demand movement through numbers of social situations. In the quest for power, for instance, people must move through situations to obtain their resources, to participate in exchanges, and to develop an extensive network within which these exchanges can take place. The "context" of behavior refers to this totality of situations; sensitivity to this context—the ability to understand or "read" it—can be developed over time. Although context was not frequently given an exact label by the respondents to the survey, many referred to it in various ways. One congressional staffer with over ten years' experience in Washington, D. C., said, "A lot of the most influential congressmen do not have an area of expertise such as taxation, the national defense, or health care for the elderly. Their genius is that they can look at a proposal prepared by someone else and judge whether or not it will move through the legislative process given current priorities, concerns, and budgets." Put another way, the legislators can read the context in which they are working to determine if a proposal is politically and economically acceptable at the time.

In the book *Social Situations*,[18] Michael Argyle and his colleagues propose a nine-point check list that is useful as a starting point for the analysis of situations and contexts. People who are good at reading situations have developed an intuitive feel for these points, even though they may not consult a checklist or use the terms. According to their book situations involve:

1. Roles, which involve the people who participate in various ways, and the expectations others have about the people's behavior.

2. Goals, or outcomes desired by the participants.

3. Rules, or shared beliefs concerning what is proper and improper behavior.

4. A repertoire of elements, or actions that can be undertaken.

5. Sequences of behaviors, or the arrangement of the elements in time. One example of Points 4 and 5 has been previously reviewed. People invest a resource (4) with expectations of reciprocity (5).

6. Concepts, or the ideas and shared knowledge experienced people have. Sometimes these concepts are summarized in the "rules of thumb" that experienced people use to maintain power and acquire more.

7. Language and speech. The concepts often are summarized in a special language or jargon that is known only to the initiated.

8. Environmental settings, which include boundaries to situations as well as to the props people use within them.

9. Difficulties and skills, or challenges in the situation that require the acquisition of new abilities *or* the inclusion of people with each of the necessary abilities.

Each of the nine points deserves further consideration.

1. Roles

For newcomers to a social situation, it is important to identify who has power and influence. Sometimes this is a straightforward matter, and sometimes it demands the skills of a detective. Take the example of a meeting with about thirty people present. The person who speaks most frequently may have the most power, but this is not always the case. Frequently there is a quieter person who is actually in charge; the talkative individual is simply a spokesperson. Some cultures institutionalize this distinction. In Samoa there are chiefs and talking chiefs, and the former have the real power. When observers conclude that the loquacious are not the most influential, there are several ways they can identify the actual source of power. Whose ideas seem to be summarized at the end of a meeting? Whose short speech causes a move from idle chitchat to serious discussion? Who is given rapt attention during the times that they add to the group discussion? Does a meeting seem to break down into nothingness if a certain person is called out?

Other general hints have been suggested for observers of day-to-day life in organizations. If a person is handed a fistful of "while you were out" slips of paper summarizing telephone messages, whose call is returned first?[19] Whose phone calls are allowed to interrupt meetings, and whose cause people to tell their secretaries, "Say that I'll call back later!"? Whose late requests cause people to postpone already-scheduled lunches and business meetings? Where do people seem to go for advice or guidance concerning big decisions in either their personal lives or in their organizations? Who controls the flow of money? The answers to these questions will frequently reveal which people have major impact on important matters within an organization.

The concept of roles also includes expectations about the behavior of people in powerful positions that *others* hold regarding them.[20] The term can be thought of in its theatrical sense. A playwright creates a drama with a number of characters or roles. Many people can play those roles, and the actors have to stay within the confines of their roles or they will be dismissed. An actor playing Hamlet, for instance, cannot suddenly become decisive and forthright in his actions during the first act. Similarly, powerful people are expected to behave in certain ways, and if they do not, they risk losing influence. Given the number of people desiring powerful positions, there is no shortage of replacements for a person whose influence is waning. Powerholders are expected to be confident, knowledgeable, and sophisticated about the use of their resources. If they constantly have to say "I don't know" and must clumsily turn to subordinates for the answers to questions, they lose the respect of their peers and subordinates.

Powerful people must also take on tasks for which they have had little preparation. While the folklore about the role of a CEO includes careful and thoughtful planning about the future, Henry Mintzberg found the CEOs had so many day-to-day demands on their time that long-range planning was a rare event.[21] They were also expected to participate in many ceremonial events: ribbon cuttings, presentations of gold watches to long-term employees, hearty welcomes to high-status visitors and especially valued customers, and attendance at testimonial dinners for community leaders. If CEOs do not engage in a certain number of these ceremonial obligations, they can lose the goodwill of subordinates and other influential people who interpret noninvolvement as intentional snubs. I have over-heard employees complaining about CEOs who did not attend ceremonial events such as office parties and presentations of awards, with comments centering on the CEOs' lack of concern for human relations in the organization.

2. Goals

Like the process of identification of powerful people, the process of articulating the goals of a social setting may be straightforward or it may be difficult. Goals may include making a profit, expanding the organization, designing innovative products, contributing to knowledge, or passing on information to future generations. At times an easily observed goal can mask hidden agendas. People may act in an affiliative manner because they know it can advance their power need. People may pay lip service to their supervisors' goals and then do exactly what they want during their work hours. One of the key issues managers must always face is the integration of the organization's goals with the goals held by its most intelligent and creative employees.[22]

On the organizational level, the public's view of goals may differ from reality. Nonprofit organizations that receive grants from the government and from foundations frequently have continued funding as their major goal. Critics often charge that the funding goal can subvert the organization's expressed purpose for existence. Organizations that claim to train the handicapped for employment, for instance, may work with only the most attractive and teachable of the potential client population rather than the most disadvantaged. These organizations can then point to their clients' accomplishments when placed in public-sector jobs as a justification for further funding. Given their actual goals, then, the people who need help the most remain unreached.

Another set of problems is associated with purposeful obfuscation of goals. Professionals involved in evaluating public service organizations often charge that the goals of these organizations are not at all clear. Consequently, the evaluators cannot discover whether the goals are being achieved. Administrators in the organizations know this and purposely keep the goals unclear so that they cannot be targets of good evaluation studies.[23]

3. Rules

Organizations have explicit and implicit guidelines that provide direction for day-to-day behavior, and the guidelines that are implicit often take a long time to discover. One respondent said, "In a complex organization, people have to keep their mouths shut for about a year and observe what is going on. This is hard for a lot of people since they want to speak up. But this length of time is necessary to learn the rules." Rules guide diverse decisions such as how best to approach people who already have power, when to expect a return for past favors rendered, and how to deal with outsiders who want information about the organization. Baseball player Ted Williams had career-long difficulties with the press in Boston. In his autobiography, *My Turn at Bat*, he described some early encounters.[24] Since he achieved superstar-level success at a very early age, the press flocked to him. Members of the press would ask Williams probing questions, and given his youth and inexperience in public speaking, he did not handle himself well. In his book he mused about these early years and wished that an executive from the Red Sox organization had sat down with him and given him a set of rules for dealing with the press. Since no one did, he had to muddle through on his own.

One problem with any discussion of rules is that they are frequently idiosyncratic to an organization, and to add complexity, they change over time. The rules can only be learned through day-to-day experience in an organization. In the U.S. Senate, numerous rules guide behavior prior to the final vote on a bill. One technique used is called "pairing," a procedure that allows senators to cancel each other out.[25] Suppose two senators on opposite sides of a bill want to be away from the Senate floor on the day of a vote. They may both have well-paying speaking engagements, or they may want short vacations. They can "pair" their vote, registering themselves in the record as to how they *would have* voted. Given their absence from the floor, they play no part in the deliberations or maneuverings prior to the vote. If future opponents challenge their nonaction on the vote, they can respond that their position is recorded. "Should my opponents care to do their homework and examine the records, they will see that my position is clearly there." The opponents can then try to make a distinction between voting and being registered, but since this is so extraordinarily dull, neither the press nor the public will bother to listen and the whole issue will likely be forgotten. Incidentally, people who arrange pairings are performing a service for which they expect a return at a later date.

There may not be a procedure similar to pairing in other organizations, but I guarantee that there are rules as complex and as seemingly zany.

Many of these rules were established to meet the needs of generations in the distant past and are kept because people have become accustomed to them. To change the rules is to change the status quo with which people have become comfortable, and this is always difficult regardless of the quality of the proposals for change.

4. Elements

The actions that are proper and improper in situations are examples of elements. During the learning period, when people are becoming accustomed to new organizations, they should be attentive to the behavior of their experienced colleagues. Newcomers can observe the behaviors that seem to lead to success when performed by their colleagues, and they can also list the behaviors that seem to cause difficulties. For example, newly hired assistant professors at a college can be expected to teach, do research, publish, bring in outside funding, recruit students, and render community services, but the expectations for a proper *balance* among these activities varies widely across colleges, and this is learned by observation.

At times there are invisible elements. I once tried to change a policy in an educational organization located in Hawaii. The status quo was that people would come to Hawaii to engage in studies of international topics. I argued that this limited the opportunities for the people who might come, since Hawaii does not have experts in all relevant study areas who might attract the best students. I wanted to open up the funding so that the students could choose their mentors at a number of excellent institutions (e.g., in California or in Japan), as long as the proposed study had an international focus. Clearly there were problems due to limited resources: there would be a change in the amount of money flowing into Hawaii. But another problem involved symbols. Many political figures who might have supported the policy change had the image of Hawaii as a growing "crossroads of the Pacific" where people from Asia and the United States meet. In addition there was a deceased but still highly respected political leader who had supported (and may have developed) the image. So I was fighting money, old symbols, and respected elders, and consequently I did not progress very far.

5. Sequences of Behavior

Once proper behaviors are known, attention can be given to the best ways in which they should be ordered. For example, people may want to propose a new idea at an organization's regularly scheduled monthly meeting of executives. Rather than introduce the idea "cold," they can often follow a set of intelligent preliminary steps, which can be arranged in a sequence. Should the title of the proposed idea be put on the published agenda for the upcoming meeting? If so, there has to be communication with the person who prepares the agenda. This can be an important step, since a listing on the published agenda can give dignity to the proposal. If the proposal is controversial, it may be best to leak key details so the people can voice their objections before the meeting. Knowing about the possible criticisms, the person presenting the proposal can add material to counter objections.

Returning to the example of the activities expected of assistant professors, faculty members at universities where extensive research and publication are expected face a difficult first few years. While it might seem that young faculty members should spend their first year preparing courses so they will be effective teachers, this is usually not the best use of their time. At these universities they have to start as soon as possible to establish a research program, to secure outside funding for its support, and to attract the best graduate students as research assistants. Callous though it may seem, the most helpful advice at "publish or perish" universities is to prepare classroom materials and pay attention to teaching during stolen hours of the day *and* night. Since young professors are often starting marriages or raising young children at about this time, the early years of a university appointment can take a toll on family life.

6. Concepts

Experienced powerholders always have clearly developed rules of thumb for the acquisition and maintenance of power, and these often mirror well-established concepts developed by behavioral and social scientists. A frequently seen example is the use of an outgroup to rally people around a cause. When people feel that they have a common enemy, they solidify their ingroup feelings and direct energy away from internal squabbles toward an external threat.[26] In Israel, tensions among religiously observant and nonobservant Jews diminish when a common enemy, such as the Palestinians, demands their attention. In the United States, Democrats put aside considerable internal differences when they focus on heartless Republicans who want to cut off welfare benefits to widows and dependent children.

Many powerful people have an understanding of contrast effect, even if they are not able to use the exact term.[27] An action can be more attention grabbing if it occurs against a background of complementary or contrasting behaviors. If the political ranks are full of candidates with matinee-idol good looks and blow-dried hair, a plain-looking candidate can attract attention because of his or her distinctiveness. If large numbers of middle-level executives are proposing expansions of product lines in a company, the few executives who argue for better quality control of existing products can stand out from the crowd.

Other rules of thumb have been discussed in previous chapters: develop a valued resource; use it in exchanges; be careful to return favors; keep disagreements within the ingroup; and demonstrate loyalty to the outside world. Many more will be discussed when strategies and tactics are reviewed in Chapters 4 and 5.

7. Language and Speech

Important concepts are sometimes summarized in unique vocabulary terms, and in combination the terms become a jargon or argot. Membership in ingroups, or the feeling that "these people belong," is dependent upon knowing and using the jargon. International organizations frequently use the phrase "hands across the sea." Applicants to graduate programs in social work have to deal with their "desire to help people." CEOs refer to their belief that "the business of business is business."

As people become more and more involved in an ingroup and its activities, the language they use refers to more and more differentiated features of a concept.[28] The ability to differentiate, or to make fine distinctions, marks the expert. Medical doctors know the distinctions among many penicillin derivatives; investment bankers distinguish among various types of bonds; college faculty members who work extensively with foreign students know about different types of visas. While these concepts are "penicillin," "bonds," and "visas" to outsiders, the ability to make distinctions among them is necessary for people desiring ingroup membership. Inappropriate use of fine distinctions shows a lack of social grace. Readers have probably experienced such differentiations at parties where people were discussing details of their personal computers. This topic of the 1980s replaced the 1970s concern with the details of one's running shoes.

Knowledgeable people sometimes use the inability of others to make fine distinctions as a tactic in dismissing their criticism. Even though the questions raised by the others are reasonable, the people being challenged can respond with comments such as, "To answer that question, I would have to refer to classified (or proprietary) details that cannot be made widely known."

8. Boundaries

People must know where one situation ends and another, with different roles and rules, begins.[29] The most commonly used terms referring to boundary problems are "turf" and "turf battles." People must know when their activities tread on a valued situation over which someone else has control. A classic example in business is when people in product development make suggestions about marketing, which makes people in marketing feel that their expertise is being questioned. In government there are both elected officials and long-term civil servants, and the civil servants feel that they ought to be consulted if a proposed policy touches upon their carefully carved out areas of influence. In a university a senior professor may lay claim to a certain research area, such as studies of depression. Young assistant professors may have to choose other research areas if the senior professor wants the exclusive right to investigate depression. While there is no "law," the senior person can make life difficult for newcomers if the informal boundaries are not maintained. As will be discussed more fully in Chapter 4, this exclusivity is often shortsighted and can decrease the influence of the person who claims the territorial rights.

People must also know that they are in one situation rather than in another. This seemingly commonsense observation has important implications. At times people think that they are in one situation with a certain set of rules when actually they should think of themselves in another situation with a different set of rules. I interviewed a successful musician whose primary instrument is the banjo. He and I have studied the instrument for many years and know its history, its place in folk music from the Appalachian Mountains, and its role in modern country and bluegrass music. He makes his living with his music, performing almost exclusively to urban audiences. He once said to me, "Rich, these people are too busy for folk music," meaning that his audiences are not primarily interested in an evening of banjo and folk music, though they *are* interested in an evening of entertainment. Put another way, my friend is competing for the entertainment dollar, not the banjo/folk-music dollar. There are people who *do* try to compete for a share of the latter market, but it is so small that no one can make a living at it.

9. Difficulties and Skills

My friend's distinction between himself as an entertainer and himself as a banjo player reflects an awareness of the difficulties to be found in social situations. When faced with an unfamiliar social setting, a good question to ask is, "What in this situation will be difficult, and what skills are necessary to overcome the difficulties?" Some situations are difficult because the people involved have many different interests and want different outcomes. There are skills demanded in these situations that are not possessed by everyone: cutting deals, forging compromises, and encouraging people to pursue outcomes in which as many participants as possible emerge as winners. If potentially powerful people have the self-insight to know that they do not possess certain needed skills, they can give attention to recruiting colleagues who do have the skills.

Newcomers to an organization can ask experienced colleagues about difficulties that have caused problems for people, as well as for advice on how the difficulties can be overcome. The answers to these questions are not always found in textbooks or learned in college classrooms. For example, highly educated women enjoy interacting with equally well educated men. Difficulties arise when they marry and when both want responsible and challenging jobs in the same community. If they are fortunate enough to find such a community, further difficulties arise when the two try to maintain a balance between their professional and personal lives. Since only a few people have parents who have successfully maintained the balance, individuals in the current generation have to develop the necessary skills by trial and error.

AN EXAMPLE OF SITUATIONAL FACTORS

A useful exercise consists of analyzing a complex situation using the nine factors. All powerful people have to deal at one time or another with the press. Assume that three reporters are interviewing a C.E.O. and that the subject is a possible change in a well-known organization. The *roles* are occupied by three people asking questions and obtaining answers from the respondent. One of the reporters may have the reputation of being an aggressive questioner, while the other two may be willing to settle for prepared handouts. The *goals* include front-page coverage for the reporters and either positive or negative coverage of the possible change for the respondent, depending upon his or her views. The *rules* include how many quotations can be attributed to the respondent. If one rule, carefully set at the beginning, is that the interview is a "backgrounder," then the reporters cannot quote the person directly. They have to use a phrase like "A high ranking official said, . . . "

The *actions* include distribution of prepared handouts, questions and answers, preparation of the story, and creation of a headline. The latter activity is more often performed by editors than reporters. These actions usually follow the above *sequence*, but there can be additions if the reporters agree to call the respondent back to review any direct quotes or explanations of complex ideas. Other additions can include later responses to the original newspaper article from people affected by the possible change.

Concepts refer to shared knowledge. Reporters and the experienced, powerful respondents realize that they are "using each other." A reporter wants a story that will generate a good deal of interest so that more people will notice the byline at the top of the article. The respondents want coverage of certain points and downplaying of others depending upon their needs: to attack the change, to punish enemies, to promote themselves, or to test the waters to see if the time is ripe for a different policy. Some of the concepts are summarized in *language* known to insiders. Both reporters and the respondents know the importance of the lead, or main idea, emphasized at the beginning of a printed story. They all realize that many readers proceed no further than the first paragraph. The respondents often try to control the lead by imagining what reporters and their editors will find flashy and exciting, and then including those ideas in their own handouts.

The *environmental setting* includes the site where the interview takes place, but more importantly, it includes psychological concepts that are far less visible. If one reporter expects the interview to be an exclusive, then he or she will be upset when two other reporters from competing newspapers show up. Reporters also have to decide how to carve up their own territory without irritating each other. If entertainers perform regularly for local political functions, the story may be one that could be covered by either the city desk or the arts desk. Given their knowledge of newspaper rivalries, sophisticated respondents play the egos of reporters against each other. They may give one reporter a juicy piece of information with the expectation that this resource will be reciprocated by favorable coverage; if the expected coverage does not appear, then the exclusive tidbits are given to another reporter.

Many *difficulties* have already been described: controlling the lead, establishing the type of attribution for quotations, and manipulating reporters for favorable coverage. Another difficulty is cutting off negative coverage. Reporters like to publish an account of one person's attacks on another; they can then pursue another story featuring the reactions of the person who was attacked. In many cases the attacked person should not respond directly to the provocation and should make a statement like "I believe that the people will be best served if we stick to the issues that affect their everyday lives." The danger of responding in kind to a provocative attack is that the original accusation sticks in the minds of people as they read about the charges and countercharges. The necessary skill is to grin and bear the attack, not an easy task for many people, and to keep in mind that the public has a very short memory[30] for most of the colorful stories that appear in the newspapers.

If people do not respond to attacks, they are demonstrating the more general strategy of cutting their losses. No would-be powerholder comes out the winner after every encounter with opponents. Long-term damage to their reputations is minimized, however, if they are skillful at using the strategies that successful powerholders use, and a wide variety of such strategies are covered in the next chapter.

NOTES

1. Interpersonal skills are reviewed in a later part of this section dealing with personality traits. Other treatments include M. Argyle, "Interaction Skills and Social Competence," in *Psychological Problems: The Social Context*, edited by M. P. Feldman and J. Orford (New York: Wiley, 1980), pp. 123–150.

2. B. Woodward and C. Bernstein, *All the President's Men* (New York: Simon & Schuster, 1974).

3. R. A. Caro, *The Years of Lyndon Johnson: The Path to Power* (New York: Knopf, 1982).

4. Various features of resources are discussed in H. Mintzberg, *Power in and around Organizations* (Englewood Cliffs, N.J.: Prentice-Hall, 1983); also M. Harrison, *Diagnosing Organizations: Methods, Models, and Processes* (Newbury Park, Calif.: Sage, 1987).

5. R. S. Lazarus, "The Stress and Coping Paradigm," in *Models for Clinical Psychopathology*, edited by C. Eisdorfer, D. Cohen, A. Kleinmen, and P. Maxim (New York: Spectrum, 1981), pp. 177–214.

6. Colleagues and I have discussed cross-cultural differences in the ability to disassociate criticism of one's ideas from criticism of oneself as a human being. H. Triandis, R. Brislin, and C. H. Hui, "Cross-Cultural Training across the Individualism-Collectivism Divide," *International Journal of Intercultural Relations* 12 (1988): 269–89.

7. The ability to attribute problems appropriately to external factors is beneficial to mental health. D. Meichenbaum, *Cognitive-Behavior Modification: An Integrative Approach* (New York: Plenum, 1977). Other good treatments of handling problems can be found in M. McCormack, *What They Still Don't Teach You at Harvard Business School* (New York: Bantam, 1989); and S. Helmstetter, *Choices* (New York: Simon & Schuster, Pocket Books, 1989).

8. S. Moscovichi, "Towards a Theory of Conversion Behavior," in *Advances in Experimental Social Psychology*, vol. 13, edited by L. Berkowitz (New York: Academic Press, 1980), pp. 209–39.

9. P. McGhee and J. Goldstein, eds., *Handbook of Humor Research* (New York: Springer-Verlag, 1983).

10. W. Gudykunst, ed., *Intergroup Communication* (London: Edward Arnold, 1986).

11. H. Ehrlich, *The Social Psychology of Prejudice* (New York: Wiley, 1973).

12. R. Burns, "To a Louse," in *The Poetical Works of Robert Burns*, vol. 2, edited by G. Aitkin (London: George Bell & Sons, 1893), p. 11.

13. Self-monitoring is a related concept, and its effects are discussed in M. Snyder and W. Ickes, "Personality and Social Behavior," in *The Handbook of Social Psychology*, 3rd ed., edited by G. Lindzey and E. Aronson (New York: Random House, 1985), vol. 2, pp. 883–947.

14. I. Janis and L. Mann, *Decision Making* (New York: Free Press, 1977).

15. A good overview of charisma can be found in E. Hollander, "Leadership and Power," in *The Handbook of Social Psychology*, 3rd ed., edited by G. Lindzey and E. Aronson (New York: Random House, 1985), vol. 2., pp. 485–537. See also J. Hagberg, *Real Power: The Stages of Personal Power in Organizations* (Minneapolis, Minn: Winston, 1984).

16. D. Magnussen and N. Endler, eds., *Personality at the Crossroads: Current Issues in Interactional Psychology* (Hillsdale, N.J.: Erlbaum, 1977)

17. People choosing situations, the difficulties found in complex situations, and the competencies needed to overcome the difficulties are discussed in J. Wright and W. Mischel, "A Conditional Approach to Dispositional Constructs: The Local Predictability of Social Behavior," *Journal of Personality and Social Psychology*

53 (1987): 1159–77. See also the section on difficulties and skills at the end of this chapter.

18. M. Argyle, A. Furnham, and J. Graham, *Social Situations* (Cambridge: Cambridge University Press, 1981).

19. C. Felker, eds., *The Power Game* (New York: Simon & Schuster, 1969).

20. S. Stryker and A. Statham, "Symbolic Interaction and Role Theory," in *The Handbook of Social Psychology*, 3rd ed., edited by G. Lindzey and E. Aronson (New York: Random House, 1985), vol. 1, pp. 311–78.

21. H. Mintzberg, "The Manager's Job: Folklore and Fact," *Harvard Business Review* 25 (July-August 1975): 49–61.

22. R. Schoenberg, *The Art of Being a Boss* (New York: Mentor, 1980).

23. T. Cook and W. Shadish, "Program Evaluation: The Worldly Science," *Annual Review of Psychology* 37 (1986): 193–232.

24. T. Williams, *My Turn at Bat* (New York: Simon & Schuster, 1969).

25. B. Baker, *Wheeling and Dealing: Confessions of a Capitol Hill Operator* (New York: Norton, 1978).

26. M. Sherif, *In Common Predicament: Social Psychology of Intergroup Conflict and Cooperation* (New York: Houghton Mifflin, 1966).

27. H. Helson, *Adaptation Level Theory* (New York: Harper, 1964).

28. H. Triandis, *Interpersonal Behavior* (Monterey, Calif.: Brooks/Cole, 1977).

29. R. Sommer, *Personal Space* (Englewood Cliffs, N.J.: Prentice-Hall, 1959).

30. It has been suggested that negative information about another person is stored in an area of memory separate from that for positive information. Cutting losses, then, includes keeping that negative part of people's memory small in comparison to the positive part. S. Fiske and S. Taylor, *Social Cognition* (New York: Random House, 1984).

4

STRATEGIES FOR POWER
ACQUISITION AND
MAINTENANCE

Experienced powerholders know that they do not win every competition for resources. None of them prevail in every argument, successfully introduce each desired policy shift, support only successful politicians, or win every lawsuit. They do, however, increase their chances of success by employing a number of strategies. Put another way, success in the competition for scarce resources involves probabilities—people win some, and they lose others. Good poker players know that they cannot play every hand dealt to them and come out a winner at the end of the evening. Frequently, they have to look at their cards and fold immediately. Their probability of ultimate success can be increased through the employment of various strategies, such as withdrawing early when the case is hopeless.

For the purposes of organization, I have grouped the strategies used by powerholders into several broad categories:

1. Working with others who are at a similar or lower level within their organizations;

2. Working with powerholders (bosses, community leaders);

3. Dealing with the general public;

4. Surrounding oneself with positive images;

5. Learning complex bureaucracies;

6. Thinking into the future.

As with all organizational schemes, various people will rightfully point

out that there is overlap and that specific strategies can be considered
under more than one heading. For instance, strategies for developing positive images (4) are useful for working with colleagues (1) and with people
who have power (2). However, there are more advantages than disadvantages to a system for organizing disparate information, as long as people
realize that the categories are not to be reified.

WORKING WITH OTHERS AT SIMILAR AND LOWER LEVELS

Power does not consist solely of one person telling others what to do,
with subsequent behaviors of the multitudes following the powerholder's
instructions to the letter. More often, power involves complex combinations of behaviors involving superiors, colleagues at about the same level
within an organizational hierarchy, and subordinates.

One of the most important activities of would-be powerholders is to
develop a network of helpful people. While some network members will
(and should) be successful powerholders who are widely known, there are
only so many of these people in a community. The largest number of people
in one's network will usually be at a similar level of influence and power
to oneself or at a lower level. Members of a network are different from
close friends.[1] Good friends have strong emotional ties with one another
and count on each other's help in times of need. People in a network
however, maintain contact for each other's benefit. One person may have
information about tax law to share and may exchange it within the network
for help in getting on television. Another person may be willing to put in
time and energy on a fund-raiser for a charity in exchange for introductions
to people who have leads on good job opportunities. Still another may
exchange the names of influential people ("contacts") from his Rolodex
for someone's free lecture at a service organization's monthly meeting.
People within a network are cordial, gracious, and good-natured but do
not necessarily have warm feelings about each other. While people within
networks *do* occasionally develop true friendships, they more often maintain relationships as long as they accrue benefits to themselves. People in
a network sometimes drop from view for a few years and then rejoin when
participation is likely to benefit them. In such cases, however, they must
be careful not to gain reputations as "takers" who only want membership
to gain benefits. They must be willing to return favors when it is their turn
to do so.[2]

The ideal network consists of people with many areas of expertise: law,
communications, athletics, entertainment, finance, taxes, medicine, elected
politics, education, international affairs, and so forth. Where might these
people be met? While more answers will be found in Chapter 8 a few will
be apparent if we ask ourselves where influential people spend time. An-

swers to this vary across communities, and the resulting information is an example of what newcomers should learn during their initial period, when they should be observing, listening and learning the rules of their organization (Chapter 3). In communities I have known, powerful people could be found at activities sponsored by the local symphony orchestra or ballet support group, either of the major political parties, service clubs such as Rotary International, the golf course, churches, voluntary organizations attached to museums, interest groups such as a bridge club, alumni organizations for various colleges, parent-teacher organizations at schools, organizations devoted to activities for children such as Little League baseball, and support groups for nursing homes.

The last two may seem out of place, but they are good examples of meeting grounds for potential network members. Many influential people have children between the ages of 6 and 16 and recognize the value of organized athletic activities for them. They support these activities with their time, energy, and money, and often can be found taking roles as coaches, umpires or referees, and fans.

Similarly, influential people sometimes have elderly parents who must receive around-the-clock care in a nursing home. They support the homes in various ways and can often be found there. Years ago I had my first extensive interaction with a U.S. Senator at a nursing home. I had volunteered to give a banjo/folk music concert; he happened to be visiting his mother, and we struck up a conversation. The basic piece of advice for the development of a network is "Don't stay at home—get out into the community!" In some places people actually use the word network, telling their spouses, "I'm off tonight for a fundraiser—network time!"

Coalition Formation

Once a network is formed, one can begin to learn the values, preferences, and goals of the other members. With this information, coalitions can be organized to pursue policies of interest to many. Powerholders look at proposals more seriously if the interests and efforts of many people are involved. It is much easier to dismiss one isolated individual than a united coalition. Given knowledge of others' interests (including knowledge about the resources for which they are competing), an ambitious individual can incorporate as many of these interests as possible into a proposal so as to gain their support.

What steps should be taken? The first is simply to ask people, "What would you like to see done around here? What would you like changed so that the organization will prosper? What can you add to make my draft proposal better?" People love to be asked! Most people are not asked for help in this manner, and they are complimented if someone cares about their opinions.

The greatest untapped resource in American organizations is the knowledge and know-how of workers intimately familiar with their jobs, and one of the most puzzling unanswered questions of this century is why their knowledge and energy is not better harnessed. One of my oldest friends runs a successful consulting firm in Washington, D.C., and also teaches a university-level course in policy studies. He assigns his students to interview a high-ranking civil servant about policy options in his or her area of expertise and influence. The students inevitably complain, "But these people are so busy that they won't have any time for a nobody–college student like myself!" My friend answers, "They are busy, but chances are that no one has asked them for *their* opinion on anything in months. Many are so surrounded by paper that they haven't *spoken* with anyone in two weeks! They'll be delighted that you care to listen to them." None of his students have ever experienced difficulty in finding high-ranking civil servants willing to be interviewed.

When people give input to a draft and see that their ideas are represented in subsequent drafts, they begin to feel a sense of ownership. They want to see the proposal accepted by powerholders and subsequently implemented by all concerned because something of themselves is in it. The person who writes the proposal and incorporates the suggestions of others has to learn to develop ideas in win-win terms. It is easier to understand this concept by reviewing an example of a win-lose situation first.

Win-Win Instead of Win-Lose Thinking

One of the most frequently studied problems that has strong possibilities of win-lose solutions is known as the prisoner's dilemma. Two male criminals are apprehended and are charged with committing a serious crime. They are separated and interrogated by experienced police officers. Each is promised lenient treatment if he cooperates so that a case can be built against the other. However, if each agrees to testify against the other, there is no advantage to the police to cut deals and both will be prosecuted with vigor. Complexity is added by the fact that other types of evidence for prosecution of the major crime are nonexistent. If both maintain their innocence and do not "break ranks" and squeal on each other, they will only be prosecuted on the lesser charge of owning unregistered handguns. In pictorial form, the dilemma appears in Figure 4. Two psychologists analyzed the problem in the following way:

Put yourself in the place of one of the prisoners. It seems easy enough to keep your mouth shut and receive a light sentence for a minor crime. Yet, if your partner confesses, you will pay dearly. On the other hand, you can confess to gain a lenient sentence and worsen your partner's position relative to yours, but again you run the risk that you will both suffer. The Prisoner's Dilemma is a mixed-motive

Figure 4
The Prisoner's Dilemma

Person B

		maintains innocence	turns against other
Person A	*maintains innocence*	A-2 years on lesser charge B-2 years on lesser charge	A-20 years in jail B-6 months in jail
	turns against other	A-6 months in jail B-20 years in jail	A-8 years in jail B-8 years in jail

situation precisely because the action that is the best choice for each individual separately will, if chosen by both individuals, result in a losing outcome.[3]

One possibility is a win-lose outcome. One criminal will win since he receives a light sentence, while the other will lose by spending 20 years in jail. Many problems in life are win-lose. If two people are courting someone with the goal of marriage, only one can win. If there is limited funding for new product development, together with many proposals for use of the funds, some will win and some will lose in the competition for support of their ideas.

Too often, however, problems are perceived in win-lose terms when a little creativity would lead to the development of win-win solutions. In such solutions, everyone involved perceives that they have received benefits. While many long-distance races could emphasize one winner, or a few winners divided according to age groups or gender, some successful charity fund-raiser races emphasize that "everyone is a winner." All who finish a ten mile race have accomplished something important: the exercise has contributed to their good health; their entry fees help an important charity; and they all get to wear a T-shirt indicating their active participation.

Designing win-win solutions is admittedly an art, and there are no hard and fast guidelines. Basic questions to ask are: "What do people in my organization or network want? How can aspects be added to my proposal so that all come out feeling that they have benefitted—that they are winners?" One reason why pork barrel bills are so popular in national and state legislatures is that all the legislators involved go home to their constituencies looking like winners—they have a building program, or a highway, or a dam to wave in front of the voters. Of course, influential legislators who control pork barrel allocations trade their ability to designate resources for fellow legislators' votes. Pork barrel designators (such as finance committee members) expect the recipients to give their votes to projects favored by the most powerful in the legislature.

Win-win solutions have been part of important events in history. To gain the necessary support of the states for ratification of a new constitution for the United States in 1787, a compromise was devised that split the legislative branch into two parts. The upper chamber would have two representatives per state, and this protected the interests of the less populated states. The lower house had differing numbers of representatives per state based on population. With this compromise, the delegates to the constitutional convention could return to their states, large or small, claiming that they had been the winners in the negotiations.[4]

Designing win-win solutions requires extensive knowledge of the organizations in which people work, as well as the people's specific needs and desires, and so I can give examples only from organizations that I know well. I believe, however, that the general principles are similar across organizations and that they focus on ways to benefit all the people involved.

Assume that there are five ambitious assistant professors in the same college who desire good careers. At the college the norms for tenure involve either excellent teaching or excellent research publications, although outsiders have long suspected that professors with good access to sources of funding also are favored during tenure negotiations. Professor A is very interested in undergraduate teaching, feeling that this aspect of the college experience has been underemphasized in the "publish or perish" grind; Professor B enjoys being the boss of projects and enjoys hobnobbing with high-status people; Professor C wants to be a well-known, nationally recognized researcher in psychology; Professor D enjoys working with foreign students from a variety of countries; and Professor E is interested in scripting and producing television programs.

One or more of these five people can develop a win-win proposal. The proposal would call for a Center for Undergraduate Teaching Excellence. Every college dean and president will have to give a good proposal serious attention or else risk the severe criticism that they are downplaying the importance of undergraduates on campus. "Deans Dump On Disappointed Undergraduates Again!" is a headline that will almost certainly appear in the local papers, and the parents of 18 through 22-year-old students will not keep their phones on their hooks. Professor A would be able to work directly with undergraduates who come to the center for special tutoring. Professor B would run the administrative structure, interacting with the dean and college president, and with potential funders who could contribute to the college general fund. Professor C could start a research program on the special needs of undergraduates and their professors, such as the issues involved in translating complex research findings into principles that can be grasped by students and used in their other courses. There are fine academic journals where good research on such problems will find a sizable audience. Professor D could add a program for the special needs of students from other countries to the proposal—how they can best compete for grades when they are using a less familiar language, or how they can cope with culture shock. Professor E could produce videotapes focusing on successful outcomes. For instance, widely distributable videotapes could be produced that would present reports on complex scientific research findings, followed by lectures on the tapes by a skillful college teacher presenting the findings to enthusiastic students in a clear manner. Note that all the people involved are gaining benefits—they can look upon the proposal as producing a "win" for them. Note also that it should be relatively easy to recruit other supporters—the undergraduate student government, the audio-visual center, the foreign student advisers' office, and so forth.

Communications and the Absence of Enemies

During the time when a proposal is being developed, and during its aftermath following acceptance by powerholders, people should maintain communications with their peers and with their subordinates who participated in its preparation. It is easy to fall into the power-intoxication pattern described in Chapter 2, with its associated arrogance and smugness, so this should be consciously avoided. The help of others will be needed so that the current project will receive constant attention and at the same time future ventures will be developed. If others feel "dropped" from communications networks, they will be less likely to help during future times of need.

In her account of the turmoil at the Bendix Corporation and of her relationship with William Agee, Mary Cunningham[5] admitted (and later regretted) that she had not maintained good communication links with her peers. Cunningham was young, bright, and attractive. She developed a close professional relationship with the influential senior executive Agee, who acted as her mentor in the world of big business. Cunningham was promoted within Bendix at an early age, and with fewer years in the company, than other mid-level executives. This created jealousy, and this emotional reaction increased when Cunningham did not keep up good communication links with the other executives. When the tremendous upheavals occurred at Bendix, these others were not eager to help Cunningham.

When people develop ties with powerholders, they should consider sharing the information they gain with their peers who do not have access to the same circles. Obviously there will be proprietary information that cannot be disseminated, but there will be much that can be widely shared and that will interest others. People love gossip, tales of intrigue, rumors, and juicy tidbits about possible future deals. This fascination accounts for the continued popularity of soap operas, a contemporary literary genre that has its antecedents in folk ballads sung or recited six hundred years ago. One hears about the foibles of the rich and powerful in these old ballads, just as one sees them on television shows like "Dynasty" and "Dallas." If the favored pass on information, they are sharing a scarce resource and can expect gratitude in return. People like to feel privy to company insider information, and the person who can pass on gossip and high-level executives' musings will be popular.

If people keep up communication networks, they find themselves in the company of grateful colleagues rather than among enemies. Powerholders make as few enemies as possible. There will be so many occasions for the formation of coalitions in the future that it is stupid to make enemies today. As several respondents pointed out, "People may be adamantly against your proposal today, but it is unwise to make enemies of them. Tomorrow there may be issues on which you can agree. Their help may be welcome."

There are many variations on this piece of advice. Newly elected congressmen are told by their elders, "Get along with people who disagree with you on the issues closest to your heart." A colleague of mine was named vice president of a university without having previously held any administrative positions. I was surprised, and asked for the reactions of a person who had known him over a 25-year period. He suggested, "The new vice president has long had a talent for not making enemies."

Still, people occasionally have to take a strong stand and declare that someone else is so vile, corrupt, and incorrigible that there has to be as little contact as possible. But before an enemy is made, one should think about the matter long and hard. "Will the momentary pleasure of purposely snubbing, humiliating, or denouncing this person be wise in the long run? Or will more benefits accrue if the person is kept in my network?" If the objectionable person is influential, purposeful exclusion can lead to distancing from that same objectionable person's entire network. The loss of potential access to that network may make the exclusion unwise. Also people who gain a reputation in a community for making a lot of enemies find themselves denied opportunities that are offered to their more level-headed peers. Person A is unlikely to introduce Person B to influential people if B is likely to make enemies of them. Such behavior would reflect badly back on Person A, who would be seen as someone who did not have the ability to size up others accurately.

Speaking of the need for scientists and explorers to check on each others' works and claims, the explorer David Livingston said that "we are made wise by our peers." Similarly, people who want to be powerful must derive their status through interaction with others in overlapping networks. If they have poor relations with too many others, they will find themselves dropped from influential social circles.

WORKING WITH POWERHOLDERS

At some point, one's proposals will be reviewed by various powerholders to determine whether they will be accepted or rejected. These powerholders may be one's direct supervisors, the company board of directors, local or national politicians, or a faceless set of outsiders who will determine whether the proposal will receive government or corporate funding. Occasionally, the powerholders are not only faceless but invisible to any sort of scrutiny. I once tried to introduce changes at a state university and only much later found out that resistance had come from one member of the board of regents. This regent was not the chairperson but was by far the most colorful and quotable of a rather staid group. Newspaper and television reporters went to him for stories. His talent with the media, and the fear of other regents that this talent could be used against them someday, made him a formidable foe.

The Mentor

The importance of recognizing faceless and invisible opponents is the sort of knowledge gained through close relationships with experienced elders, most often called mentors. While this word seems to have been usurped by up-and-coming business executives born after World War II, the mentoring process is much more widespread. In any culture, senior people take on apprentices and pass on skills that are rarely found in the culture's written record. Native healers pass on the secrets of plants; bishops give selected younger priests advice on combining financial soundness with the saving of souls; full professors pass on an unwritten lore concerning how best to work with the editors of prestigious journals; and CEOs pass on their extensive networks.

The benefits to the people who have good mentors are clear; they include inside information, access to networks, first-hand observations of decision making in action, rules-of-thumb for dealing with various organizational problems, guidance on how to obtain important but currently unavailable information, the norms for resource exchange, and tacit knowledge limited to insiders. The benefits to the people who act as mentors are less frequently discussed. If they can help people on the way up society's ladder eventually the mentors can expect these favored individuals to pass on benefits from their eventual lofty perches. Since younger people often have more time and energy for network development, senior people can benefit when the names of key individuals (e.g., potential clients) are passed on. At times the younger person will meet an influential individual, and the mentor will later follow through on the contact. "I understand that you were able to help John Edwards. We are very proud of the way he is developing here.

Is there anything I can do for you?" The mentor has more impact on this other person, given his or her greater status and seniority; but the contact would not have been made without the younger person's efforts.

Psychological dynamics, including the satisfaction from seeing one's work continue into future generations, need to be taken into account when considering the role of mentor. Robert Schoenberg collected the following analyses in his interviews with senior executives:

I enjoy working with people, having people to supervise. The biggest kicks in business come in selecting people and seeing them come along. I get a great deal of satisfaction out of watching them grow.

That's your motivation: to be able to take the product of your years of experience and success and pass this baton on to younger people so that they can capitalize further. You can leverage your own experience through other people, and that's a *big* motivation.[6]

Mentors gain a great deal of satisfaction from seeing that others use their accumulated wisdom. Another of Schoenberg's respondents referred to younger people as a "living monument" to the mentor.[7]

What should young people look for when choosing a mentor? Obvious qualities are knowledge, influence, visibility in the community, and a willingness to share. Less frequently mentioned is that the mentors should *not* put a stamp on young people. A mentor who insists that everybody else should recognize certain young executives as "my people" may do a great deal of harm. The young people gain the reputation of being mere clones of the mentor and may never develop an identity of their own. The best mentors are willing to work quietly with their selected people and do not insist on constant public recognition. Further, they do not insist that their people always do things the way the mentors would. Good mentors pass on knowledge and skills but realize that people must combine these resources in their own unique ways.

Mentors also look for certain qualities when choosing younger people to whom they can pass on their wisdom. The young people should possess a resource for exchange, and they should be socially skilled, congenial, and imperturbable when faced with difficult situations. These are the qualities described in Chapter 3. Mentors look at these factors, since mistakes made by chosen younger people reflect back on the respected elders. "What kind of people is that old fogey tossing at us?" might be the reaction to a mistake-prone youth who tries to enter influential networks. Further, enemies made by the younger people can cause difficulties for the mentor. In general, then, a mentor chooses people who will lead influential others to conclude that the young up-and-comers were sponsored by a wise individual.

Anecdotes abound concerning the selection of young people for the fast path to eventual influence. Prestigious organizations hire summer interns from fine colleges. The organization does *not* expect any productive effort. Since they have good records at widely known schools, the organizations assume that the interns have basic intelligence and a resource based on knowledge (e.g., law, taxation, accounting, or the media). Executives want to see who has the social graces, who mixes well at cocktail parties where the guests are mostly strangers, who remains calm during meetings where their views are strongly challenged, and who can think quickly when faced with a difficult question. People who pass the summer test are offered permanent positions. Another benefit of choosing gregarious people who mix well is that the young people will talk favorably about their mentors. "She's been so helpful and unselfish with her time!" Others then begin to look even more favorably upon the mentor, and opportunities may be forthcoming since her name is on people's minds when the possibilities of new ventures are discussed.

There is a place for strong, silent types who keep to themselves and do not engage in frequent conversations with colleagues during the workday, but the place may not be within power-wielding circles. Silent people may not engage graciously in enough social activities to develop a network, and they may not be chosen by potential mentors, since there will be little favorable word-of-mouth advertisement in widely disseminated networks.

The fate of people who do not engage in resource exchange (especially the paying-back of favors) was discussed earlier. There is no angry outburst on the part of the powerholders; rather, the nonparticipants are simply dropped from opportunities for further interaction.

The outcome is similar for the socially ungraceful who argue too much, become upset too frequently, or irritate powerholders. Nobody sits down with these people to have a chat about their shortcomings; instead, they are dropped from further opportunities to develop a good network with a powerful mentor. This silent removal from future opportunities becomes the mentor's revenge on young people who irritate too many powerholders.

Reading the Traits of Powerholders

It is easy to become irritated with powerholders. Assume that an individual is involved in pushing a recommendation for a certain decision regarding an important policy matter. In making the final decision, the powerholders have to balance so many economic, political, historical, and psychological factors that they will seem to shortchange any *one* interested individual. The individual in question can easily say, "These executives are tunnel-visioned anachronisms who are owned by special interests." While it is momentarily pleasurable to express this sense of moral outrage stemming from certainty about an ideal world, if this person's bitter remark becomes public, he or she may be dropped from opportunities for power acquisition. A better strategy is to assume that the powerholders make their decisions for good reasons and from noble motives, and then to figure out the exact reasons and motives. By so doing, the individual is more likely to be able to make future recommendations that incorporate the powerholders' preferences, priorities, and values.

Questions should be asked concerning what powerholders want out of their jobs. Do they want new products, quality control of existing products, self-serving publicity for accomplishments in their organization, increased short-term profits, long-term growth? Many powerholders want a lasting monument to their names, often in the form of a building erected during their tenure—this is sometimes called the edifice complex. For instance, political appointees to high-level posts in Washington, D.C., stay the surprisingly short time of less than two years (on the average).[8] Within that time, they often want to accomplish something that has their name on it: a policy, a program, a change, a building or the like. If they take over a government office with good programs and hard-working employees, they receive little credit for *continuing* the first-rate efforts that were started by others. They make reputations for themselves as movers and shakers only if they introduce a major change or begin an innovative program. But they don't have time to do the work on such innovations themselves, given the day-to-day pressure of telephone calls, endless meetings, mail to be answered, political fund-raisers to attend, and so forth. The people who can actually *do* the work necessary for the innovation earn the gratitude of the powerholders. If there is success, the powerholders return to their home communities after their two-year stints in Washington with reputations as "doers" with "good connections in the Fed."

Given knowledge of powerholder goals, the task for up-and-comers is to link their efforts to those goals. If the linkage is made, the powerholder then uses his or her influence to push the program through the bureaucracy. One respondent, the executive director of a professional membership organization, had the goal of hosting an international conference in a major North American city. The basic theme of the conference was to be the importance of international experience in understanding today's business world. One young member from the city volunteered to be the local coordinator of the conference. She invited many influential figures in the city who were known to be good speakers and who had lived in other countries. The executive director was well served by a conference at which excellent speakers gave interesting presentations. Since the speakers had good reputations, they attracted a large number of participants, who paid hefty registration fees. The local coordinator made extensive contacts with these speakers, as well as with others whose calendars did not have the appropriate open dates. She now makes a handsome living acting as a consultant on international matters to the organizations where the speakers have high-level positions. Note the win-win nature of these outcomes: the executive accomplished her goal of hosting a good convention; the people invited to be speakers were complimented, even if they could not attend; and the local coordinator developed a network and thereby secured a living as a consultant.

People also want to take into account the idiosyncrasies of powerholders. Are there some times during the day or week when particular powerholders are best approached? Do they like people to "drop in" with new ideas, or do they prefer to read a memo so they can think about it carefully before responding?[9] Are there people whom the powerholders do not like very much and who should not be included in a proposal? Does the powerholder want to be treated like *the* boss, or does a more informal style ("Please call me by my first name!") prevail.[10] Does the powerholder value following tight rules and regulations, or is bold "cutting through the red tape" admired? Does the powerholder enjoy knowing the names of other influential people who will benefit from the proposal? Does the powerholder want to see that negative consequences of the proposal have been carefully considered, or is there a preference for attention to only positive aspects in the first few drafts? The answers to these questions are of great assistance in developing new ideas into a formal plan.

At times it will be wise for young people to give credit for the organization's accomplishments to the powerholders. Executives are often part of the public image of an organization, and they should be in the limelight when praise and honors are bestowed. If each major contributor insists on receiving public credit, the number of names becomes dull and confusing and there will be the risk of no publicity. Consequently, when the ribbons are cut for the grand opening, or when the formal gathering is held to signify the start of a new venture, the powerholders should often be the ones who pose for the photographers. The younger people who did all the work will be in the background, and in so doing they are giving a resource to the powerholders for which there should be an eventual return. If the other guidelines previously presented are followed, such as maintaining good communication networks, the important people will know who deserves credit for accomplishments. Incidentally, wise CEOs often host gatherings at a later date where the contributions of various people are publicly recognized *within* the organization. By being careful to give credit to their subordinates, powerholders encourage the subordinates to continue their hard work on projects that bring credit to all concerned.

Communicating with Powerholders

As very busy people, powerholders do not always know exactly what their subordinates are doing. While there are some exceptions, most become somewhat aloof from their subordinates and *do not* travel from door to door within their organization to find out what is happening. They do not just drop in and say, "How are things going? Anything I can do to help?" In the absence of direct inquiries from powerholders, young people have to make a point of keeping their superiors informed concerning their progress and accomplishments and the benefits they bring to the organization. Occasionally, powerholders can be asked for their opinion or advice without the subordinate's communicating a sense of helplessness. If the occasional request for help takes place against a background of previous hard work and accomplishments, the powerholder is flattered to be asked.[11] Even though they spend most of their time on managerial, budgetary, and administrative matters, powerholders continue to believe that they are the best possible resource in their original area of specialization. All CEOs who were once engineers believe that they still have insights into difficult design problems. All college deans believe that they could still write an influential book in their original academic specialty if they only had the time. I have seen many young people advance by appealing to these beliefs.

Some of the better popular guides to career success advise people to strike a balance between long work weeks and communication with powerholders.[12] This advice was also given by the respondents during my interviews. Many young people put in 70-hour weeks but find that their superiors do not know about their contributions. It may be better to work a 60-hour week and to spend the other 10 hours making sure that powerholders know about one's accomplishments. Memos can be sent; receptions for powerholders can be attended ("hobnobbing" and "rubbing shoulders" are frequent recommendations); and photocopies of letters of praise can be placed in superiors' in boxes.

The creativity needed to find ways to keep powerholders informed can provide a pleasant change of pace from normal day-to-day (now 60 hours per week) efforts. In fact, the stimulation that people derive from the rescheduled 10 hours can make the 60-hour week even more productive. I have known young people who have taken advantage of their resource as good public speakers. They give speeches at membership organizations that *friends* of the superiors attend. These friends then pass on compliments. "You've got a real up-and-comer. She gave a fine speech at the meeting." People who are skilled with the media can plant stories, mentioning their own names and accomplishments as well as those of the distinguished powerholders "who are truly responsible for setting the climate so that the organization's mission can be accomplished." Others become involved in supportive work within national membership organizations (e.g., of accountants, managers, lawyers, psychologists). Usually they work on committees that engage in unglamorous but necessary tasks such as membership drives. These efforts are often noted by the elite within the membership organization, and praise is passed back to the people's direct superiors. Since these communications come from members of the elite in other cities, their impact can be quite significant. Note that all these activities also contribute to the young people's networks.

When powerholders behave in ways that deserve praise, they should be treated like human beings; that is, they should be complimented for their efforts, since everyone enjoys recognition. Their subordinates do not have to behave like fawning sycophants—a simple statement that a speech was well presented or that a statement of organizational purpose was forcefully written, will suffice.

Perhaps an aside at this point will not be distracting. While I mentioned above that most powerholders do not visit their subordinates door to door, the exceptions benefit from the practice. One of my friends became a college dean at an early age, passing over professors senior to her in terms of age and experience at the college. I pressed her for the reasons for her success. She mentioned that she makes a point of "dropping in on people" and asking them what they are doing. This allows her to show interest in their work, to offer encouragement, to make suggestions that will (over time) bring their work more in line with overall organizational directions, and to obtain details that can be later passed on to the college president. When people feel that their efforts are appreciated, they are willing to work long and hard.

WORKING WITH THE GENERAL PUBLIC

At some point potential powerholders must decide how much time they will spend with the general public.[13] Certain people must spend a great deal: politicians seeking elected office need voters; young lawyers not attached to a well established firm need clients; salespeople must seek customers; reporters must seek stories; doctors must seek patients; and so forth. Others do not have to spend as much time with the general public: college professors can exist in relative isolation on their campuses; people interested in politics who do not seek elected office can work behind the scenes; some investment bankers work with a few wealthy clients rather than with the general public. Even with these latter, however, there can be *phases* in people's lives during which they need to be concerned with the public's reaction. Young college professors are often assigned the introductory courses in their disciplines and must work with freshman and sophomore students who differ widely in their interests and abilities. Behind-the-scenes politicians have to show their usefulness to the party before they are given any status, and this usefulness may include canvassing the public on behalf of a certain candidate. Investment bankers do not interact with the wealthiest clients during their first years of employment. They receive such plum assignments after years of proving themselves with more typical investors. While this section on working with the general public will be more important for some kinds of potential powerholders than others, much of the material will apply to at least some period in a person's career.

A Theatrical Style

Many would-be powerholders should consider developing an entertaining, theatrical style of presentation to the public. The public is so deluged with people to whom it could pay attention, especially in the mass media, that those who are not interesting in some way will not be remembered. The criteria for being interesting include enthusiasm, a confident manner, a forceful voice, the ability to discuss complex points in a clear manner, good anecdotes, good organization of the ideas to be covered, an attractive appearance, and the ability to respond well during question-and-answer sessions. See the section on imperturbability in Chapter 3.

Politicians I have interviewed admit that they have to "put on a show" when they work with the public or else their efforts will not compete well with television, sporting events, the time people spend with their hobbies, and so forth. The same "need for a show" was discussed by consultants to organizations who are contracted to give workshops on topics such as leadership, stress management, and the promotion of good mental health in the workplace.

College professors who teach large classes have to work on an interesting lecture style or lose the students' attention. Many colleges have a system of teacher evaluation that allows students to rate their professors. Typical items on the questionnaire, filled out at the end of the semester, ask the students about the professor's "enthusiasm in communicating the concepts of the field," "coverage of the material in an interesting manner," and "use of examples to clarify complex points." Professors who take a pure view of their discipline, believing it to be so interesting that the material will inevitably engage the interest of their students, receive low teacher ratings. This can delay if not damage their negotiations for promotion, pay raises, and tenure.

Some people with highly specialized training have the ability to communicate complex concepts to the general public. I have known young lawyers, accountants, psychologists, stockbrokers, and veterinarians who go on the "service club lecture circuit" to meet people who might become clients. They offer free talks as the guest speakers of the Rotary Club, Lions, Elks, American Business Women's Association, and so forth. In exchange they receive exposure among people whom they otherwise might not meet. The more dynamic and interesting their talks, the more clients they are likely to attract. Imagine the predicament of a parent whose child has a sick pet rabbit. Who might the parent call? "Oh, yes, I heard an interesting talk by a vet about two months ago—what was his name?—Sullivan." So young Dr. Sullivan, just starting his practice, receives a call.

I have also seen certain accountants, lawyers, psychologists, and physicians attract large clienteles through regularly scheduled commentaries (minute-long segments) on local TV news shows. There, they combine a dynamic speaking style with their God-given gift of looking good on television. They are probably poorly paid for the television appearances, but the benefits they accrue are considerable, since their names become widely known.

How long do these appearances before the general public have to continue? There will obviously be differences depending upon the people involved, but a common estimate is about two years. Power and influence do not occur overnight—a long period of time is necessary to get one's name before the public, to turn some members of the general public into members of one's network, and to later develop close working relationships with a few members of the network. Unfortunately, the need for this considerable time investment occurs, while many people are marrying and starting families. Their unwillingness to put time and energy into presentations to the public, and to network development, is one reason why these people cease their quest for power. They frequently decide that they want to emphasize other aspects of their lives, such as their families, hobbies, community services, and churches. As discussed in Chapter 2, power leads to happiness only for certain people. Others are happier seeking goals more in line with an affiliation or achievement motive.

Accepting Criticism and Saying No

Once people do acquire some visibility in their communities, two events begin to occur on a regular basis. One is that these people will be criticized by members of the general public, for a whole host of reasons, including jealousy, differing opinions about the contributions these powerholders have made, and the desire for status acquisition on the part of the people doing the criticizing.

A colleague and I attended a lecture by a well-known businesswoman. We both thought that she was extremely well prepared and insightful, but we also heard some intense grumbling from junior-level people in the organization. I asked my colleague, "Why do people feel the need to do that?" His response was that people acquire status in their own minds by taking potshots at well-known figures. My guess is that he is right; individuals who develop a solid reputation in their communities will inevitably be the targets of negative commentary by people seeking status. Readers may want to consider whether they know of powerholders who escape criticism—I have not been able to think of anybody.

Powerholders attempting to respond to critics who have less status must have a thick skin, as previously discussed. Responding in a firm manner runs the risk of escalating ill feelings or making the high-status people appear to be bullies. The hard facts of life are that members of the general public can criticize powerholders, but the attacked have to be very careful about their responses. This seems to be a price that powerholders must pay.

The other event that will happen regularly is that people will make requests of the powerholders for their time, money, contacts, and other resources. Given their own limits, the powerholders' response will often have to be no. Powerholders have to learn to say no graciously. They must communicate that they are not able to give resources, but at the same time they do not want to make enemies. Saying no with as little offense as possible is an art worth developing. One approach acceptable to some but not all requesters is to give the reasons for the negative decision. Another is to form a bureaucracy around oneself that can be blamed for unpopular decisions. A committee of unseen individuals can be formed to review requests, and this anonymous collection can be blamed for negative actions. A third approach is to develop procedures that allow people to make a case for their request. If people feel that they have had a fair hearing on all aspects of their request, rather than an opportunity to make only a few points, they are more likely to accept a negative decision.[14] One reason is that they appreciate the attention from powerholders; another is that, through skillful questions and comments made by the powerholders during the presentation, requesters often learn that the powerholders receive more appeals than can reasonably be granted.

Some powerholders develop a substitute response to requests. The best-known folksinger in North America, Pete Seeger, has written that he receives over two hundred audio tapes a year from aspiring songwriters. He admits that he simply does not have enough time to listen to them, but since he reads music, he will answer letters that include one song written in standard musical notation.[15] He responds to people sending tapes with the alternative that he will read and answer their letters. I have not heard any widespread gripes that Pete Seeger is unhelpful to young songwriters.

Giving Attention

Some powerholders can interact with the general public in a style that makes individuals feel that they are the centers of the universe. For example, the powerholders may give public presentations, often at service organizations, and then respond to questions and comments. While making their comments to the powerholder, the people are made to feel that the speaker is giving them his or her total attention. One of the respondents remembered an address to a large group by Senator Edward Kennedy. "Kennedy would give people who commented his rapt attention. He would gesture to an aide to write down certain points, and the aide would flip out a pen and notebook. People felt that even though they didn't get a chance to comment, Kennedy *would have* given them his total attention if they *had* spoken out. It's a magical style of communication when done well.''

This style has not been analyzed in detail so as to make it easily teachable. If it were, large numbers of people could adopt the style and it would lose its value because it would be commonplace. People able to use the style often have some charismatic qualities (Chapter 3). They give attention to others not only with their eyes and face but also with their entire bodies. That is, they lean slightly toward the others and also keep their entire bodies a little tense, since tension signifies interest. There is also a rhythmic quality to their facial expressions. They move their eyes, eyebrows, forehead, and mouth to correspond to points made by the commentators. They also pause for a moment after the others finish, as if to signify that the points the others made were good and that they demand careful consideration prior to a response. The style is very effective when done well, and it is probably worth searching within one's network for models who might be emulated.

DEVELOPING A POSITIVE IMAGE

I once attended a meeting at which marketing experts were discussing ways of measuring the public's perceptions of large organizations. The organizations being discussed were from the *Fortune* 500 and included General Motors, IBM, Proctor & Gamble, and so forth. Possible perceptions included whether the companies were "personable," "reliable," "generous in their communities," and "safety conscious." One executive spoke out: "These possibilities are much too specific. The general public thinks that these companies are big, hope that they don't cheat people too much, and that's about it." Others at the meeting accepted his analysis, and future discussions built on his point.

Another way of expressing this executive's insight is to say that the public has a very simple image of large companies. Images consist of short, concise summaries that focus on only a few aspects of people, places, organizations, and things. Images can often be summarized in a picture that comes quickly to mind or in a short phrase that can be placed on a bumper sticker. For instance, when the words "fast-food restaurant" are said, some people will see an image of themselves standing in line rather than being served at their tables; others will call the words "hamburgers" and "chicken" to mind, rather than "filet mignon." Images are simple summaries that allow people to think that they have an understanding of a complex world. Politicians often have images associated with them that badly oversimplify their positions on issues and their possible contributions. Hubert Humphrey "couldn't be his own man." Walter Mondale "wanted to raise our taxes." George Bush is a "prep-school product." Edmund Muskie "burst into tears under pressure."[16]

With one of the respondents I discussed my father's advice (Chapter 1): "Have good ideas and work hard." (My brother, the city editor of a large metropolitan newspaper, remembers it as, "Work hard and do the right thing.") The respondent pointed out that this advice may have been quite correct when my father was young. "Your father grew up before television, before nuclear weapons, before computer technology, and before Japanese buy-outs of American companies. Life was less complex then. People in a community may have had more detailed knowledge about the abilities and contributions of others. Now the world is so complex that people need simplifying images."

Reviewing these comments, I analyzed an aspect of my own life. I have been able to write a number of books for the academic market and to have them published by companies with good distribution networks. As a result of the books, I have been invited to give a large number of workshops and lectures at organizations in North America, Asia, and Europe over a fifteen year period. At first I naively thought that the people issuing the invitations had read the books and would want to hear about research and analyses that had been done since the books had appeared. But after a long period of time I figured out that most people didn't have a clue about what the books contained—they were too busy with their day-to-day work to spend the time reading them. People had the image of "he writes books," and this was the entree to invitations from various organizations. If during my graduate school studies my professors had told me that books led more to people's imagery than to their substantive reading, I would not have believed them. Another fact I would not have believed is that far more money is made as a result of workshop/lecture invitations that follow the publication of books than from book royalties. In a complex world where there is far more information than people can digest, shortcuts are needed. Images serve this purpose. "He writes books; he must know something; let's invite him in to tell us what's important."

People may want to consider developing a positive image that surrounds them and becomes part of others' thinking. There are certain strategies that can be adopted.

The Image of a Winner

Everyone loves a winner. If people disagree, I suggest that they visit any field or gymnasium where organized children's sports are played: basketball, baseball, soccer, football, or whatever. If they visit about three-quarters of the way through the season, they can observe which teams attract a crowd of enthusiastic and cheering parents and which ones do not. With few exceptions, the teams that attract crowds will have winning records. In people's adult lives, the term "winner" is used to designate individuals who start projects and finish them successfully. They do not whine about difficulties and do not blame others for failures. They take on projects and see them through to a successful completion. With their reputations enhanced, they are able to take on ever more challenging tasks.

Karl Weick[17] has suggested an approach to people's work and community activities that can lead to the image that they are winners. An exercise may help to communicate his advice. Assume that there are people in a community who want to become more influential, more powerful, and a force to be reckoned with when powerholders make decisions that might affect them. Members of the group feel that if they show their usefulness, they will be taken more seriously. They consider five projects:

1. Identifying candidates for local office who are about thirty points behind in the polls and supporting them. If they are elected, the candidates should appreciate the support given to them during their underdog days.

2. Starting a fundraiser to buy $100,000 worth of computer equipment for the local high school (enrollment of school: 600).

3. Cleaning up an unused, swampy area and developing it into a community playground.

4. Collecting used books for the community's small library by asking others to donate hardback books that they don't use very often, if ever.

5. Converting a church, no longer used since the consolidation of two congregations last year, into a shelter for the homeless.

Which project should the group undertake? Weick recommended a strategy called "small wins." He suggests that people undertake projects that are do-able and that will almost surely lead to success; this will develop their reputations as winners and as movers and shakers who can get things done. With success, these people *themselves* internalize an image of "we're winners" and will become more confident about taking on other projects. Since others love winners, the group will receive a great deal of attention, and many in the community will want to join so that they will receive the benefits that group membership is clearly bringing. Given its reputation, entrenched powerholders will then take the group far more seriously.

This advice leads to the selection of Project 4: books for the library. This project will almost surely be successful. Almost everyone has a few old books that they would be happy to donate to a library, knowing that they will have access to the books there. If there is a college nearby, all people have to do is go door-to-door within a campus office building carrying big boxes. All the professors I know have books that they no longer use and that are just taking up space, but they don't have time to seek out a worthy recipient for their donations. People who come to their offices take care of the problem. After collecting the books, someone can build them into a pyramid. The group can then pose in front of this structure, in the company of the librarian, and the picture can be distributed above the caption, *"Group Builds Pyramid of Knowledge."* This will be covered by local newspapers, and the pyramid will create an image that may stick in people's minds.

The other four projects may seem more important and glamorous, but all are fraught with tremendous potential difficulties. There are too many possibilities that the projects will fail and that the people will become known as "losers." They might then internalize *this* image and become discouraged about engaging in future projects.

Just a few difficulties might be mentioned for each of the other four projects. Regarding Project 1, the feelings of the electorate do not turn around so quickly that candidates can overcome a thirty-point deficit in the polls. There are well publicized exceptions, but these are just that: exceptions. The far more common outcome is that people badly behind in the polls lose elections.

In the case of Project 2, there are so many fund-raisers that communities become tired of them, and raising $100,000 for a high school is a task likely to fail. In an organization of 300 reasonably generous individuals that I know, fund-raisers do well to raise $10,000 once a year for the United Way drive.

As for Project 3, clearing swamps often leads to run-ins with people who claim ownership of the land. The claims may or may not be valid, but it is expensive to petition the courts for a decision. Environmentalists frequently become involved, claiming that the swamp is the only home of some unfamiliar insect, fish, or bird.

Finally, with regard to Project 5, shelters for the homeless also involve legal restrictions. Various local and state agencies have to inspect the shelter for safety, sanitation, and treatment facilities for physical and mental health delivery systems. Insurance costs to protect the organizing group against liability can be prohibitive.

Accomplishing the goals that a group sets for itself is satisfying and contributes to a number of psychological needs, including achievement, affiliation (since the work is done with others), and status. When a group finds itself ready for large projects, the strategy of small wins suggests that large tasks should be subdivided into smaller, do-able steps. For each step there is a visible goal, and the attainment of that goal will be a clear sign to the larger community that the group is doing well. One way to plan the steps is to think of reasons for celebrating. If a party can be held to celebrate the attainment of a reasonable goal, then people will be more likely to continue to be involved, seeing themselves as making steady progress toward the eventual accomplishment of the large task. The party is another visible sign, along with goal attainment in and of itself, of the group's progress.

For example, in projects that involve building new facilities, such as churches, playgrounds, and additions to schools, planners can subdivide the large task into "winnable steps." The accomplishment of each step will signify an appropriate time for some sort of celebration: a speech by a local celebrity, a sit-down dinner, a newspaper story, and so forth. Projects that involve new buildings involve at least the following steps:

1. Identification of a good site;
2. Clearance of legal obstacles for use of the land;
3. Fund raising;
4. Purchases of the most important elements;
5. Ground breaking;
6. First use of a partial facility (e.g., a church that does not yet have a roof but can be used on a sunny day);
7. Final completion;
8. First use of the completed facilities for a normal function (e.g., first children's game; first meeting of students and teachers).

After the accomplishment of each step, a celebration can mark a "win" by the group.

In recent years, many psychologists have taken a broader view of intelligence than the older position that linked intelligence to the abilities necessary for school success.[18] Many now consider intelligence to consist of the variety of abilities needed for successful adaptation to the environmental settings in which people find themselves. People adapt in different ways to different demands. Some work with the type of intelligence that leads to good grades in school; some work with their musical skills, adapting to the tremendous expectations that people have for professional musicians; others work with their social skills and mold the disparate talents of diverse people into a smooth-functioning team.

One skill necessary for adjustment to the demands of career development is that of identifying projects that can be successfully accomplished. Intelligent people examine their skills to determine what they do well and what they do less well. They then use their well developed skills to formulate projects that can be successfully accomplished. If chemists are interested in the development of new products for a drug manufacturer but do not have the social skills to work with the egos of high-strung scientists, then they will probably not be good administrators of their company's research and development branch. They will do much better in their career development if they identify a patentable product that they can develop by themselves or with just a few coworkers. With success, they develop reputations as winners and benefit from the status given to people who are useful to the company.

People should also learn to phrase their goals in "winnable" terms. A recently hired insurance salesperson, after considering her skills, territory, and experience, might decide that she can sell $750,000 worth of life insurance during her first year on the job. She tells her superiors that this is her goal. But she sells $600,000 and is considered a loser in her company. What if she had set her goal at $500,000? Then she would have exceeded expectations and would be viewed as a winner. One odd fact about human nature is that the actual event or accomplishment does not cause the final judgment people make about others. The judgment is caused by the difference between expectation and reality.[19] Because people expected $750,000, $600,000 is a disappointment. But if they expected a lower amount, then the actual figure of $600,000 would mark a winner. Powerholders have an intuitive understanding of such quirks of human nature and employ them in their dealings with people.

Avoiding Negative Images

Another fact that powerholders know is how hard it is to "shake" negative images. Once images are established in the mind of the general public, they are extraordinarily resistant to change. Edmund Muskie will always be the candidate who cried amidst the snows of New Hampshire. For Americans, Nikita Khrushchev will always be the Russian leader who backed down when challenged about missiles in Cuba. On a more local level, graduates of the University of Hawaii complain that when they interview for good jobs in the continental United States (called the Mainland in Hawaii), they have to overcome an image of playboys and beach bunnies who went to a party school and mellowed out in the sun while putting in minimal efforts on their degree studies.

The best way to deal with negative images is never to let them enter people's minds. While this is not totally under the control of individuals, a few strategies are helpful in the avoidance of negative images. One strategy is to avoid situations where the unpleasant aspects associated with any *job* come to be seen as part of the *person*. The person–job distinction is an aspect of the helpful but rather abstract principle that "there is never total discounting."[20] An example should help clarify the principle.

John is a 22-year-old student who has strong positions on a number of social issues. One is abortion—he is intensely against the practice. John is taking courses in psychology and interacts frequently with a Dr. Jacobs. A few months ago, Dr. Jacobs was very kind to John's 18-year-old sister during a family crisis. Dr. Jacobs knows that John is well read on the abortion issue. He approaches John for help and says, "For a research project on student attitudes, we need to have essays written about various social issues. I could do it, but I might not be able to capture the way students talk about issues. Could you write a proabortion essay for me?" Since he admires Dr. Jacobs's research and remembers the help given to his sister, John writes a convincing, well reasoned proabortion essay. If outsiders had all the information contained in this paragraph, what would they conclude about John's attitudes regarding abortion? If outsiders believe that John is anything but strongly opposed to abortions, they are showing that there is not total discounting. It was mentioned that John is intensely antiabortion, but that he wrote the proabortion essay for a research project and because of the help given to his sister. However, outsiders have a difficult time totally discounting these other factors. They are likely to conclude that John has *some* proabortion sentiment that allows him to write a good essay.

Discounting is part of the process of considering all possible reasons for behaviors and focusing on those that seem to be most influential while eliminating others. But given the fact that most people are extremely busy and are faced with all sorts of information on any given day, they cannot do a good job of considering and discounting reasons for all the behaviors that they observe. They are likely to consider that individuals do things because "that's the way they are," not because there are social factors external to the individuals that could provide a good explanation for their behaviors. Consideration of external factors is hard and time consuming. It is easier to focus on the qualities of the people performing certain behaviors.

Powerholders have an intuitive understanding of these facts and so are careful not to be seen as the primary reason for behaviors that might cause offense. When firings have to be carried out in an organization, someone other than the CEO often does the job. When the U.S. Senate appears to be coalescing against a nominee for Supreme Court Justice, someone other than the president is likely to tell the candidate to withdraw as gracefully as possible.

Perhaps a personal example of a rather foolish behavior will illustrate these important points. I had been working with a graduate student who was applying for a handsome grant. Even though I had limited influence concerning exactly which students received the grants, I was perceived by many as a member of the funding organization. Approximately four months before the awards were to be announced, the student asked me to informally review his credentials. I did so and told him that, in my opinion, his formal test scores (on the Graduate Records Examination) were not as high as those of his competition. He would do much better to not depend on this grant and to spend the four months between then and the grant-announcement date on finding other sources of money.

My goal was to assist the student to use the four months to his best advantage. However, he stopped interacting with me after my suggestions, and I believe, in retrospect, that he held me at least partially responsible for the final negative decision about his grant application. He did not discount. He did not view me as just one person who had limited influence over the grants. Rather, he saw me as a member of the granting organization, the only such person he knew, who had influence over decisions. He did not consider my reason for giving him early feedback or even consider the idea that the four months would be better spent looking for money than just waiting for a decision.

I talked about this case with a colleague whose relation to the distribution of grants is about the same as mine. He said,

I think that your analysis is correct. I don't think I'm as honest as I used to be with people seeking grants. I used to give them the same sort of information as you did, to help guide them to the best funding source. But they blamed me for any sort of negative decision. In addition, they would talk about me negatively to *their* colleagues. So now I just say things like, 'Your credentials are excellent, and there are many excellent applicants. Not all these superb applicants can receive grants due to the number of awards available, but you can submit your application and wait and see.' Since the final decision comes in the form of a very bureaucratic letter from an unknown administrator, I'm no longer linked to any negative decisions. This is all too bad, since the people waste a lot of time waiting for the final decision and do not get feedback on aspects of their applications that can be improved.

Powerholders, as much as possible, try to avoid negative images that might stick to themselves. As my colleague pointed out, one way is to blame negative decisions on a faceless bureaucracy with its seemingly endless offices, rules, and regulations. This is just one way a knowledge of bureaucracy can be used.

LEARNING THE BUREAUCRACY

Power is made use of in complex bureaucracies. People who know how the bureaucracy works and where its potential benefits can be found possess a tremendously valuable type of knowledge. John Gardner, a former secretary of health, education, and welfare, pointed this out when discussing the most complex bureaucracy in the United States, the federal government.

The most far-flung set of organizational arrangements in any modern society is government. In a democratic society the sovereignty of the people gives power an innocent face but the reality is there. Every government grant program generates power: favors to give, favors to withhold. Every government licensing procedure generates power: the capacity to grant, delay or deny. Every contracting office generates power. Our federal government is the biggest carrot-and-stick warehouse in the world. No wonder the power junkies gather.[21]

Gardner goes further to give examples of people who master a bureaucracy or aspects of it. Lyndon Johnson had an encyclopedic knowledge of the complexities and technicalities of procedures within the U. S. Congress. He used these to his advantage and rose to be Senate majority leader over colleagues with far more seniority. There are top sergeants within the U. S. Army who know the "regs" so well that no recent graduate of an officer candidate school or West Point can possibly give an order if the sergeant thinks the order is unwise. Certain Washington, D.C., insiders make a handsome living as "consultants" by pointing clients to the appropriate person or office within the massive bureaucracy who can deal with a certain issue. Gardner feels that those who do not pay attention to bureaucratic procedures decrease their chances of effectiveness.

It is a familiar failing of visionaries and of people who live in the realm of ideas and issues that they are not inclined to soil their hands with the nuts and bolts of organizational and social functioning. Often there is a snobbish element involved. They are inclined to think that the people who work in the sub-basements of power and understand the organizational machinery are lesser people.... [Mastery of bureaucratic detail] in itself is not evidence of leadership, but when linked with leadership gifts it is potent. Good leaders don't ignore the machinery. Every leader needs some grasp of how to "work the system."[22]

Paper and Money Flow

In everyday life, the questions to ask of a bureaucracy include, "Who controls the flow of paper?" I knew an administrative assistant within an organization who could bring any executive's work to a halt because of her knowledge of paper flow. This included travel requests, travel reimbursements, budget forms, procedures for subcontracting, permission to pay overtime, and so forth. No executive with any sense whatsoever would dare get her the least bit angry. It was far more intelligent to work closely with her, to do what she recommended with no deviation from her guidelines, and to reap the benefits of efficient paper flow.

Another question is, "Who controls the money?" Its related query is, "Who has influence with the people who control the money." Answers to the second question often lead to individuals who prefer to exist in relative anonymity "behind the scenes." These could be former mentors of today's chief executive officers, people who were with the executives during the lean and not-so-thrilling days of yesteryear, congressmen who control pork barrel allocations that might benefit an organization in the private sector, and senior members of the law firm who have dealt with the organization. These are the people that a potential powerholder should contact to determine what preferences, priorities, and recommendations they have. Then, any project or proposal can be phrased in win-win terms that benefit both the upcoming powerholder and these members of the established power elite.

One image I have found helpful in understanding bureaucracy is a some-what folksy adaptation from studies of primate behavior. When gorillas claim a territory, they urinate all around its borders. The resulting olfactory signal tells other gorillas to keep away. If the signal is ignored, there will be aggressive acts. A similar process occurs in bureaucracies. People claim a certain territory, whether it is an office, a set of procedures, a collection of materials, a set of policy interpretations, or work in a certain topic area. These people then become very upset when others tread upon their ter-ritory. It is much more intelligent to work cordially with these people and to acknowledge their value whenever aspects of their territories are needed for one's projects and proposals.

Understanding Probabilities

Another way to use the bureaucracy is based on the realization that it is inefficient and often makes either mistakes or very arbitrary decisions. Take the example of applying for grants, licenses, or contracts. In the following discussion I will assume that the applications are well thought out, well written, identify competent people to carry out the proposed work, and meet the basic guidelines established by the granting agency. The bureaucracy will consider many applications and will favor some and disapprove others.

The favored are not necessarily the best. Criteria such as attention to minority applicants, distribution of resources around the country, political pressures from influential congressmen, whether or not the application caught the fancy of reviewers, and the mood of the bureaucrats who read the proposals can all affect decisions. Favorable reviews are based partly on probabilities. The "odds," very much in the sense used in Las Vegas gambling casinos, may not work in the favor of a specific applicant. For instance, there may be many applications from New York City and only one from New Mexico. To spread resources and to not be seen as the pawn of big cities, the bureaucracy may approve the proposal from New Mexico and only one or a few from New York City.

The response to disapproval should be, "We'll try again." The people writing the proposals should not conclude that they do inferior work. The fact is that only so many applications can be approved, and some very fine proposals have to be turned down. People should enter the grant-appli-cation sweepstakes again and try to be the beneficiaries of probabilities the next time. During the next review of applications there may be a more even spread of proposals from big and small cities in which case applicants will not be downgraded simply because they live and work in a certain place. The odds will be more even, since the big-small city criterion will not be used against any of them.

One of my respondents was the head of an organization that sponsored overseas exchange programs for students. He told me that much of his time was spent securing funds for the programs. "About one in ten applications gets funded," he said, "and so I figure that if I write 100 applications a year, I get about 10 grants, and that will support the programs." Incidentally, he later joined the State Department and now has the rank of ambassador. Of the many qualities he possesses that have led to his success, just two are his knowledge of how bureaucracies work and his willingness to submit multiple applications so that his probability of success is increased.

Another example is from my own work. A very good scientist from the Philippines applied for a grant to support her research plan. I recommended approval, but she was "unlucky" that one year. There were many good Filipino applicants (far more than in an average year); I had been successful with six recommendations the previous year (far more than my share); and for political reasons [23] the bureaucracy was favoring other countries in Asia that year. She was not accepted *that one year*. I wrote to her explaining all this, even though I am not supposed to, and recommended that she apply again the next year. "Chances are," I wrote, "that there won't be so many good Filipino applicants and you'll be at or near the top." She wouldn't do it. My guess is that she internalized the disapproval and felt that it was aimed at her and her abilities. She was not able to take into account the external factors of an unusual year for Filipino applicants, the fact that it was not "my turn" to have recommendations accepted, and the fluctuations in bureaucratic response to different countries. Instead, she must have focused only on her own abilities, and this was unwise. As discussed previously, the ability to take into account various external factors found in one's environment is very important in career development and power acquisition.

One reason the ambassador had success securing funds in his previous job was that he did not internalize rejections of his applications for funding. When turned down nine out of ten times, he did not focus on his own shortcomings. Rather, he said to himself that the competition for funds is tremendous and that a good record is one acceptance for ten proposals. "If I keep writing proposals, the odds will catch up with me." This sort of attitude does not permit internalization of failure and is useful in encouraging continued efforts on projects so that success will eventually occur.

The ability to view one's continued efforts as increasing the probability of eventual success is of widespread use. One supersalesman respondent said that when he was starting out he figured out how many doorbells needed to be rung before he made a sale. He concluded that it was one out of twenty, and that each sale netted him $200. He divided $200 by 20 and obtained a figure of $10. So he would go up to a door, paste an imaginary ten dollar bill above the doorbell, and ring it. If he was met with refusal, he would take the imaginary ten dollar bill off the house and put it in his pocket. The next doorbell would then have two imaginary ten dollar bills placed above it. Using this technique he did not become discouraged, since he knew the odds would eventually catch up with him and he would make a sale. Over time, he improved his skills as a salesperson and increased his ratio of doorbell-rings to sales.

THINKING INTO THE FUTURE

At this point, it is assumed that our potential powerholder has a good network, a resource that is of use within that network, and a set of social skills that gives him or her a reputation for being congenial. There comes a time when this person has to wonder whether things are moving fast enough, and whether the resource that made him or her useful within the network and organization is still the correct resource for moving upwards.

For instance, I have known people who *entered* the ranks of the powerful because of a skill that was useful, but that did not contribute to their *advancement*. For instance, one person was very skillful writing speeches for powerholders. Company presidents and other high-level executives rarely have time to write all their own speeches, and so people who can prepare solid first drafts are rendering a valuable service. The danger, however, is that these people can go on writing speeches for years and not advance out of that role.

One of my younger colleagues who has an unusual amount of self-insight told me that her original resource was that she was articulate and looked good on television. "I became the spokesperson for an organization and explained its policies to the general public. But I was not allowed to participate in the formation of those policies." Since she was ambitious, her response was to leave the organization and develop other skills. She enrolled in a master's degree program at a large university and is developing resources that should lead to an executive-level position.

I have lectured at a number of such programs, most often in courses geared toward master's degrees in business administration, which universities have established to take the work schedules of older students into account. The programs meet on weekends, during evening hours, and sometimes during a two-week summer session, for which students are expected to take vacations from their regular jobs. The students are successful people who used their skills to secure comfortable positions, but who now feel the need to acquire more resources to continue their advancement. Students with whom I have worked include a television news anchorperson who wants to be a station manager, a civil engineer who wants to be company president, a nurse who wants to be a hospital administrator, and a salesperson who wants to move into the acquisition of companies for a large conglomerate. In all cases, these able people are developing new skills (e.g., financial analysis, supervision, computer literacy) that will be useful in the directions they are pursuing.

Another way to move up within an organization is to request new challenges for past services rendered. If people are useful to powerholders, they will eventually build up debts that the powerholders feel obliged to return. Rather than the more familiar request for a raise in pay, the suggested return might be for more challenging assignments. If they are successful in these new assignments, these people will be seen as having used more skills than the powerholders previously thought existed. They will move beyond their images as good speechwriters or articulate spokespersons.

Many times, however, a person has to leave an organization to have an opportunity to use newly developed skills. Various odd facts about human nature are discussed throughout this book, all of which are intuitively understood, if not explicitly known, by powerholders. One is that people are prophets without honor within about three hundred miles of their organizations. They become overly familiar, old-hat, and comfortably broken-in when they are seen every day. Outsiders brought into the organization seem more fresh, vivid, exciting, and knowledgeable. Perhaps the image many people still have is that of a white knight coming to town and cleaning up all the problems, such as destructive dragons and other evil demons. Clinging to this myth they may feel that newcomers can contribute more than established individuals who know the organization's problems and prospects.

One of my colleagues was a professional hockey player (for the Detroit Red Wings) who later became a college professor in the northern United States. He is a superb teacher. He tells me that nobody within three hundred miles of his home asks him to give hockey clinics for youngsters, although thousands of them play on organized teams. He has to travel north into Canada, where a far superior game of hockey is played, to give clinics. Near home he is overly familiar; in Canada he is fresh and exciting.

Applied to potential powerholders, the suggestion is that people may have to move to another organization to pursue more challenging and important tasks. At the other organization, *they* will be the fresh faces with up-to-date knowledge coming in to slay dragons. The ability to move will be greatly aided if people have long maintained a good network. Information about the availability of good jobs is more often gathered from members of one's network than through open listings in newspapers and professional periodicals. If people invite various members of their networks to lunch, they may be able to find job leads. They may combine the strategy of maintaining their networks with the use of certain tactics, such as calling the lunch to discuss investment possibilities and instead casually slipping in questions about the job market.

Tactics are behaviors that assist people in obtaining their goals in specific settings. They are more limited in scope than strategies. For instance, if the strategy is to develop a positive image, a politician's tactics might include being photographed in front of a city's symbolic buildings. There, various pronouncements might be made that are linked, in the public's mind, to the symbols. Tactics do not work well unless the basic strategy is well established. People cannot use various tactics to call upon others for help unless they have long used various strategies to develop a broad and influential network. A number of the tactics powerholders use will be discussed in Chapter 5.

NOTES

1. E. Berscheid, "Interpersonal Attraction," in *The Handbook of Social Psychology*, 3d ed., edited by G. Lindzey and E. Aronson (New York: Random House, 1985), vol. 2, pp. 413–84.

2. Developing a network and understanding the unwritten rules for giving and returning favors is difficult for outsiders. H. Triandis, R. Brislin, and C. H. Hui, "Cross-Cultural Training across the Individualism-Collectivism Divide," *International Journal of Intercultural Relations* 12 (1988): 269–89.

3. L. Wrightsman and K. Deaux, *Social Psychology in the 80's*, 3d ed. (Monterey, Calif.: Brooks/Cole, 1981), p. 240.

4. C. Collier and J. Collier, *Decision in Philadelphia: The Constitutional Convention of 1787* (New York: Random House, 1986). Win-win thinking is described in S. Covey, *The Seven Habits of Highly Effective People* (New York: Simon & Schuster, 1989). A good general treatment of negotiation is G. Nierenberg, *The Complete Negotiator* (New York: Nierenberg & Zeif, 1986).

5. M. Cunningham, *Power Play: What Really Happened at Bendix* (New York: Simon & Schuster, 1984). The importance of frequent communication with co-workers is treated in M. Kennedy, *Powerbase: How to Build It, How to Keep It* (New York: Macmillan, 1984).

6. R. Schoenberg, *The Art of Being a Boss* (New York: Harper & Row, 1978), p. 236.

7. Ibid.

8. H. Heclo, *A Government of Strangers* (Washington, D.C., Brookings Institution, 1977).

9. The distinction between "dropping in" to an executive's office for an informal talk about a new proposal and its submission in writing is one that I have found very important in my own work. It is important to discover the preferences of powerholders and to respond with oral or written proposals, as appropriate.

10. Working with people who have different expectations concerning the social distance kept between supervisors and subordinates, as well as with people who have differing amounts of respect for rules and regulations, has been analyzed in G. Hofstede, "Cultural Differences in Teaching and Learning," *International Journal of Intercultural Relations,* 10 (1986): 301–10.

11. People build up "idiosyncrasy credit" when they perform well for an organization. They can later request paybacks given their credit, such as help on complex projects. E. Hollander, "Leadership and Power," in *The Handbook of Social*

Psychology, 3d ed., edited by G. Lindzey and E. Aronson (New York: Random House, 1985), vol. 2, pp. 485–537.

12. W. Crisp, ed., *Winning Strategies for the Woman Manager* (Brooklyn, N.Y.: Omni Litho, 1985).

13. S. Bullitt, *To Be a Politician* (Garden City, N.Y.: Doubleday, 1959).

14. T. Tyler and K. McGraw, "Ideology and the Interpretation of Personal Experience: Procedural Justice and Political Quiescence." *Journal of Social Issues* 42 (1986), no. 2, pp. 115–28.

15. P. Seeger, "Appleseeds," *Sing Out!* 33 (1988), no. 2, pp. 53–56.

16. The search for images is one aspect of "satisficing." Given the amount of information people encounter each day and the number of decisions they must make, they have to perform satisfactory examinations of available information and alternatives without enough time to do excellent analyses. Images help cut through massive information so that a satisfactory outcome is possible. H. Simon, *Administrative Behavior: A Study of Decision Making Processes in Administrative Organizations* (New York: Macmillan, 1957).

17. K. Weick, "Small Wins: Redefining the Scale of Social Problems," *American Psychologist* 39 (1984): 40–49.

18. R. Sternberg and R. Wagner, eds., *Practical Intelligence* (Cambridge: Cambridge University Press, 1986).

19. The differences between expectations and reality cause major problems in adjustment when people live in cultures other than their own. R. Brislin, K. Cushner, C. Cherrie, and M. Yong, *International Interactions: A Practical Guide* (Newbury Park, Calif.: Sage, 1986).

20. There is a discussion of discounting in M. Ross and G. Fletcher, "Attribution and Social Perception," in *The Handbook of Social Psychology* 3rd ed., edited by G. Lindzey and E. Aronson (New York: Random House, 1985) vol. 2, pp. 73–122.

21. J. Gardner, "Leadership and Power," Leadership Papers no. 4, Washington, D.C., Independent Sector, 1986, p. 9.

22. Ibid., pp. 12–13.

23. People frequently use the terms "political factors" and "political considerations." These can remain vague and unhelpful in the analysis of complex decisions unless they are asked to be more specific. Here the political considerations follow the introduction of new governments in Asian countries. To be seen in a favorable light by the new governments, various countries may direct special attention their way in the form of foreign aid, grants for overseas study, invitations to capital cities to interact with high-status officials, and so forth.

5

TACTICS IN POWER ACQUISITION AND MAINTENANCE: GAINING SUPPORT

Strategies consist of careful plans for the successful accomplishment of long-range objectives, such as multiple job promotions and professional visibility. Tactics consist of employing specific skills and resources to achieve short-term goals, such as an impressive presentation at a regularly scheduled meeting. The distinction is similar to that proposed by Richard Wagner and Robert Sternberg in their discussion of the tacit knowledge that the successful have but the less successful do not. Strategies are similar to a "global orientation," which "refers to a focus on one's long-range, career-related goals when making work-related judgments and decisions." Tactics are similar to a local orientation, which "refers to a focus on the short-term accomplishment of the specific task at hand, with no consideration given to one's reputation, one's career goals, or the 'big picture'."[1] For example, opening a new sales territory would be an example of a global orientation to one's work, since it could be part of the "big picture" leading to career success. Designating time in one's day-to-day busy schedule to work on this important task would be an example of a local orientation, which demands the application of various specific tactics.

People are most effective when they develop tactics that complement their strategies. Tactics for calling attention to one's proposal at a company meeting will be ill timed if one has not developed long-range strategies for career development, such as having a valued resource of use to the organization. Strategies, such as the development and maintenance of a positive and memorable image, are enhanced if people use cooperative tactics in the development of joint proposals. A positive image, a strategy, is damaged if people do not seek out the contributions of others, a tactic, and simply impose their own viewpoints and demands.

The tactics to be discussed in this and the following chapter can be organized according to seven broad categories:

1. Gaining the support of others;
2. Face-to-face interaction with supporters;
3. Working with subordinates (or people who have less power);
4. Anticipating the nature of the opposition;
5. Distracting the opposition;
6. Negotiating with opponents; and
7. Recognizing difficulties (especially sabotage) and avoiding them.

Some of the tactics to be discussed are very congenial to those who have positive views of human nature and seek to maintain effective communication with respected peers and subordinates. On the other hand, many of the tactics are manipulative, controversial, and cunning. Some even border on dishonesty, and many readers will feel that a few "cross the line" from cunning to immoral. The reason for covering these is not to recommend their use but to make readers aware of the darker tactics in case they are used by others against them.

This chapter covers tactics that can be used with potential supporters of one's work; Chapter 6 covers tactics that can be used with opponents and adversaries.

GAINING GENERAL SUPPORT

Power is used most effectively when the talents, time, and energy of many people can be enlisted in the pursuit of similar goals. While it may give a person a sense of temporary satisfaction to be "a voice crying in the wilderness" (Mark 1:3), that same person will be far more effective in the quest for worldly power if his or her efforts lead to the formation of a committed coalition.

One tactic is called "taking the high road." The task is to identify general goals that cannot be attacked by others with impunity. If the goals are attacked, the critics expose their own ignorance, insensitivity, selfishness, or other negative qualities. For instance, in large American universities great amounts of attention are given to research and to the education of graduate students. The reasons for this include the desirability of developing and maintaining scholarly reputations, which are linked to research productivity. Graduate students play major roles as research assistants, and many projects would be impossible without their hard work. As a result of this attention, the education of undergraduates is often short-changed. Professors who take the high road and link their proposals to "the better education of our undergraduates" cannot be attacked with impunity. Can anybody envision a serious attack on proposals calling for more attention to the needs of undergraduates? There might be claims that one proposal is better than another, but the general goal of better undergraduate education is as unassailable as the goal of social security for the elderly. No sane person who wants to remain powerful will launch a vigorous attack on these goals. Other examples of people taking the high road are politicians who claim to run clean campaigns without negative advertising against their opponents and plant managers who seek to add safety features to insure the continued good health of workers.

Agenda Setting

Taking the high road can assist in the use of another tactic called "agenda setting." An agenda is a general plan, and the clearest example is a list of issues to be treated at an upcoming meeting. If chairpeople control the agendas of meetings, they can list only those issues they want to see addressed. Agenda setting is practiced by powerholders who call upon the hardest working and most articulate people to defend favored issues and ask poor public speakers with mediocre reputations to discuss unfavored proposals.

Agenda setting also takes place in arenas much larger than company meetings. Given limitations of time, money, and other resources, powerholders have to set priorities. President Reagan had an agenda of lowering inflation, building up the military, and eliminating what he thought were wasteful government programs. He could take the high road with such statements as, "It is important that working people know that a dollar earned through their hard work this year will buy a dollar's worth of goods next year," or, "There is nothing more important than a strong military to insure the continued security and peace of mind of the American people."

With this agenda, fewer resources go to other worthy issues, such as continued attention to civil rights and affirmative action, and job-training programs for the inner-city poor. If the deep interests of individuals working in Washington, D.C., do not mesh well with the president's agenda, they will experience a great deal of frustration. They may leave government service and be replaced by others more sympathetic to the agenda. The presence of these new people insures that important issues outside the agenda will continue to take second place in the competition for the nation's attention.

In the more mundane world of company meetings there are cunning tactics powerholders can use to avoid discussion of certain issues. If a subordinate wants a certain issue treated, the powerholder might schedule it as Item 7 on the agenda. If Item 1 or 2 is a "high road" issue like improved insurance programs for employees, then there can be few gripes about the placement of this new agenda item. If the meeting is scheduled at 11:00 A.M. there is little chance that Items 1 through 6 will be discussed before people will want to adjourn the meeting to leave time for lunch. I have been at very few meetings where people were willing to give up their lunch break and their midday meal to discuss a new item.

There can also be control of decisions through agenda setting. Assume that an employee petitions to use her vacation benefits in a way that is not clearly treated in company policy. If the managers do not want to approve the employee's request, they may agree to discuss the matter at their regularly scheduled meeting. Instead of discussing the merits of the individual petition, however, they first discuss the policy and make a clarification of it. Since they agree that the policy does not permit approval of a certain category of requests for the use of vacation time, the employee's petition is then covered by the clarified policy and the managers can vote no. Subsequently, they announce to the employee that company policy does not permit approval of her request. Most managers find it easier to turn down petitions by appealing to a policy than to rule on the merits of the individual case. Very few employees know enough about tactics to realize that they are being turned down because of agenda setting: the policy to deal with the petition was covered first, then the specific request. Over the last thirty years in the United States, fewer and fewer employees have been members of unions whose leaders might recognize such tactics and intervene appropriately.

"There's More on the Inside"

During the days I accompanied my father as he organized carnivals for the Rutland State Fair, we would travel to other cities. There were several reasons. One was his intrinsic interest in this art form, and another was his need to prepare himself for the carnival's arrival in Rutland. Other cities had less pristine standards for attractions they would and would not exhibit, and my father could be prepared for the worst by observing them on other fairgrounds. One of the toughest fairs was in Tunbridge, also in Vermont, where the price of admission was said to be "a bottle of liquor and someone else's wife." The same attractions would show in Tunbridge and then later try to set up in Rutland.

There was always controversy surrounding the side shows, with their dancing girls and human oddities.[2] To be truthful, gentle reader, I would run ahead of my father and to try to observe these as long as possible before he came along. The pitchman would appear on the bally stand and ask a dancing girl to come out and present herself to the passersby. She would be clothed in garb far more modest than the swimsuits found at the most conservative beach in present-day America. She'd move around a little bit, and the pitchman's last appeal was always, "There's much more on the inside!" Hopefully, passersby would become paying customers and would enter the tent to see these promised entertainment treasures.

Successful people create a sense that they have a lot to offer and that there is much more on the inside. That is, there is much more that others can learn or accomplish *if* they include these people in various plans, proposals, and ventures. In international negotiations, for instance, there is great value in learning approximately a hundred useful phrases in the local language for greeting, inquiring about safe conversational topics, and covering the basics of organizing a meeting. ("Shall we meet at your office or at my company's boardroom?") If people know a hundred phrases, others will feel that they know much more. I know American business-people who have used this tactic and who are considered native speakers by citizens of other countries. So few American businesspeople bother to learn the language of their customers in other countries that the ones who do stand out and command attention. When the native speakers begin to introduce material that the hundred-phrase businesspeople do not know, the Americans can retreat, appear uncharacteristically modest, and pay a compliment at the same time. "Your English is so much better than my Nepalese! Could we take advantage of your skills and negotiate in English?"

Other examples of "more on the inside" tactics occur during negotiations with adversaries. Members of one side can appear at the meeting early, so that the other side has to be ushered into *their* established presence. In addition, the first side can appear well prepared with a series of color-coded briefing books. Both of these features generate respect among the members on the opposite side, together with a sense that "they must really know their stuff concerning negotiation methods." The other side may be less likely to try cunning tactics themselves, recognizing that they are ne-gotiating with a sophisticated opponent.

Various status trappings can lead to a sense that people have a lot to offer. Handsome offices in attractively designed buildings, framed diplo-mas, bookshelves of bound volumes, and pictures of individuals with well-known personalities all create respect and admiration. One respondent feels that Americans are especially susceptible to manipulations based on status and status trappings. He negotiates for contracts involving multi-million-dollar mineral rights, representing third-world countries that en-tertain bids from various industrialized nations.

For all their claims of coming from a class-free society that discarded the pomp of an upper crust with the Declaration of Independence, Americans love status. To loosen American negotiators up so that they will make concessions, just arrange to have them introduced to the country's king, queen, or prime minister. They fall apart in awe.

Perhaps the more-on-inside effect works because the Americans observe that the country's negotiators have easy access to heads of state. If the negotiators have the ability to arrange introductions and meetings with these people on short notice, they must have great authority and ability.

Messages Must Mesh

To generate support for their efforts, successful people have to use various types of messages. These include interviews on television, write-ups in newspapers, face-to-face interactions, and word-of-mouth messages that *others* communicate about the successful people. While there can be no guarantees concerning the exact final content of all these messages, successful people do exert some control. Newspaper and television reporters are busy and have many stories to cover. If individuals can develop key ideas around which the stories can be written, then they are both providing a service and exercising control over content. If the individuals learn to write and talk in the language of newspaper and television reporters, they will reap benefits. For instance, newspaper reporters look for first sentences that grasp the essential aspects of stories. People who know how to write such sentences can use them to introduce their own press releases. If the first sentences and the rest of the stories are good, my experience is that reporters will make few if any changes.

Television reporters look for visual aspects that can be shown to viewers. I have observed politicians spending long periods of time at the site of their TV interviews. They carefully examine their surroundings to find visual aspects that will televise well. TV reporters also look for interesting and vivid "sound bites" that can be inserted into 30-and 60-second stories. Sound bites are eminently quotable chunks of a speech that can call attention to people, their images, and also their substantive proposals. Successful people often spend large amounts of time with pencil and paper trying to develop pithy phrases that will be attractive to TV reporters and eventually to the show's viewers.

At times, the same basic message or content has to be stated in very different ways. During my graduate studies, one of the most helpful exercises I was ever asked to do consisted of communicating the results of the same medical research to two very different audiences. One was scientists and physicians who read highly technical material like that found in the *New England Journal of Medicine*. The other was the general reader who would be exposed to the information in *Reader's Digest*. For the first I had to detail the method and results so that the work could be replicated by other scientists. For the other I had to appeal to the layperson, and one technique for doing this is to apply the research findings to a specific hypothetical case. "There has been a medical breakthrough that will be of help to Louisa and others like her throughout the world." Successful people have to interact with others from extremely varied backgrounds, and exercises like this can help them focus on ways of appealing to the interests and viewpoints of others.

When different messages are employed, they must mesh into a meaningful, positive image. If not, there will be confusion among audience members, and instead of putting effort into sorting out contradictions, they are likely to take their attention elsewhere. Recalling the discussion of status introduced in the previous section, there is also no question that television coverage can give prestige to the people on camera. With this prestige can come a sudden demand for additional information. One of my respondents is head of the international programs office at one of the Big Ten universities. Over the years he had developed excellent programs to encourage international understanding, for instance by encouraging greater involvement of foreign students in campus life and providing overseas study opportunities for American students. He had had his share of successes but was always fighting for program expansion, a more generous budget, and so forth. One year it became his turn to be the focus of a halftime segment during a televised Big Ten basketball game. During halftime, many broadcasts introduce the two universities competing in the game and later focus on one office or program within each university. The international programs director came on the screen and talked about opportunities for foreign students and how Americans can become more international in their outlook through more extensive interaction with students from other countries. He told me that in the two weeks following the telecast, he received more inquiries than he had in the previous five years. The key point, for this discussion, is that he had good messages that followed up the telecast, so that the positive image was reinforced. When people asked for printed materials, he had attractive and informative brochures. When people asked permission to pay a visit, he could show them an attractive set of offices with an obviously enthusiastic and dedicated staff. If the program chairpeople of local service organizations called and asked for a guest speaker at an upcoming meeting, he could suggest a number of people and supply their phone numbers. All the messages worked together, and his total program benefited.

Negative Messages about Others

During every election year, analysts talk and write about the place of negative messages in political campaigns. Their concerns focus on communications that attack opponents personally rather than deal with their ideas or proposals. It is very hard to give general guidelines concerning the use of negative messages, since the vague rules for their appropriate use change so rapidly. During one campaign year a negative message seems to be part of the "fair play" of rough-and-tumble politics, but during another campaign year, the same message is seen as degrading to the political process. Only sophisticated political strategists can make an informed judgment about the advantages and disadvantages to a campaign, and these analysts are often wrong. Other technical analyses, as of the mutual benefits of negative messages for the people exchanging them (e.g., both receive publicity; excitement is added to a previously dull campaign) should be made only by people with many years of experience in the specific sort of campaign in question. Again, judging from the results of political campaigns where negative messages are a staple, these high-priced experts are frequently incorrect.

My judgment is that for most readers of this book, negative messages will have more disadvantages than advantages. I am not referring to communications about important policy recommendations. In these latter type of communications, there will always be an implicit, if not explicit, rejection of alternative proposals as individuals build up a case for their recommendations. When cautioning against the use of negative messages, I am referring to communications that attack people on a personal basis. Negative messages make enemies; they can contribute to a repugnant image of "surly," "whiney," or "mean-spirited" for the person delivering the messages; and they cut off possibilities in developing a wide network. Assume that a user of negative messages meets other individuals who might be very helpful in the pursuit of mutually held goals. Those other individuals might easily say, "This person is always mouthing off with criticisms and attacks. If I get involved, I may be the target of similar stuff someday. I'm going to keep my distance."

"The Speech"

Many successful people are good public speakers. In addition, they seem to be able to give a decent, if not excellent, speech on very short notice. This skill makes them useful to executives, program chairpeople of membership organizations, and television talk shows. All of these individuals sometimes need last-minute speakers when others cancel. "Who can substitute on short notice?—Sarah—she always has a lot to say and says it well."

I have tried to analyze aspects of this skill. One day the governor of Hawaii was faced with an unexpected delegation of hairdressers celebrating their national day of recognition. On thirty seconds notice he gave a fine welcoming talk to the group that went on for about fifteen minutes. One observer said, "Here's a real political trouper—a guy who can give a talk like that to a specialized group on short notice!" I asked one of the respondents, an experienced political participant, how it was done. Her answer was that executives have one basic speech. Then they add a few lines about how the group on hand contributes to the theme of the speech. In Hawaii "the speech" is about the Aloha Spirit, or sense of sharing, pleasantness to others, and good-naturedness among people of all races, creeds, and colors. After some words on this theme, ways that hairdressers contribute to the Aloha Spirit are inserted. For instance, their contributions to people's attractiveness and pleasantness can be mentioned. "When we look good, we feel good, and this feeling is communicated to others."

In other states, speakers can always talk about the natural beauty of "the place where we have all chosen to live or visit." More specific presentations could start with images that people in a state have long held. In Tennessee, the theme might be the spirit of volunteerism; in Vermont, self-sufficiency would be emphasized. If the group of visitors is clearly Republican, the joke in Vermont about the inability of the Democrats to hold a convention there for lack of a phone booth large enough to hold them can always be used. In Alaska, an executive would refer to his hearers as members of, or visitors to, America's last frontier.

Timing

The user of tactics for the acquisition of power must be sensitive to the time at which they are introduced. Professional politicians are often skillful at judging the appropriate time for various tactical moves; the same tactic can be considered an intelligent move at one time and a mistake at another.

One aspect of timing involves recognizing the position in which people find themselves on the swinging pendulum of public opinion. Direct military intervention by U.S. combat forces in the jungle of Central America may be a tactical move considered by Pentagon strategists. Given the history of military involvement in the jungle of Vietnam, however, the American public may still be likely to become outraged at such action. Whereas the "pendulum swing" might have been toward the involvement of American influence and righteousness during the 1960s, the general public was more modest and gun-shy about military involvement in the 1980s. The pendulum swung back toward a position that advocated quiet diplomacy without the presence of fighting forces. Whether America's involvement in the Persian Gulf Crisis will lead to another pendulum swing during the 1990s, or whether Americans recognize clear differences between jungle warfare and a military presence in the Gulf, remains to be seen.

Another aspect of public opinion sensitive to pendulum swings concerns the place of massive government intervention into domestic social problems. In the 1960s many influential people felt that government programs could have a major beneficial impact on poverty and the problems of inner cities. Feeling that there had been only modest gains for the massive amount of money spent, and in light of the rigid bureaucracies that grew up around social problems, people later became less sanguine. They secured themselves to the swinging pendulum, which moved toward a more modest view of what government intervention can accomplish.

The practical point for potential powerholders is that they must recognize such shifts. If individuals call for massive government spending in the early 1990s, they may be dismissed as unrealistic visionaries who are unaware of history and public opinion. The two pendulums of faith in direct military intervention and faith in government spending may swing back by the year 2000, and if they do, some people will acquire power by riding a shift back to the position current in the 1960s. One of my colleagues advises,

Never throw away any of your old speeches. You can use them on thirty-year cycles. Educators wrote speeches after the Russian launching of Sputnik in 1957 that decried the state of science education in America. These speeches can be dusted off a little and used to address the challenge in science and technology due to the better education received by Japanese and Korean students.

Timing is important, not just in the heady heights of public policy, but in everyday career moves. Since I have been involved in international educational programs for twenty years, I frequently counsel young professionals who want to enter the U.S. Foreign Service. The Foreign Service is extremely selective, taking no more than 5 percent of all applicants. There is an extensive check into the background of applicants who pass the first few screening tests.

Many of the young professionals who would apply for the Foreign Service grew up in the late 1960s and early 1970s, a period when experimentation in drug use was common. During the late 1980s, the pendulum swung *away* from a belief that experimentation with drugs marked a normal, intelligent person with a healthy degree of curiosity. Vivid headlines proclaimed that Supreme Court nominee Douglas Ginsburg had admitted using drugs into the late 1970s. Nancy Reagan made the fight against drugs her personal cause in her role as First Lady.

When providing information about themselves, Foreign Service applicants have to assume that the follow-up security clearance will be thorough enough to find purposeful inaccuracies. I have told people who ask that in my opinion, if they experimented with drugs early in life, this is not a good time to apply to the Foreign Service. I would not be at all surprised to learn that an informal memo has been circulated to selection boards, emanating from the White House, suggesting that candidates who admit to drug use be excluded. Imagine the headlines if a person were admitted into the Foreign Service and then made a mistake: 'Admitted Drug User Fouls Up State Department!' To avoid the problem, the service can choose others, since the selection rate has long been about 5 acceptances out of 100 applicants. My recommendation to those who ask is to use their time, energy, and talents on other career moves. Maybe the pendulum will swing back in a few years toward a greater tolerance of past experimentation with drugs.

Why do these pendulum shifts take place?[3] One of the many reasons is that the memories of people fade, and they forget what happened twenty and thirty years before. Also, the people who developed certain policies retire, to be replaced by younger people who have no experience with the solutions to problems that were attempted before these policies were implemented. An interesting point to ponder is that in the 1990s there will begin to be congressmen and congresswomen who will have no significant personal memories of the U.S. involvement in Vietnam.

Another reason for these shifts is that politicians seem to get more votes by promising "new ideas." Since a candidate who promises continuation of the status quo will appear insensitive to obvious social problems, there is a tendency to suggest actions that are just a little different from the current pendulum position. Over time, these small movements may add up to a noticeable shift. Still another reason is that opinion shapers, such as influential journalists and television commentators, cover the "news" and not the "olds." The events covered in the "news" are those that are slightly different from the familiar products of the recent past. In public opinion, again, small changes over time can add up to significant pendulum swings.

FACE-TO-FACE INTERACTIONS WITH POTENTIAL SUPPORTERS

After encouraging the general support of others through the use of various tactics, potential powerholders will want to identify a smaller number of individuals with whom they will have more intensive interactions. These encounters will almost always take place in face-to-face sessions, during which these people can have a great deal of control over topics of communication, the emotional tone of the interactions, and even the exact behaviors in which the *others* engage.

Firsthand Experience

Assume that people want to generate support for a policy change involving reallocation of tax dollars, with the ultimate goal being amelioration of a social problem. To gain the support of others, these people should arrange for others to have extensive firsthand contact with the problem and with the proposed policy. While firsthand experience is not the only way people develop attitudes toward individuals, policies, products, and ideas, it is one of the most important.[4] Reading about an issue in a magazine, seeing treatments of it on television, or hearing a lecture about it from an influential professor can be informative, but these often take a back seat in people's minds to their own firsthand encounters with various aspects of the issue in question.

Perhaps a summary of a conversation I had will make the point clear. I was discussing decision-making strategies with a consultant to one of the Big Three automakers in Detroit. I told him, "I own two cars, both Nissans from Japan. The reason is not their flash, or horsepower, or even their comfort. The reason is that they are reliable and stay *out* of the repair shop. My experience confirms this, as does that of my friends, and our conclusions are supported by independent rating services such as *Consumer Reports*. Why can't Detroit make a reliable car that stacks up to those made by the Japanese? Surely we have the technology and the intelligence! What's going on?"

My colleague, also a psychologist, said that he had also thought about the matter for a long time and had concluded that the top executives had never experienced the problem—they don't have experiences with cars that might break down.

They get a new car every year, so they don't have the risk of breakdowns you and I have with three- to four-year-old cars. When their cars need service, they can give the keys to their secretaries, who run the cars over to the nearby maintenance shop set up for the executives. They don't have to rearrange their days to bring their cars in for servicing, arrange for alternative travel to work, hang around in ugly waiting rooms, wait for two weeks while the repair shop works through its backlog, bicker about bills, and so forth. They don't have direct experience with the problem of unreliable cars. Addressing the problem of unreliability, then, is not a priority in their decision making.

The distance between the personal experiences of policymakers and the social problems they might address is frequently discussed in analyses of powerholder inaction and ineffectiveness. Critics contend that policymakers do not address the needs of the homeless, the inner-city poor, or single mothers with children. Since people who might direct policy actions are unaware or insensitive to the needs of these groups, given their lack of firsthand experience, they turn their attention to other matters with which they are familiar because of their own day-to-day experience (e.g., taxation and the middle class). The occasional powerholder who has a background in one of the ignored groups, such as a Black executive who once lived in a rundown neighborhood, is swamped in the competition for resources by the much larger number of people familiar with middle- and upper-class concerns.

Powerholders sometimes distance themselves and become inattentive even to middle-class concerns. In one city where I have lived there are three major highways that bring people into their workplaces from the suburbs. These become a frustrating tangle at rush hour. High-level politicians and civil servants who might attend to the matter, however, avoid the problem. They live in high-rent districts close to their work, are able to set their own hours to avoid traffic, or have chauffeurs. Since the last option allows them to have meetings or phone conversations as they travel to work, even in rush hour they become oblivious to the traffic around them. Observers are convinced that if these decision makers had to experience rush-hour traffic like everyone else, the problem would be addressed quickly and efficiently.

Anecdotes abound concerning the use of firsthand experience as a tool for involving others in one's concerns, even though it is rarely given by powerholders as the underlying reason for beneficial outcomes. One respondent has worked with managers who live in countries other than their own. The managers are often on two- and three-year assignments from the home base of a multinational organization. As part of their work, they often supervise citizens of the country (called the "host country") to which they have been assigned. I asked the respondent, "Are there any managers who have a particularly good reputation at being able to work with host-country subordinates? It can be a difficult task, given the differing expectations that supervisors from one country and subordinates from another bring to the job." The respondent answered,

I can think of one person. She was especially good at communicating in ways that could be understood. She worked for a manufacturing organization (*Fortune* 500) that used a great deal of flammable paint during several production steps. Workers were careless around the paint, frequently smoking. Great deals of money were spent on signs, carefully translated into all the languages and dialects of the area, warning people about the hazards of smoking around the paint. These did no good.

She took five paint cans and asked all her workers to accompany her to an infrequently used area in the parking lot. She loosened the tops of the paint cans, spilled just a little around the parking lot, and then flipped a lit cigarette into the pile of cans. There was a big explosion that blew a big hole in the parking lot. The problem of smoking near the paint disappeared from that moment. There were understandably a lot of complaints from the top brass, but these died down when a cost-benefit analysis was presented to them. It cost $700 to fix the parking lot, but this was a fraction of the cost for the signs.

In the language of this chapter, the manager gave the workers a firsthand experience with the problem. Since they could see, hear, feel, and smell the outcome of cigarette use, rather than just imagining possibilities after reading a sign, their behavior was affected. The incident in the parking lot also became a frequent topic of conversation among workers supervised by other managers. The explosion provided the type of exciting, colorful image that people talk about. In contrast, the dull signs that had been posted were not the type of material that forces people's attention and causes them to talk about an issue.

A respondent associated with the U.S. military services told me about another example of using firsthand experience as a tactic. A contracting firm wanted to sell simulators to the Navy to train antiaircraft gunners. The simulators attempted to present realistic combat conditions through a combination of film, sound effects, and various moving parts. There were various levels of difficulty to which the simulators could be set. For instance, to add in the evasive actions of skilled enemy pilots, the simulators would be set at a higher level of difficulty. Whenever the admirals came to examine the simulator for possible recommendations about purchases, the contractors would set the simulators at the easiest level. The admirals would then shoot for a high score. Of course, the admirals thought that any machine on which they could obtain a high score must be worthwhile for the Navy. Subsequent to the admirals' inspection, the contractors always received an order for a large number of simulators.

In Hawaii, sunny days are a major selling point for the tourist industry. A drawback, however, is that the bright sun causes glare on the windshields of automobiles. A number of accidents have been attributed to this glare. During one legislative session, a lobbyist for a manufacturer persuaded several senators to introduce a bill that would make tinted windshields mandatory. The bill passed both houses of the legislature. The opponents of the bill, however, persuaded the governor to drive around the city in a car with tinted windshields. As they hoped, the governor decided that the tinted windshields cut down vision, and that this drawback was more severe than the sun's glare that reflected off traditional windshields. He vetoed the bill. Giving the governor firsthand experience provided him with information to make his choice about signing the bill or vetoing it.

The tactic served other purposes as well. Providing firsthand experience to people frequently leads to the types of visual stories that television stations prefer. In this case the governor received a great deal of coverage as he got into the car, drove around the city, and emerged from the car to give a few preliminary comments to the media. The people who arranged for the firsthand demonstration earned the governor's gratitude for the media coverage, and they earned a reputation as winners who know how to get things done. Other opportunities were presented to these people during later legislative sessions.

Giving firsthand experience to decision makers is a powerful technique. I have to admit that I have lost battles for budgets because my competition for money used the tactic and I failed to do so. My competition would identify the decision makers who had control over the budget (or who had influence on those who actually made final decisions) and would then involve them directly in the proposals for funding. Assume that a group of people wants a certain program funded that would benefit an identifiable set of clients, whether those clients be foreign students seeking college degrees, kidney dialysis patients seeking transplants, or young middle-class couples needing affordable housing. Those wanting funding would invite decision makers to address the group that would be affected by the budget. A walking tour (e.g., of the kidney dialysis unit at a hospital) would be arranged during which various people would approach the decision makers to ask their advice on different matters. As discussed previously, people are flattered that they are asked for advice and are impressed to see their opinions and suggestions incorporated into the final proposal. Dinners would be arranged at which the decision makers would sit at a prestigious table. The most attractive, articulate potential recipients of the program would speak about the benefits that would be attained by approval of the budget request.

Any of these experiences have more impact on decision makers than the dry, stolid prose of a formal written proposal. The direct experience also provides a pleasurable break in the workday of decision makers, most of whom are inundated by paper that arrives in the mail, by progress reports from subordinates, and by the reports they have to prepare for *their* superiors or governing boards. The contrast provided by the firsthand experience becomes memorable, since it occurs against the dull backdrop of a seemingly endless flow of paper.

Finally, a pleasurable firsthand experience provides a contrast to the inevitable negative aspects of the decision maker's life: criticism from people who don't like certain decisions, complaints about the behavior of subordinates, and directives from governing boards to do more and to do it faster. I have known people who wait with their pleasurable firsthand experiences until the decision maker has had a bad day or even a bad week. The people then enter the scene with their positive experiences, together with the sorts of flattery and status-giving suggested above. In contrast with the decision maker's recent annoyances, the pleasant experiences become even more memorable and impactful.

Working with Others' Current Knowledge and Images

In addition to providing decision makers with firsthand experiences, potential powerholders can tailor their persuasive messages and choose specific experiences based on knowledge that others already possess. This knowledge, sometimes summarized by images, provides a solid "container" for new information in people's minds. The word for this container used by psychologists who study learning, memory, and attitude change based on persuasive communications, is "category."[5] When potential powerholders know the nature of someone's categories, they can shape their message to fill those established places in that person's brain.

The danger of not engaging in this selective presentation is that the information presented will pass into people's consciousness but will not find a permanent place of residence in their memories. Adolescents, for instance, do not seem to have a category that includes information about their own mortality. Consequently, appeals concerning threats to their longevity, frequently used in antismoking and antidrug communication, do not find a welcome place in their minds. People who have never lived outside their own country, necessitating that they adjust to cultural differences, have no category for the plight of foreign students, refugees, and overseas businesspeople who are trying to settle in their communities.

When categories do exist in the minds of an audience, communicators with a relevant communication and set of recommendations can reap benefits. In *The Triumph of Politics*,[6] David Stockman argues that Ronald Reagan has a category that permits quick understanding of the "Laffer curve." Part of the economic analyses of Arthur Laffer, the curve indicates a point where taxation becomes so burdensome that people do not bother continuing to work hard. If they continue to work and earn money beyond a certain income level, so much money has to be paid in taxes that there are few benefits accruing to the individuals themselves. The recommendation emanating from this analysis is that there should be tax reductions to stimulate more productivity. Reagan has a relation to the Laffer curve based on memories of his Hollywood film-making days. During the height of his popularity as a movie star, he made a great deal of money from work in four films a year. But if he made a fifth, even though he had the time to do so, the taxes on the additional income would have left him little money to take home. Consequently, he would stop working after the fourth movie. He agreed with the recommendation about tax cuts, realizing that in his own life he would have made more money and would have been more productive as a film star if the tax burden had not been so onerous.

Good communicators try to link their messages to others' existing categories. A colleague and I were being interviewed by a reporter from the *Los Angeles Times* about Japanese ownership of companies in the United States. My colleague is particularly good at explaining complex concepts by relating them to the categories that listeners already have. The interviewers began to focus on whether Americans can expect to be promoted to the highest levels of Japanese-owned companies, or whether the top spots will be reserved for Japanese nationals. The interview proceeded as follows:

Q: Will there be limits placed on Americans' advancement to the very top of Japanese-owned companies?

A: There are cultural differences that lead to a "yes" answer. The Japanese executives considering Americans for promotion may be looking for a deep-seated feeling of company loyalty.

Q: Don't Americans have this?

A: Not to the extent of the Japanese. There is a value placed on long-term affiliation with one company in Japan and a lesser value placed on "job-hopping." The value placed on loyalty versus job hopping is often the opposite in the United States. For example, if the *New York Times* called you tomorrow and offered you a $10,000 raise, you would be very tempted to take the offer. Your close friends at the *L.A. Times* might applaud your move to New York, realizing that the *L.A. Times* management might have to look at its salary structure to prevent more defections of good reporters. In the United States, a person who works for one company for 25 years is often considered a drone, or as an unimaginative person who won't take risks.

Q: So the Japanese might feel that Americans will leave the company and take secrets with them?

A: Trust is a quality expected of the people with whom we surround ourselves. There is a greater sense of closeness or "family" in Japanese companies than in the United States. If your editor brought you and other reporters together and said, "We are going to have a close, family-like atmosphere here," you and your colleagues would later probably make a series of snide remarks. In Japan there actually is this sense of closeness, and workers in a company spend a great deal of time with each other during the evening, sometimes ignoring their spouses and children in the process. When Americans do not participate in the "company-closeness," the Japanese are less likely to develop the feeling that the Americans can be thoroughly trusted.

Q: Is anyone at fault for these difficulties?

A: There are no "good guys" and "bad guys," or people with white hats versus people with black hats. The Japanese are familiar with one set of behaviors that they have learned in their country, and the Americans are familiar with another set of behaviors that have brought them rewards in *their* country. The difficulties arise only when these two systems come together because of extensive intercultural contact brought on (in this case) by Japanese presence in the United States.

Linking Japanese-American intercultural relations to the reporter's existing categories of job-hopping, family atmosphere, and the good guy–bad guy distinction helped clarify important points. My experience has been that if communicators use categories in this way, the reporters are likely to repeat them in their final published stories. If the categories assist the reporters, they are also likely to assist the eventual readers of the newspaper or magazine.

Personifying the Problem or Program

The issues competing for the attention of newspaper readers and television viewers are so complex that communication about them is aided by working with people's existing categories. Another tactic is to personify the issue of the intervention that is meant to alleviate a social problem. This is done by attaching identifiable people to the problem or program, making them the spokespeople or symbols that capture the essence of a social issue. Appeals for contributions to charity frequently use this tactic.[7] It is easy to dismiss an appeal for a kidney transplant unit at a hospital a hundred miles away. The people who ignore the appeal are not heartless, but they receive appeals from so many charities that they are unlikely to notice any one specific request. It is much harder to turn down an appeal from the family of an attractive two-year-old child who needs a kidney transplant to reach his or her next birthday.

In national and international affairs, the issues facing informed citizens are so multifaceted that few have the specialized education or training to understand them. Fair and efficient taxation, protest movements in other countries, foreign trade policy, and the nuclear arms race are just a few examples. Such issues are often simplified by summarizing them in the figure of one person. There are many union leaders in Poland who have risked their lives in protest against their government. The complex issues are simplified by focusing on the movements of one person: Lech Walesa. Centering attention on one person has served the interests of protest movements in Poland, assisted the media in reporting newsworthy events, and provided a basis for understanding for the citizens of various countries who want to remain informed. If the movements and policy recommendations of too many of the people involved in similar protests were covered, there would be great confusion and a subsequent lack of attention. One reason why citizens of the United States had difficulty agreeing about a policy on Nicaragua under the Sandinistas was that there was a lack of individual figures who summarized a certain stand or a vision of the future. There was no attractive figure, such as Walesa, to summarize a political position around which supporters in other countries would rally. One reason Americans were initially sympathetic to President Bush's policies after Iraq's invasion of Kuwait, is the presence of a clear villain to oppose: Saddam Hussein.

In any set of communications prepared by potential powerholders, consideration should be given to including material on how the positions advocated will affect specific people. In addition to comments such as, "Services will be delivered to 40 percent more people," it might be well to supply descriptions of how the services will affect three designated individuals. There is admittedly a "soap opera" quality to these communications. The key to soap opera popularity is that people are interested in the trials and tribulations of others and are pleased when there are happy endings. An interesting exercise is to read newspaper and magazine accounts of various policy interventions, conflicts in other countries, and acts of God such as floods or fires. There will almost always be direct quotes from individuals, or some aspect of the story that describes the effects of these larger events on select people. Without such quotes or treatments of individuals, the commentaries would come across like journal articles, which are notorious for their lack of impact on the vast majority of potential readers and policymakers.

Starting Small and Working Up

If people begin with small requests that are granted by powerholders, they may acquire a "foot in the door" [8] for the pursuit of larger favors at a later date. One reason why powerholders may grant the subsequent, larger request is to protect the investment they made when they first allocated their resources.

In *The Power Broker: Robert Moses and the Fall of New York*,[9] Robert Caro described how this technique could be used. As construction coordinator for the City of New York, Moses would go to the legislature with a proposal to build a 50-mile superhighway at what seemed like a reasonable cost. Money would be voted, since Moses would be careful to build in benefits for various influential groups: unions, legislators whose districts would be served by the superhighway, and machine politicians who would have patronage jobs to dispense. The money, however, might run out after ten miles had been built. Moses would then request funds for the highway's completion. To protect the ten miles already built, the politicians would almost always vote to approve the larger request. They did not want to be mocked by the media ("How the Legislature Approved the Ten-Mile Road to Nowhere"), and they wanted to fulfill their promises to constituents who would benefit from the additional 40 miles.

The desire to protect initial investments can be seen in more everyday behaviors. Most readers have probably owned a car that was about three years old, but was beginning to have problems. The carburetor might need an overhaul: $300. Two months later there is a problem with a piston: $600. Three months after that the clutch might need replacement. When this $800 problem comes up, what should the owner do? Assume that there is money in the owner's bank account, but that there are various potential uses, such as vacation plans or home remodeling possibilities, besides the $800 car repair. There is a strong temptation to invest the $800 in the car, believing that "this has to be the last big repair—the car will now run smoothly." Besides the initial purchase price of the car, there is the amount of the first two repair bills to protect, so there is less of a tendency to say, "All right, it's time to cut my losses. I'm going to give up on the car and put the money into the downpayment for a new automobile!"

One of my colleagues insists that the tactic of starting small and then increasing requests was used to establish a medical school at a large state university. He was on the faculty senate at the time of the planning and implementation. Realizing that there were severe budget restraints that would prevent a comprehensive medical school, select faculty members began by requesting a program for the first two years of medical training. After those two years, the students would transfer to other universities to finish their schooling. In return, the state university in question would accept veterinary and dental students from cooperating institutions, the latter students to be placed in existing and successful programs. The two-year proposal was accepted. After about four years, the same people came back to the faculty senate with a request for a fully accreditable medical school at which students could receive their M.D.'s. "The two-year transfers are settling in the states where they finish up their schooling, and we are not receiving the benefits of our initial investment." Appeals were also made to the prestige that accompanies state universities with good medical schools. The request was approved, and the university now has an elaborate program in which doctors can pursue a number of specialties.

Another reason why the small request–large request tactic works is that upon granting the first request, the people granting favors begin to think of themselves as big enough, sophisticated enough, and forward-looking enough to support large investments of money. They want to continue this positive self-image when faced with the larger request.

When people use the small request–large request technique, they have to do so in a poker-faced, shameless manner. If they know that the small request is only the Trojan horse needed to get into the fortress, they cannot let this be known at the time of the initial meeting with powerholders. Although they may have to shed some mock tears at the time of the later request, they will eventually be seen as winners in the competition for scarce funds. As they receive the congratulations of others while holding their celebrations, the *way* they won will often be forgotten in the flush of victory. For most people, my guess is that if they decide this tactic is consistent with their moral principles, they will still only be able to use it infrequently. In a small community, people who use the tactic often may develop a reputation as careless incompetents. With such a reputation, they will not be granted the *first* request during subsequent encounters with powerholders.

The Barnum Effect

P. T. Barnum never actually said, "There's a sucker born every minute." He did, however, take advantage of people's curiosity and occasional gullibility. At the Barnum Museum in New York, he once became upset that people were milling about for long periods of time in front of particular exhibits. Without a reasonable turnover of patrons, the people waiting on the street could not pay their admission fee and enter. So he had a sign painted, with an arrow, that said, "To The Egress." People followed the arrow, went through a door, and found themselves on the street outside the museum. [10]

In the analysis of personality, psychologists have studied a phenomenon called the "Barnum effect."[11] People are given complex tests; psychologists appear to go through a great deal of trouble scoring them; and information is then given back to the test takers. In actuality nobody bothers scoring the tests, and all the people receive the same insights about their personalities, such as the following:

"You have a strong need for other people to like you and for them to admire you."

"While you have some personality weaknesses, you are generally able to compensate for them."

"Disciplined and controlled on the outside, you tend to be worrisome and insecure inside."

"You pride yourself on being an independent thinker and do not accept others' opinions without satisfactory proof."

The people are then asked to rate the quality and insightfulness of the analysis. Even though they all receive the same analysis, they tend to report that it is an excellent summary description of themselves. This is the Barnum effect: people accept the same general description as a precise depiction of themselves because it is seemingly based on formal tests. The Barnum effect is undoubtedly one reason for the historical and continuing popularity of astrological forecasts. The "insights" given by the astrologers are worded along the same lines as the Barnum statements that people think are such amazingly precise descriptions of themselves.

Barnum statements can be used as a tactic. Potential powerholders who want to gain supporters can use the Barnum phenomenon during discussions with others. Imagine this scenario: An individual who wants to form a coalition interacts with a number of potential supporters. After a few discussions, the individual schedules a series of one-on-one meetings with each supporter. During the conversations, the individual makes statements such as the following:

"It's clear that you have a great deal of untapped potential that executives with whom you've worked haven't allowed you to use."

"You prefer a certain amount of change and variety and become dissatisfied when hemmed in by restrictions and limitations."

"If you are asked to contribute to important projects, you are the sort of dependable person who has the ability to get the job done."

"Given your insights into difficult problems, you are an important asset to any team."

These Barnum statements *seem* insightful and sincere, but they are the sorts of generalities that people tend to think are accurate depictions of themselves but not necessarily of large numbers of others. People hearing these statements feel that the individual who presents them is intelligent and perceptive. They feel that they are being treated in a unique manner, and they are likely to throw their support to the one who is sensitive and knowledgeable enough to have such detailed information.

Giving Oneself a Role

Use of any of the tactics discussed above assumes that people are mixing freely with others, working together in meetings, interacting at parties or other social gatherings, finding themselves together for a few moments after a public lecture, and so forth. But what happens to those who are not able to mix freely? What if a person does not know anyone at the social gatherings, or is shy and does not easily approach strangers at parties, or feels that no one who possesses status will take him or her seriously?

Such people should give themselves a role.[12] The importance of this tactic was discussed by one of the respondents, who was associated with the policy that brought the first wave of Mainland Chinese students to the United States in the 1970s. While the presence of Chinese students on U.S. campuses is commonplace today, in the late 1970s they were a symbol of a major change in international relations. The president of one of the earliest receiving universities was scheduled to meet the first of its students as they got off the plane, the ceremonies having been arranged by the university's public relations officer. The advent of Chinese students was such a publicity-generating concept, however, that others wanted to become involved: the governor, U.S. senators, and other public figures. Given the presence of these other luminaries, the importance of the university president began to fade. The public relations officer changed the arrangements so that the state's governor and senior senator would greet the students. My colleague and respondent, another administrator at the university, told the public relations officer: "You are going to get fired! The president is not good at mixing when he does not have a clear role. You have taken away his status if he is just standing there at the airport, one of many people. You had better arrange some clear duties for him." The public relations officer then gave the president a role as a dignitary in the receiving line, and as the person who would present the first bouquet of flowers. The president was content with these duties, and the officer survived to arrange other ceremonies.

The tactic, then, is to have a role that allows smooth mixing with others. A good approach is to volunteer to write stories for a newspaper, whether it is an in-house mimeographed sheet or a low-circulation weekly that serves a small community. Then the individual can approach just about anyone at a public gathering and say, "I am writing a story for a newspaper and I'd like to interview you." Very few powerholders will say no to such a request, even though the newspaper in question may be quite modest. If they do say no, given a bad history of being misquoted, at least the request serves as an ice-breaking introduction, and a pleasant conversation may ensue. When the story appears, copies can be sent to all the people who were interviewed. If this is done regularly, the individual will meet and become known to large numbers of people. One colleague told me, "I used this approach. I started a company newspaper—just a few sheets to keep people informed about the goings-on in various divisions. I could go into any executive's office to interview them, and I was able to talk to far more senior people than others at my level within the company."

Another role is as coordinator of a lunchtime speaker series. People are invited to bring their brown-bag lunches to a room where they will hear various community leaders present their views. The coordinator can move freely at social gatherings and within large organizations while talking to powerholders and scheduling them for talks. When he was a staff aide to a member of the U.S. House of Representatives during the 1930s, Lyndon Johnson used this technique and was able to mix freely with the senior senators and representatives as he scheduled them for a speaker series.[13]

WORKING WITH SUBORDINATES

Many of the tactics already discussed can be adapted to interactions with subordinates. These can include genuine attempts to increase communication, such as working with existing categories or providing firsthand experiences. Work with subordinates can also be based on more manipulative tactics, such as starting small and then increasing requests, or the use of Barnum statements.

Joint Ownership

Another positive approach, taught in virtually all human relations courses within business schools, is encouraging a sense of ownership of ideas and plans.[14] Executives should listen closely to the views of their subordinates, take their suggestions into account, encourage genuine participation in final decision making, and delegate responsibility and authority to see that the plans become implemented. With these steps, their subordinates will feel that they are part-owners of the plans, and they will be more likely to follow through to implementation, since *their* egos, and their sense of self-worth, will be invested. Encouraging a sense of ownership contrasts with simply handing down orders. There may be a seemingly deferential acceptance of a directive, but there will often be lackluster efforts to implement it. Without a sense of ownership, people do not put a high priority on directives from above. There may be *some* effort, but no more than the routine attention given to the other everyday requests that fill people's in boxes.

One reason for Japanese economic success is that in Japanese companies a great deal of participation in decision making about plans, products, and policies takes place. From the viewpoint of Americans, the amount of time the Japanese take to make decisions may be annoying. But once the decisions are made, they are implemented quickly because the people involved feel that they have had important input. Since others in the company feel the same way, any individual can call upon the resources of others to assist in the introduction of key steps for the plan's implementation.[15]

An Aloof Presence

Several other manipulative tactics are used with subordinates. My guess is that since use of these can eventually irritate people, they may be effective only in certain settings. For instance, if highly productive people can easily move to other jobs, given the demands for their talents, superiors certainly would not be wise to use potentially irritating tactics. Tactics that might cause ill-feeling can only be profitably used in communities where there are not large numbers of good jobs and where people would have to put a great deal of effort into finding employment elsewhere.

One of these manipulative tactics is to ignore the advice in Chapter 4, where the advantages of frequent informal communications between superiors and subordinates were discussed, and become an aloof presence, rarely talking with or consulting subordinates. An executive using this tactic calls in subordinates, or visits them in their offices, only as a reward for behaviors of which the executive approves. Since talks with such a powerholder are a rare event, subordinates would discuss them with each other and wonder why the talks took place. These executives' assumption is that the subordinates identify the behaviors that led to the talks and incorporate similar behaviors into their own work. Another benefit is supposed to be that since the talks are uncommon, the few people blessed with the powerholder's presence have their egos enhanced. They can talk to others and say, "The boss said this . . . and then I said . . . and I told . . . and the boss thinks the company will . . . " This granting of ego enhancement becomes a resource the powerholders can use (at no monetary cost) and for which they can later expect a return.

All presidents of the United States have used this tactic. Given the number of people presidents *could* consult, any particular individual favored with a one-on-one meeting is likely to feel extraordinarily complimented. If the president calls in one of the 535 members of the U.S. Congress and says, "I need your help on this matter," there are few legislators who will not seriously consider the president's request.

Making Rewards out of Rights

Managers willing to keep an emotional distance from their subordinates can often manipulate the rights and privileges associated with a job. Or there may be certain expectations associated with a job that previous managers have encouraged but that can be changed by a newcomer. The first step is to list subordinates' rights and reasonable expectations. These will vary from company to company, but a typical list will include vacation time, travel to professional meetings, office space associated with seniority, and amount of secretarial help. Then the managers decide who they do and do not want to favor with these rewards. For instance, all employees can take vacation time, but not all can take it during their most preferred months. These managers will distribute the preferred time, June for beach lovers and January for skiers, based on what employee behaviors they want to reward. They will withhold rewards for behaviors they want to punish, such as feisty disagreements during public meetings or unwillingness to adopt the priorities set by the managers. Another reward for desired behaviors is travel to desirable places. Many employees want to travel, at company expense, to exciting cities such as San Francisco, New York, and London. Fewer want to travel to small towns with a reputation for rolling up their sidewalks at 8:00 P.M. Managers can approve or disapprove travel requests based on acceptance of their power, of their right to make decisions for the company, and of their right to direct employee behavior. If they fear union reprisals, these managers can take the high road when explaining these decisions. "I realize that they requested vacations in June, but during the summer months we receive the sorts of requests from clients that they are able to handle especially well. The company will depend on them."

I observed this tactic at an organization for which I worked. There was an office of 20 people, who all had some degree of job security protected by a union. A new director came in who clearly wanted a turnover of about five individuals so that he could bring in "his own people." There could not be a direct confrontation because of the union protection and because the director realized there would be debilitating ill will if five people were directly encouraged to leave. So, over time, approximately five people were targeted for disfavor. They did not receive their first requests for their most desired vacation dates. Their travel requests to professional conferences were turned down. ("There is an extremely prestigious visitor coming during that time whom I want you to meet.") Their pleas for additional secretarial help were not granted. At the same time, a number of other people received all the benefits for which they applied. After about a year, the unfavored five "got the message," realized that their careers would remain at a standstill if they stayed with the company, and sought positions elsewhere.

Since not a single identifiable grievance could be claimed against the director, the union remained uninvolved. The director was seen as an aloof individual by the rest of the office but was not actively disliked. From my observations of him, he had a high need for power and a low need for affiliation (Chapter 2). Consequently, he was not particularly bothered by his office reputation. In fact, it fit his needs and goals: "We are going to do things my way. If people work hard and accept my directives, they are welcome. If not, they may be able to pursue their career goals more effectively in another organization."

An important point is that this summary of his needs and goals remained unarticulated. The conclusion he wished to have his subordinates draw was the implicit message that certain employees discovered after observing the director's actions for about one year. Certain tactics presuppose that people use them but must not talk about them. People reap the benefits of these tactics only when they keep their own counsel. The need for silence is similar for a poker or bridge player who holds four aces: the cards are most effective when their holders do not tell others what they have. When asked about her gentleman friends, Linda Ronstadt, who at one time was dating Governor Jerry Brown of California, answered the question, "Can public figures have a private life?" with, "Yes, as long as they don't talk publicly about it."

Taking Advantage of Naivete

A number of jobs have a romantic, optimistic quality to them that, over time, becomes quite unpleasant. Powerholders need to see that these jobs are filled. Because of the initial romantic notions associated with the jobs, there are many applicants for the positions. Further, the powerholders do not have to pay these employees good salaries, since there is a great deal of competition for the jobs—it is a buyer's market.

The examples I know best are jobs associated with the international exchange of high school and college students. Foreign-student advisers work with people from a number of countries, helping them obtain their degrees and participate in opportunities to become acquainted with students from many other parts of the world. The jobs encourage the romantic connotations of "hand across the sea," "the world's people," and "bridging barriers." Since there are thousands of young college graduates desirous of these jobs, the administrators do not have to pay foreign student advisers high salaries. The administrators hire 22-year-old college graduates and ask them to substitute their dreams and visions for a reasonable monthly paycheck.

After about three years, the foreign student advisers become frustrated. Much of their work is spent on the processing of visas and on enforcing the rules for foreign students who want to remain indefinitely in the United

States. The advisers do not always work with pleasant and successful students who thank them frequently. Rather, they work with students who have a large number of problems and are not gracious with those who offer help. As the young advisers begin to ponder their futures and consider such steps as starting a family, they begin to wonder about salary needs. They leave their jobs at about age 25, but this poses few problems for the administrators, because there is always a large number of newly graduated 22-year-olds who will assume the responsibilities of the jobs, again investing their vision of a better world.

While some administrators are quite aware of this process, in many cases they are not evil powerholders who consciously take advantage of young people's optimistic vision. Rather, the entire social system sometimes supports the cycle of low salaries, frustration, job change, and the hiring of new visionaries. I have known a number of social workers who began their college studies with the goal of "helping people." This fervent desire takes them through their college graduation into the workplace, usually in a low-paying job with a city or state department of human services. There they are given a case load of situations that are extraordinarily resistant to their desire to help: child and spouse abuse, alcoholism, adolescent crime, homelessness, and so forth. Social workers complain that the amount of legally sound documentation needed to intervene in just one possible child abuse case is so overwhelming that they cannot keep up with their total case load. So much time is needed to *write up* interviews with clients that there is limited time to offer services. They become frustrated and leave the profession, and they are replaced by younger graduates of social work training programs who still have their vision of a better world intact.[16]

It is hard to identify a point in the system where intervention would be possible. The U.S. legal system is meant to protect the individual who might be a target of court proceedings, not the social worker concerned about possible abuse within a person's home. Taxpayers are unwilling to pay social workers a reasonable salary or to vote for legislators who make a campaign issue out of the need to create more positions. Experienced social workers are so busy with their own case loads that they do not have the time or opportunity to provide more realistic job orientations to newcomers. Further, the romantic notions of newcomers provide a buffer (until it wears out) against the inevitable stress associated with their jobs. Many experienced people feel there are more advantages than disadvantages to the buffer.

The tactics covered in this chapter are useful in developing support for one's power acquisition from colleagues, superiors, and subordinates. Many of these tactics are cunning and manipulative, and I have dealt with them not to recommend their use but to permit readers who become their targets to recognize them. Another set of tactics can be used when people discover opposition to their proposals and plans: these tactics, used against adversaries, opponents, and enemies, are covered in the next chapter.

NOTES

1. R. Wagner and R. Sternberg, "Tacit Knowledge and Intelligence in the Everyday World," in *Practical Intelligence*, edited by R. Sternberg and R. Wagner (Cambridge University Press, 1986), p. 64.

2. D. Mannix, *We Who Are Not as Others* (New York: Simon & Schuster, 1976).

3. F. Klinberg, *Cyclical Trends in American Foreign Policy: The Unfolding of America's World Role* (Boston: University Press of America, 1983).

4. The writings of Alan Elms have been especially helpful to me in analyzing the importance of firsthand experience. A. Elms, *Social Psychology and Social Relevance* (Boston: Little, Brown, 1972).

5. A good analysis of current thinking about categorization, applied to people's conceptions of personality and the behavior of themselves and others, can be found in W. Chaplin, O. John, and L. Goldberg, "Conceptions of States and Traits: Dimensional Attributes with Ideals as Prototypes," *Journal of Personality and Social Psychology* 54 (1988): 541–57.

6. D. Stockman, *The Triumph of Politics: Why the Reagan Revolution Failed* (New York: Harper and Row, 1986).

7. J. Sommer, "Voluntary Action and Economic Development in Third World Countries," in *Cultural Relations in the Global Community: Problems and Prospects*, edited by V. Bickley and P. Philip (New Delhi: Abhinan, 1981), pp. 135–53.

8. J. Freedman and S. Fraser, "Compliance without Pressure: the Foot-in-the-Door Technique," *Journal of Personality and Social Psychology*, 4 (1966): 195–202.

9. R. A. Caro, *The Power Broker: Robert Moses and the Fall of New York* (New York: Random House, 1974).

10. I. Wallace, *The Fabulous Showman: The Life and Times of P. T. Barnum* (New York: Knopf, 1959).

11. M. Diamond and M. Bond, "The Acceptance of "Barnum" Personality Interpretations by Japanese, Japanese-American, and Caucasian-American College Students," *Journal of Cross-Cultural Psychology* 5 (1974): 228–35.

12. B. Biddle, *Role Theory: Expectations, Identities, and Behaviors* (New York: Academic Press, 1979).

13. R. A. Caro, *The Years of Lyndon Johnson: The Path to Power* (New York: Knopf, 1982).

14. P. Drucker, *Management: Tasks, Responsibilities, Practices* (New York: Harper & Row, 1973); C. E. Larson and F. M. La Fasto, *Teamwork*, (Newbury Park, Calif.: Sage, 1989).

15. R. Christopher, *The Japanese Mind* (New York: Fawcett Columbine, 1983).

16. Meg Greenfield has analyzed the short-term careers of visionary young people as they come to Washington, D.C., as political appointees: M. Greenfield, "Victims of Good Fortune," *Newsweek*, December 28, 1987, p. 68.

6

TACTICS IN POWER ACQUISITION AND MAINTENANCE: DEALING WITH OPPONENTS

Every important decision has both positive and negative aspects. Good roads allow people to travel freely, but in order for them to be built, some individuals have to move, because the land they own has been earmarked for highway construction. The closing of educational facilities may lead to significant financial benefits for the government, but some parents will be greatly inconvenienced when they have to transfer their children from the beloved neighborhood school. The vast majority of a community's dentists may recommend that flouride be added to the water supply, but an opposition group is likely to form around questions concerning long-term adverse effects of flouride in people's bodies. Previously powerless minority groups whose members marshall their forces to elect representatives will gain a tremendous boost for their causes, but these efforts will be seen as threatening by those preferring the status quo.[1]

The constant presence of negative aspects means that there will frequently be opposition groups that must be faced by powerholders who want to see certain decisions implemented. If for no other reason, there will be an opposition group claiming that it did not receive a fair share of society's resources (e.g., government funding, status brought on by newspaper coverage). Or there will be an opposition group whose members claim that its proposal for some benefits (e.g., Medicare) was passed over in favor of a slightly different (and of course inferior) proposal for the *same* benefits that had been put forward by another group. Even though Medicare becomes widely available, one group is seen as a "winner" for proposing the benefits and the other group is seen as a "loser."

Certain tactics are useful for dealing with the opposition, and these are discussed in this chapter. These tactics cover four broad areas: anticipating the nature of the opposition, distracting the opposition, negotiating with opponents, and recognizing difficulties early so as to avoid them.

ANTICIPATING THE NATURE OF THE OPPOSITION

Realizing that there will always be opposition of one form or another for any proposal, powerholders use certain tactics to discover the nature of others' criticisms and complaints.

The Trial Balloon

One way to find out opponents' criticisms is to launch a trial balloon. The ideal trial balloon contains the essence of a proposal but is presented in such a way that it can be disavowed if necessary. The disavowal will be made if the powerholders discover that the opposition is too widespread, too strong, or too well organized. Powerholders, it should be remembered (Chapter 4), have to cut their losses early and put their efforts into new battles that can be won. In national politics, a favorite way to launch a trial balloon is to ask *former* administration officials to appear on the TV political talk shows. They propose that Policies A, B, and C should be adopted to address a certain problem. If there are too many negative reactions from influential people, such as senators and lobbyists, the *current* administration can disavow the proposal by saying, "The person suggesting these policies is a former member of the administration who is speaking as an individual and who is exercising America's great right of free speech." If there seems to be general support, then the administration can proceed with its plans. Another benefit is that specific trouble spots in the proposals can be identified. Perhaps there is general acceptance of Policies A and B, but one aspect of Policy C receives negative commentary. With this information, the administration can improve its proposal of Policy C to better its chances of eventual acceptance and implementation.

One politician I know came up with an especially interesting trial balloon. He announced his support for a candidate on April 1. When the press responded with the general theme that "this is a terrible idea," the politician claimed that his proposal was an April Fool's joke.

I have seen people use trial balloons by writing letters to the editor or by writing opinion pieces for a newspaper (on the op-ed page). They make their suggestions and then wait for follow-up letters from others. If they have good contacts at the newspaper, they can gain access to the letters that are not printed, as well as unedited copies of those letters that *are* printed. People can then judge whether their ideas are attracting apathy, support, or opposition. If there is opposition, the exact points leading to criticism can be pinpointed and improved.

Leaks

The analysis of leaks has attracted a number of scholars, and a minor cottage industry has developed around publications that examine their uses for powerholders.[2] There are many types of leaks, and their purposes include ridicule of opponents, ego inflation for people who feel that they have insider information to share, genuine disagreements with proposals for policy changes, and the creation of distractions so that opponents must spend more time plugging leaks than pursuing policy changes.

For the purpose of anticipating opposition, leaks are especially useful in situations where trial balloons would be unsuccessful. The source of a trial balloon is usually identifiable, but leaks are anonymous. When powerholders want information to be disseminated without being identified as the source, leaking is the technique of choice. In many organizations there are individuals who enjoy gossiping with others. Put another way, there are individuals who play central roles in the "grapevines" that exist in any organization. One reason they are such stellar players in the grapevine game is that they do not reveal the sources of rumors that they hear. They can be trusted to pass on information but to respond with a phrase such as "Oh, I just heard it" when asked about the source. Powerholders, then, can mention a proposed policy shift to these individuals with the assurance that the news will spread. The sources and substance of any opposition, or the possibility of foot-dragging on the part of key individuals, can then be identified by listening for the follow-up responses. The same individuals who put the leak into the grapevine may eventually report people's reactions back to the powerholder.

In addition to allowing powerholders to anticipate the opposition, leaks have other purposes. When policy changes are to be massive and are to affect individuals in major ways, leaks can allow time for emotions to dissipate. I am familiar with an organization whose chief executive officer wanted to introduce cost-cutting measures, and layoffs of key personnel were high on his list of proposed changes. Since the executive had the self-insight to know that he did not handle emotional confrontations well, he leaked the basic information that a number of middle managers would be offered early retirement. The leak was carried out by leaving a draft of a memo, with no information to identify its exact source, near a frequently used photocopy machine. Given this leaked information, company personnel had time to internalize the basic fact that major changes would be forthcoming. Further, they had time to put their emotions in check. This served their own purposes, since emotional outbursts can interfere with settlement packages; it also served the executive's purposes, since he did not have to be on the receiving end of the outbursts.

Leaks are most frequently discussed in terms of powerholder–media relations. Powerholders want certain information conveyed to the general public; television and newspaper reporters want good stories. Both of these needs are frequently served through the use of leaks. In one case that I followed closely, powerholders wanted budget cuts. They leaked the names of the programs they were thinking of cutting. A list of programs targeted for budget cuts makes interesting television and newspaper stories, since it appeals to people's fascination with identifying winners and losers. As predicted, the proponents of the targeted programs marshalled their opposition. But it became clear that certain opposition forces were far weaker than others. With this information, the powerholders cut the budgets of the programs protected by weak oppositions and met their cost-cutting targets, the exact "bottom line" figures having been kept secret.

Working One-on-One

One cultural difference between negotiating in Japan and negotiating in the United States involves the place of open discussions at meetings.[3] In the United States it is acceptable to bring up new ideas at meetings where large numbers of people are present; in Japan this is unwise, since an issue might be raised that catches key individuals unprepared. In Japan there is not a great deal of value placed on individuals being able to "think quickly on their feet." When introducing a new idea, it is far better to ask oneself, "Who will be affected *in any way* by this idea? And especially, who might be against it?" After making a list, these individuals can be visited one by one in the privacy of their offices. At these meetings, the reasons for any opposition can be identified, improvements can be suggested, modifications can be made to incorporate others' needs, and a sense of joint ownership of ideas can be encouraged. At the later open meeting, the presentation of the new ideas is done in a manner reminiscent of a drama or story known to everyone. There are no surprises. The public announcement of the new ideas becomes a ceremony signifying their acceptance. The hard groundwork necessary to translate the ideas into company policy has already taken place. Americans often complain that it takes a long time to carry out these one-on-one negotiations. "Let's just hash it out in one or two well-attended meetings!" The time needed for policy formulation in Japan *is* long, but the time needed for implementation is much shorter than in the United States. The people involved have had their say. They feel that they are part of the decision. When they are asked to implement the decisions, they are carrying out aspects of their own contributions. They are far less likely to drag their feet, since in so doing they would be interfering with their own decisions.

While the approach of working one-on-one with probable opponents is more preferred in some countries than others, people might consider it no matter where they find themselves. One of my colleagues uses the approach by making it a point to show her proposals to colleagues who are known to be philosophically opposed to her idea. The sessions during which the others disagree with and tear into proposals may not be pleasant, but their criticisms are so thorough that there will be no questions for which the proposer will later be unprepared. There are other benefits. At times the others will be flattered that their opinions are requested. The people who do the asking may benefit from the "more on the inside" reaction. The others might conclude, "It's smart for those people to seek me out to discuss difficulties in their proposal. They must know what they are doing." Occasionally, if they are able to incorporate benefits for themselves, members of the opposition can be co-opted into the group supporting the proposal. So few individuals are *asked* to become involved, and to give their opinions, that those people who *do* decide to ask reap tremendous benefits. In his book *Man of the House*,[4] Tip O'Neill tells of the time he took a constituent's vote for granted. O'Neill told an old family friend that he felt he could count on her vote, since he used to cut her grass during the summer and shovel her sidewalk during the winter. The constituent replied, "Tom, let me tell you something: people like to be asked."

Taking Advantage of Differences

After powerholders work one-on-one with opponents, they can consider organizing a discussion with people who have widely varying backgrounds, to take advantage of their natural differences. The give-and-take of debate frequently sharpens issues, brings out heretofore unexamined aspects of proposals, adds reality to idealism, and paves the way for more efficient policy implementation. If one of the criteria for choosing members of this disparate group is that they have healthy egos, then they will likely compete with each other to prepare the sharpest, most useful alternative proposals.[5] The people selected should also have a high need for power (Chapter 2). Their need can be satisfied if they develop major policies, with their names attached to them, that have a significant impact on society. This "need to affect policy" keeps many people in Washington, D.C., and other centers of state and local government and encourages them to resist the temptations of higher-paying jobs in the private sector.

The competition among egos serves the needs of powerholders, since intelligent people are constantly generating new ideas. The mix of people should include both theoreticians and political realists. Comments like, "This proposal is intellectually sound, but it will never pass in today's political climate," will send the ideas back to the drawing board. Because of their healthy egos, the people who have prepared the ideas are likely to make adjustments so as to be judged "winners" after the next review.

Keeping Implementation in Mind

Naive observers frequently make the mistake of assuming that a change has occurred once a new policy has been formulated and accepted by powerholders (e.g., the legislature, board of directors, or well-known community leaders). In actuality, formulating policies acceptable to powerholders is a relatively easy step in the process of important social change. Encouraging others to *implement* the proposals can be far more difficult.[6] If a significant number of people are charged with implementation but are against the new policy, there are many ways that they can drag their feet. They can wait for the powerholders to move on to other positions and hope that the successors will not be interested in the policy change. They can constantly write memoranda asking for interpretations of key points, behaving according to the old policy during the clarification period. They can combine recommendations that stem from the new policy with those that stem from the old, and behave according to their preferences.

In a state university health clinic, a policy was handed down that prevented staff members from counseling female students about abortion, because administrators were worried about cuts in the *total* university budget by influential conservative legislators. Staff members combined this directive with an older one that stated, "students should be encouraged to pursue studies leading to completion of their degree work in a reasonable amount of time so that positions are available for incoming students." Since concealing information about abortion could cause a female student to lose a year of school, staff members gave the information so as to support the students' degree acquisition goals.

Other excuses for foot dragging arise from the fact that many people have a variety of matters that pass their desks. They have to decide to which matters they will give large versus minimal amounts of attention.[7] They can choose to give priority to those that have little to do with the new policy. After a period of time, a policy unenforced becomes a policy forgotten.

Another, especially interesting, possibility is that the people who do not wish to implement a policy may comply with the policy so well that they bring the organization to a standstill. In many jobs, if people followed guidelines exactly, they would spend so much time on procedures that they would accomplish little actual work. For example, the social workers I know are expected to keep careful records of their interviews with clients. If they kept records with the details called for by regulations, they could serve no more than three or four clients a week.

Returning to the issue of taking advantage of differences, one type of person to include in the discussion is the savvy practitioner of implementation. This would be a person who has observed large numbers of policy changes introduced and who has a good understanding of why some are implemented and others are not. Experts in this area may not make the most exciting intellectual contributions, but their role is very important. They can point to potential pitfalls in implementation and can identify key figures who ought to be brought into discussions at an early stage in policy formulation. Again, people who are integrated into a group and asked for their opinions feel that their worth is appreciated and that their contributions are valued. They are more likely to follow through on proposal implementation, since their egos have been incorporated into the policy.

Meetings of the disparate types of people under discussion here are frequently long, messy, and unpleasant. But such meetings are preferable to the silence and inaction that often occur when unpopular policies are not implemented by the appropriate bureaucracies.

Employing a Devil's Advocate

When time or circumstances prevent extensive communication with opponents, the powerholders may assign someone on their team to take a devil's-advocate role. This person is charged with discovering so much about the opposition that he or she can act as a spokesperson, presenting cogent arguments against the powerholders' proposed policies, outlining difficulties in implementation, and specifying the long-term problems that might be *brought on* by the proposed policies.

Presidential candidates frequently use this technique in preparing for debates with their opponents. David Stockman's first major task on behalf of Ronald Reagan during the 1980 campaign was to oppose him in mock debates. Stockman learned so much about Walter Mondale that he actually bested Reagan. Reportedly, Reagan did well in the actual debates because Mondale came across as an easy opponent compared to Stockman.[8]

The assignment of a devil's advocate is frequently recommended as a step in improving decision making. It is easy for powerholders to surround themselves with like-minded colleagues and subordinates.[9] All of us enjoy interacting with people who agree with us, who look at policy issues in similar ways, and who do not bring bad news so as to interfere with the congenial tone of meetings. But this strong human tendency leads to limits on the sorts of information that come to the attention of powerholders.

Information Gathering

All the techniques reviewed in this section can be summarized as ways of gathering key information. A number of my respondents are successful lawyers, negotiators, and politicians, and they pointed out that the people with the most accurate and extensive information have greatly increased chances of winning their battles. One type of information is the set of precedents surrounding a law or policy. Louis Nizer, the well known lawyer, was frequently asked to name the source of inspiration of his success as a trial lawyer. He replied, "Inspiration comes at 3:00 A.M. in the law library."

Information gathering is often dull and time consuming, but it is essential to the acquisition and intelligent use of power. A frequently neglected character in power acquisition is a good reference librarian, who knows the sources of key information. Good librarians can access government documents, obscure journal articles, out-of-print books, company reports, census data, and so forth. In recent years libraries have developed computer access to widespread sources of information, and this improvement makes their contributions even more effective.

Some information-gathering techniques involve a bit of cleverness. When reporters want information, they will often phone key figures and say, "I have about half the story. Do you want to present your side?" When pressed, the reporter may present one fact, thus taking advantage of the "more-on-the-inside" effect. Many figures being interviewed will then fill in the outline of the story with more information. The reporters will use this expanded information in pursuing even more from the next figure to be interviewed.

Another technique is to take advantage of people's egos. I stumbled onto this technique a few years ago. I was considering a person for a research award that would allow him to spend time at the same organization where I worked. I had heard rumors, however, that he had a history of not following through on contracts. His failure to complete one particular contract, according to the rumors, had led to hearings with officials of the granting agency. I asked his previous supervisor about this and received an evasive, noncommittal reply. Without really thinking what I was doing, I then said, "I'm surprised you didn't hear about it. You were his supervisor, after all." The supervisor was unwilling to let me think that something important had occurred in his office without his knowledge. So he told me the entire story, giving me far more details than I had expected.

DISTRACTING THE OPPOSITION

Once those in opposition have been identified through their reactions to trial balloons and leaks, various tactics can be used to distract them. A skilled powerholder who uses the tactics can keep the opposition so occupied that its members will produce no threat to his or her interests. At times powerholders can also increase the favorability of their own images through the use of select tactics.

Giving the Opposition a Sandbox

When an opposition forms, it can often be countered by giving its members a "sandbox" task. Such tasks are seemingly important, but even their successful completion will have no discernible impact on the powerholders or their organizations. Because the opposition will be investing its time and energy in the task, it will have little left over to confront powerholders on other matters. Put in everyday terms, the opposition will be taken "out of people's hair."

At universities, students complain about all sorts of matters: on-campus housing, rules and regulations, cafeteria food, professors who give dull and irrelevant lectures, inadequate job placement facilities for seniors, and so forth. Using the sandbox tactics, administrators think of a problem that has no possible solution, and then assign it to a student task force. At one institution the problem was financial support for the *spouses* of graduate students. At this school there was adequate support of students who were enrolled in courses and pursuing advanced degrees. The problem centered on support for the spouses, many of whom did volunteer work in the university and in nearby communities. The committee worked long and hard and came up with some recommendations. As might be expected, the committee recommended monthly stipends to the spouses because of their services to the graduate students and to the community. The committee members had to spend a great deal of time, since there were so few models of spouse support at other schools that they could study for guidelines and suggestions. By the time they made their recommendations to the administration, a number of things had happened. Some of the most vocal members were nearing graduation and had to devote resources to their job searches. Fads and fashions had moved away from spouse support to another "hot issue"—day care for dependents. A very visible and well publicized budget cut had been voted by the state legislature, making impossible any changes that involved new allocations of funds. The committee disbanded, having accomplished little in the way of tangible results. The administration then formed another student task force to look into the issue of day care.

At times the sandbox can be large and visible. In one state a group of activists wanted condemnation of expensive commercial land for their humanitarian programs, which would include the delivery of extensive social services. The land was owned by influential powerholders who were active in financing various political campaigns. The governor allowed the activists to hold their meetings at the state capitol. There was extensive media coverage. But behind the scenes, of course, the powerholders met to assure each other that current land agreements would stay in force. The entire procedure benefited the governor and other powerholders in the state, since they were seen as so open and so tolerant of controversy.

Some sandboxes are formed when activists are discontented but have no obvious target. They then pick a target; television is a favorite. Its inane shows may be cutting into student's serious reading time, and its violent programs may be contributing to street crime. Its glorification of the rich and elite may be interfering with the development of social consciousness. So task forces are formed that monitor television shows and make reports on their violent content, on the amount of sugar in the advertised breakfast cereals, and on the number of characters who suggest unsafe sex. The task force faces a major problem, however, since most members of the viewing public are content with television.[10] In surveys of the American public, "television" does not appear prominently as an answer to such questions as, "What do you think is the cause of major problems in the United States?" So much money is made in the television business by commercial concerns that there is little motivation to change the status quo. On occasion, citizen task forces have written enough letters to help keep certain shows on the air, but such influence is at the margins rather than at the center of power. For the most part, the activists engage in harmless activities that keep them away from important roles in decision making.

Having a Lightning Rod

Some powerholders keep the opposition away from themselves by carefully choosing a few subordinates with abrasive personalities. These subordinates take on very public roles, such as by heading task forces concerned with popular issues. If the powerholders maintain the traits recommended in Chapter 3, such as congeniality and imperturbability, then the abrasive subordinates may act as lightning rods. Frustration and criticism become directed at the lightning rods, not at the powerholders. Just one reason for the early success of Reagan's presidency was that he had people around him who were unpopular with the press and who attracted criticism: James Watt, Donald Regan, and Larry Speakes. There were others with clear images who also attracted colorful coverage. Stockman was the young and cocky budget genius; Michael Deaver was the public relations expert who cashed in on his connections. When these people attracted criticism, it did not necessarily affect the powerholder, Reagan. Critics could busy themselves attacking the lightning rods, and in so doing they had fewer resources to invest in attacking the president. The lightning rod tactic works best when the powerholder has an attractive personality and a good public image. Richard Nixon was surrounded by such unpopular individuals as Robert Haldeman and John Erlichman, but Nixon did not have the sort of positive, pleasant personality that is well served by the presence of lightning rods. Given his lack of a congenial image, Nixon himself was relatively easy to attack.

The concept of lightning rods can be seen in other arenas of life. In large public high schools there are often vice principals in charge of such matters as attendance, truancy, and discipline. They often have to take firm action against troublesome students and consequently become the targets of gripes and grievances. Since troublesome students are sometimes popular with their peers, vice-principals can develop negative images when they dispense punishment. Skillful principals can remain popular, since their subordinates "take all the flak" for the frustrations inherent in public high school education. In many school systems, principals are expected to rise through the ranks, starting as teachers and working up the ladder. The ability to handle the frustrating period during which educators take a vice principal's position is important in their career development. Some people leave the field of public education due to their thoroughly unpleasant experiences in the vice principal's role.

Lightning rods can become hatchet men (Chapter 1) when they carry out unpopular decisions. The use of hatchet men is especially cunning when, unknown to members of an organization, they are hired specifically to carry out the plans of powerholders. The powerholders remain above the inevitable complaints by using such "high road" statements as, "We have to be fair and give the vice president enough time to learn company policy and our way of doing things." When the people hired to implement unpopular decisions complete their assigned tasks, they can be removed. Since they were the chief targets of people's frustration and hostility, the powerholders may emerge as heroes for removing the hatchet men. Because there are many companies whose chief executives are desirous of quick change, people willing to be hired and fired according to a careful plan will have no difficulty finding employment elsewhere. In large organizations with many branches, people successful at the hatchet-man role can be placed in offices where their history is relatively unknown. When this is not a career specialization, the ability to take one or two hatchet-man assignments is sometimes seen as important in career development. Such people are seen as able to show toughness and even ruthlessness when necessary for the good of the company.

Having a Foil

Another type of person powerholders might consider as a member of their circle is the foil. If powerholders want certain aspects of their images emphasized, they can surround themselves with others who differ on those aspects. Foils have their effect because they contrast so sharply with the powerholders. As an example, consider civil rights leaders during the 1960s and their relation to Eugene "Bull" Conners. These leaders, summarized in the person of Martin Luther King, Jr., wanted to stress such images as the rightness of their cause, their nonviolent methods, and their reasonableness in pursuit of their goals. They confronted Conners, a burly Southern law enforcement officer, and stood up to his fire hoses and attack dogs. The unfavorable press coverage Conners received provided an important boost to the general public's awareness of the civil rights movement. In retrospect, analysts now say that Conners should be recognized as a major figure in the quest for antidiscrimination statutes in the U.S. legal system.

Conners was not the only angry White person whose efforts contributed to racial integration. In deciding where to hold demonstrations, civil rights leaders kept foils in mind. They wanted to demonstrate peaceably and to make sure that there would be ugly responses from angry and unattractive Whites. The civil rights leaders would then bring in a well educated, articulate, imperturbable spokesperson. Which unattractive, abrasive White leader would be most likely to respond by confronting the demonstrators with threats and vindictive remarks? After making their decision based on such criteria, the civil rights leaders would inform print and television reporters about the place where the next demonstration would be held. The resulting media coverage, especially reports on television, had a great impact and called a great deal of favorable attention to civil rights.[11]

The presence of foils can be seen in good cop–bad cop routines, a technique found in more social situations than those concerned solely with law enforcement. In its classic form, a suspect is interrogated by two policemen. One policeman is agitated, angry, and hostile during the questioning. He storms out of the detention cell, promising even more severe questioning when he returns. In his absence, the second policeman acts in a pleasant, caring, and sensitive manner. He explains his partner's actions by saying, "He is always this way—you shouldn't take it personally. But I'll admit he can get meaner." Given the kindness and sensitivity that he perceives, and because he clearly experiences the contrast between the two policemen, the suspect opens up and gives the good cop some key information.

Good cop–bad cop variations are seen in automobile dealerships. One salesman acts as a nice person, helping the customer to get a good price. The customer commits himself to buying a car at a rock-bottom price. But the salesperson has to clear the deal with her supervisor, and so she scurries down the corridor to another office. The supervisor returns with the salesperson, acts in a strictly businesslike rather than pleasant manner, and explains that the dealership would go out of business if they gave people such good deals. "Your salesperson fought hard for you, but we just can't do it." The supervisor then offers another price, perhaps mentioning that the salesperson will get a cash award of some kind if the car is sold. Because the salesperson has been so pleasant and friendly, in contrast to the supervisor, it is hoped that the customer will act consistently with his original commitment and will purchase the car at the adjusted price.[12] To counter this technique, I have known people who bring a friend with them when shopping for a new car. This friend is able to act in an unpleasant and abrasive manner, sometimes neutralizing the effect of the supervisor.

At times, two people act as foils for each other and both gain benefits. Muhammad Ali would have become a well-known boxer without the help of a foil, but he might not have achieved superstardom as one of the *world's* most widely recognized athletes. Howard Cossell might have been able to find steady work as a sportscaster, but he might not have become a household name. Together, they made each other famous. Cossell, who never had a career in professional athletics and who distanced himself from colleagues who did, was the tough reporter who would take a stand in favor of unpopular causes. Muhammad Ali was the good-looking, quick-witted, humorous athlete who could be counted on for quotable, sometimes poetic remarks. They played off each others' traits well and benefited from being members of a team.

Creating a Bogeyman

Although I've rarely heard cases of parents threatening children with the bogeyman to force them to eat their spinach or do their homework, this creature of terror seems to have remained part of American culture over many generations. Children use the bogeyman when interacting with others of a similar or younger age, calling upon the bogeyman to take revenge for real and imagined slights. Children themselves keep the creature alive, each group of older children passing on certainty of his existence to a group of younger children.

Perhaps the bogeymen is similar to a character invented by Bill Cosby. Why do children, generation after generation, come home with the same set of dirty words? The use of these words inevitably causes their parents to exclaim, "Where *did* you learn that?" Cosby suggests that there is a 600-year-old gnome who lives in the furnace room of every elementary school in America. The gnome's sole reason for existence is to teach children the use of words that will mortify their parents.

Powerholders use bogeymen to keep criticism away from themselves. Use of these characters is probably the most frequently employed tactic I have observed since adolescence. Members of a high-school student council vote in favor of a certain policy. Their leaders take the proposal to the school principal. He or she turns it down, not for the straightforward reason that it would interfere too much with the status quo, but because it is inconsistent with recent directives that emanated from the state board of education. In actuality, the principal has only a vague notion of how the state board of education would react; calling upon the board's views is like calling upon bogeymen. People keep criticism away from themselves by invoking a vague source of power that cannot be seen, disagreed with, or confronted. The only tangible evidence of the power's presence is the principal's interpretation of its dictums. Since the students seeking approval of their proposals have no access to the state board of education, and because they are unaware of power tactics, they see no option other than to accept the principal's interpretation.

This tactic is frequently used. Church members cannot pursue their innovative ideas because a group of prelates in another state say the plans are inconsistent with church policy. Faculty members cannot pursue a new program because the association that controls the college's accreditation has put higher priority on other matters. Musicians cannot record their preferred kinds of music because producers claim that "the general public is only buying other types this year."

Outside review panels, or hired consultants, are frequently used as bogeymen. The powerholding group in an organization wants major changes but does not want to be seen as the source of disruptions in people's lives. So the powerholders hire a number of outside consultants who visit the organization. The consultants spend much of their time talking with the powerholders. Since the powerholders are paying for their services, the consultants are likely to pay a great deal of attention to the executives' suggestions. There is an old joke that consultants are people who borrow your watch, look at it to tell you what time it is, and then submit a bill for their services. While the point of the joke is that clients should be wary of such consultants, in actuality many powerholders want this type of service. The consultants submit their report and recommend what the powerholders have always desired. The consultants then return to their home offices, usually far away from the organization that consulted them. With the recommendations of this now faceless set of consultants, the powerholders introduce the changes. When faced with opposition, they can say, "We paid a great deal of money for the advice of these prestigious consultants. We should give their ideas a chance."

Creating Outgroups

Another common way of dealing with opponents, examples of which are found throughout history, is to identify a common enemy of *both* the powerholder and the opposition.[13] To deal with the common enemy, people have to set aside their differences and merge their efforts. In the 1700s there were bitter sectional rivalries within the British colonies in North America. These were manifested in restrictive trade policies, in an inability to collect taxes for services of use to all, and in vastly different positions on the slavery issue. These rivalries would have kept the colonists bickering among themselves for years and years. However, the existence of a common enemy, Great Britain, compelled the colonists to set aside their squabbles and to concentrate their energies against an outside force. The desire for independence from Great Britain was a common goal that demanded cooperative action from groups of people who had been opposed to each other.

In Israel today there are vastly differing factions that could be engaging in bitter struggles against each other. For example, Orthodox Jews would like to see major changes in the country's laws, based on their interpretations of the Talmud. These changes would include stricter criteria for approval of new immigrants, limitations on people's movements on the Sabbath, and restrictions on the sorts of food farmers could grow and sell. Secular Jews do not want to see these changes, because they feel the proposed laws would place severe restrictions on activities in their everyday lives. The reason such conflicts are kept manageable is that both factions view the Palestinian Arabs as a common enemy. Thoughtful politicians in Israel feel that members of the different Jewish factions must begin to think of finding ways of coexisting among themselves, in preparation for the time they do not have such heavy conflict with the Arab states as a threat that demands cooperative action.

Politicians often marshal factions around a common enemy. Ideally the common enemy is a group that does not represent any votes that might be lost. Other countries are a frequent choice. Bickering elements within a political party can sometimes be united in opposition to some other country, be it Russia, Vietnam, China, Japan, or Iraq. During wartime, special efforts are put into dehumanizing the enemy, so that aggression becomes eminently justified in people's minds.

Occasionally the tactic of blaming other countries for internal problems does not work so well as politicians wish it would. In the primary campaigns prior to the 1988 election, U.S. politicians did not seem to strike a resonant chord in the public when they called for retaliatory trade legislation against Japan. Perhaps members of the average American family are happy with the quality of items they have purchased that are made in Japan. Americans may prefer to see improvements in the quality of American products, rather than legislation against exports from another country.

Returning to the previous discussion of bogeymen, powerholders can sometimes use these characters as the common enemy. After receiving the report of an outside review panel, powerholders might find a few key recommendations that are the exact opposite of what they wanted to see. They might then call their subordinates together and make a statement like the following, "I don't like the consultants or their recommendations any more than you do. But they have to be taken seriously and dealt with intelligently because the consultants will also be presenting their recommendations to the sources of our funding. Let's marshal our forces and do the exact opposite of what they recommended, and show them, our money sources, and the general public that we are doing things right!"

The outside force against which differing factions unite their energies can sometimes be a concept rather than a person or group. In nonprofit organizations, a budget deadline frequently forces people to work together and set aside their disagreements. Since all factions need budgetary support to maintain their existence, their self-interests dictate that they cooperate in intense last-minute efforts to meet the deadline. One observer called these "the eleventh-hour heroics of budgeting." If the budget has to be submitted to a funding source in another city, these people may then engage in a practice that is quickly becoming an American ritual. They travel to the post office together, purchase special delivery stamps, attach them to the package, and deposit it in the mail slot. The purchase and application of special delivery postage seems to give the budget proposal added dignity.

The possibility of severe inconvenience to the general public is frequently used as a bogeyman by union leaders who represent services such as public transportation, garbage collection, and medical care.[14] The threat of a debilitating strike at a specified date and time frequently forces management and labor to redouble their efforts at the bargaining table.

Psychologists and school officials interested in positive intergroup relations and high-quality education have used the tactic of introducing common goals.[15] The key is to find goals, desired by all, that can only be attained through the joint efforts of all concerned. In a series of studies, the psychologists found that they could achieve both mastery of school material and positive intergroup relations by dividing students into small groups. Previous to their work, students from differing ethnic groups (Black, White, Chicano) did not get along very well. The psychologists formed groups that were ethnically mixed. They gave each student a *section* of the material to be mastered. The students mastered their separate sections with the help of their teachers. Then they were expected to teach their material to the others in their work groups. The only way the students could achieve their common goal, mastery of the *entire* material and subsequent rewards such as good grades and praise from the teachers, was to work together cooperatively. They did so, demonstrating on tests administered independently that they had learned the entire lesson, and also began to show more tolerance for members of ethnic groups other than their own.

Allowing Participation in the Process

An especially intriguing way for powerholders to deal with an opposition group is to allow total participation in the decision-making process. The powerholders can allow the opposition to select representatives, who are allowed full participation in executive-level meetings. The opposition can also be encouraged to follow grievance procedures, including use of the courts. The powerholders can introduce members of the opposition to print and television reporters so that all points of view will be covered in the mass media.

A number of outcomes are likely. One is that the members of the opposition become satisfied with their treatment, if they feel that they are participating actively in the political *process*. If they feel that they are being well treated in procedural matters, they do not add up their successes and failures at the end of some reasonable period (e.g., five years) to see if they have a reasonable *record* for their efforts. The exact reasons for this finding, which has been documented in recent research,[16] are puzzling and are under active study. Several possibilities come to mind. One is that if the leaders of the opposition are well treated, some will be integrated into the established order represented by the status quo. Keep in mind that all or virtually all of the procedures for power acquisition then become available to the opposition leaders. These include introductions to members of influential networks, invitations to high-status gatherings, and courtship by the media. These aspects of power acquisition become pleasurable in and of themselves and take attention away from *outcomes* such as policy changes favoring opposition causes. Eventually these leaders may feel that participation in the established power networks provides more benefits for themselves than does their continued active membership in the opposition. Of course, this integration of opposition leaders into the status quo is a variant of the old tactic of co-opting enemies. Powerholders identify the most influential leaders and encourage them, over time, to become members of the status quo. As a result, the opposition becomes weakened because it has lost key leaders.

Another reason for the "satisfaction with procedures" phenomenon is that people enjoy being treated well. If these individuals are treated with respect, and if they are given opportunities to benefit themselves, they tend to disassociate themselves from the opposition that they once represented. There have been a number of surveys that showed that successful people make a distinction between themselves and the group of which they can be considered members. For example, a woman might agree with the statement, "Approximately 60 percent of professional women report incidents of discrimination based on their gender." But she can also agree with the statements, "I personally have not been the target of discrimination," and "Men have been encouraging and helpful in my professional advancement." If individual members of an opposition are treated well, they often begin to make a distinction between themselves and their group and do not speak out against powerholders. Tip O'Neill charged that two people with backgrounds similar to his, Ronald Reagan and Donald Regan, had learned to make this distinction.[17] Both Reagan and Regan had working-class Irish-American backgrounds, as did O'Neill. As they became successful, however, O'Neill charged, Reagan and Regan had disassociated themselves from their roots, making statements like, "If I can make it, everyone can," and "Since I did it without a lot of government handouts, so can others."

Still another reason why well-treated opposition leaders stop fighting the status quo is that the procedures central to the acquisition and use of power are often long, elaborate, and boring. Opposition leaders invited to participate frequently find that they do not have the temperament for such practices as development of coalitions, exchange of resources, participation in evening social gatherings, and so forth (Chapter 2). They find out that there are members of *other* opposition groups competing for the same scarce resources and that they have to deal with these other groups as well as with the powerful status quo. So they drop out, but they have difficulty complaining too much, since they *were* invited and encouraged to participate. During the heyday of student activism, many university administrators dealt with campus radicals by allowing them to participate and vote in faculty meetings. There is nothing more inane and insipid than a faculty meeting at an American university. Many of the student radicals dropped out because they were so bored. Or if they stayed and tried to participate, they frequently found that they were outmaneuvered by faculty members who were familiar with the strategies and tactics discussed throughout this book. For instance, individual faculty members can introduce delaying actions, realizing that they will be on campus much longer than individual students. Faculty members can also schedule key hearings on a policy during final exam week, knowing that the students will not be able to give the policy their full attention.

NEGOTIATION

At times, the previously discussed tactics for dealing with the opposition will work well to delay, confuse, or weaken their efforts. But powerholders will not always be able to set aside opposition concerns or crush competing factions. There will be times when the powerholders must sit down in the same room with competitors or opponents to negotiate agreements. These agreements might have the purpose of settling conflicts, forging compromises among competitors for scarce resources, negotiating costs of labor and materials, or determining the benefits to each party involved in joint ventures. Negotiation in face-to-face meetings has become a specialized topic that has been the subject of a number of good publications.[18] The following points, gathered from these sources and also from interviews, are especially useful to keep in mind, since they are applicable in many settings. As mentioned a number of times in this book, several of the tactics to be discussed are cunning and manipulative. I review these so that they will be recognized when used by others. The tactics I recommend are those aimed at helping individuals retain power over a long period of time when they work with the same people year after year. To retain good will over many years, people have to feel that they have been treated fairly in negotiations. If they have been subjected to manipulative tactics, they will eventually discover this fact. They will not be favorably inclined to engage in further interactions with the perpetrator.

Widening the Arena of Discourse

A number of respondents felt that when opponents present a demand, a good tactic is to widen the arena of discourse. That is the powerholders should add to the number of issues to be discussed in face-to-face meetings. This seemed to go against what I felt was common sense, so I spent a good deal of time discussing this tactic with the respondents. My "common sense" feeling was that if, for instance, union leaders come to management demanding a pay increase, management should deal with that one issue in a direct way. But these respondents said no. Management should add other issues with which it is concerned: job security, promotions based on seniority, work hours, expected output for hourly workers, quality control, and so forth. By adding issues to the negotiations, people can engage in trade-offs to reach an acceptable compromise. If management cannot meet labor's demand for an 8 percent wage increase, they may then offer a 4 percent increase and decrease slightly the expected output for workers on assembly lines. But the expected output will have to meet increased quality-control standards. In return for the wage increase and decrease in expected output, labor might make concessions on who can and cannot be promoted and how often foremen can replace workers on the assembly line if a large number of employees are ill. To sweeten the deal, an issue of interest to both sides might be added. In flextime, workers choose their own workday from a number of alternatives: 8:00 A.M. to 4:30 P.M., 9:00 A.M. to 5:30 P.M., 10:00 A.M. to 6:30 P.M., and so on. Management might favor this because it will decrease automobile traffic around the workplace, leading to a more positive public image in the community. Workers might be interested because flextime allows them more control and decision-making power in their lives.

The danger of one-issue negotiations is that there is little room for compromises. If labor goes into negotiations with an 8 percent wage hike demand, and if management begins with a 2 percent offer, one side or the other is likely to be seen as a "loser" because it will have to move away from its initial position. But with many issues to be negotiated, management and labor can develop a package of agreements with which they are both satisfied. Labor leaders can report back to union members that they are winners, and management can report back to stockholders and the company board of directors that they have won.

One respondent was involved in negotiations between representatives of a multinational organization and the government of a developing country. The negotiations dealt with the mining of precious metals. One of the major issues was the amount of money that would go to the multinational organization and the amount that would go to the government. Other issues, all of which allowed for give-and-take in the negotiations and the forging of an eventual compromise agreement, were introduced by representatives of the government. These issues were meant to insure long-term development in the country that would, over time, demand less dependence on outside multinational organizations. The issues included the number of host-country citizens who would be trained as engineers, executives, and supervisors; responsibility for the long-term maintenance of plants and equipment; development of permanent housing for laborers; and establishment of educational facilities for the children of workers.

Manipulative aspects can be added to negotiations when members of one side seem to concede on an important issue. In reality, the members may have no current interest in the issue and may engage in a dramatic presentation of their sacrifice to obtain matching concessions from the other side. If management has recently decided to increase the amount of paid vacation, for instance, its spokespeople might delay the increase until the next round of negotiations with labor in the hopes that labor will decrease its demands on other issues.

Another way of using a change to which one side has already agreed is to set a favorable tone for negotiations. If one side can first introduce an issue on which all parties agree, such as the need for more paid vacation, then a tone of congeniality, cooperation, and willingness to compromise can be established. After the initial agreement, the harder issues can be introduced. Incidentally, this tactic is similar to the practices used by well trained interviewers when conducting door-to-door surveys.[19] One reason certain questions are asked first, such as those inquiring about name, age, and length of time at current residence, is that people have no difficulty answering them. After they become comfortable with the question–answer exchange, and after they gain confidence in their ability to give answers to a stranger, the interviewer can introduce more difficult questions.

Starting High and Moving Down

Many people I have talked to feel that they do not use tactics in their work. "Tactics" has a negative connotation to them, and they feel that admitting to their use would take away from their reputations as straightforward, honest individuals. I then ask, "Haven't you ever prepared a budget in the following manner? You calculate how much you need, and then add an amount to that. You do it this way because you are sure that your proposal will be cut by the final budget-granting authority. So you add, for instance, about 20 percent, and then the administrators cut your request by 18 percent. You still have 2 percent more than the original calculation of your needs." Most people will admit to such practices, adding such comments as, "You'd be crazy not to. That's not a 'tactic!' That's common sense! The administrators have to justify their positions. They review the proposal and make a cut. They're happy that they did their jobs, and I'm happy that I have enough money."

Starting high and working down is a tactic known to almost everyone in its most straightforward manifestation. Automobile salespeople, for example, do not expect customers to accept their first suggested price, although they are delighted when customers *do* agree. The tactic is harder to see when money is not involved. To overcome censorship restrictions, Asian filmmakers have told me that they go through a series of steps. They first make their decisions concerning the content of the scenes they want to include in their work. These usually challenge the gray areas, or the limits, of the existing censorship restrictions. Then they add more violence, nudity, profanity, or criticism of the government to their scenes. These latter versions are submitted to the censors. The officials make their cuts, but these often deal only with the extra material that the filmmakers added. The filmmakers receive approval of versions similar to their original shooting scripts.

A related tactic that is familiar to most people is spending excess money at the end of the fiscal year. If people received $100,000 for a project but were efficient enough to complete their work for $80,000, they might spend the extra money nevertheless. Typical expenditures are for equipment useful in work on virtually any project, such as personal computers for the staff members. People are afraid that administrators will conclude that the work group did not need the $100,000 in the first place and will budget future projects at an amount much lower than requested.

Increasing the Number of Groups Represented

Here I will take another example from the life of P. T. Barnum. To call attention to his museum in New York, Barnum sponsored a Beautiful Baby contest.[20] He promised a cash prize to the mother who brought the most attractive, cutest baby to the museum. He thought only nine or ten mothers, a number of relatives of the babies, and some curious onlookers would show up and pay admission to the museum, but when the day of the contest arrived, upwards of two hundred mothers presented their offspring. As might be expected, each mother had one specific winner in mind. Chaos began to take over when the mothers started to argue the merits of their children. Realizing that he would make too many enemies and create too much ill will if he selected a winner, Barnum asked the mothers to form a committee and report their recommendations to him. As he expected, the mothers became so bogged down in such matters as choosing committee members and developing criteria for selection that they were unable to arrive at any agreement. They argued until the museum closed, directed their anger at each other, and spared Barnum himself from their wrath.

Powerholders can often maintain the status quo by increasing the number of groups that are represented in negotiations. Take the example of a large company involved in the development, production, and marketing of innovative consumer products. If the scientists in the research and development branch formulate a number of demands and present them to management, the executives can bring the negotiations to a complete halt. They can use "high road" statements such as, "We should obtain the views of employees in other departments to see if they can benefit from these negotiations." Representatives from such groups as the secretaries, accountants, computer specialists, salespeople, and workers on the assembly line can be asked to submit their recommendations concerning the matters to be negotiated. After their submissions, the executives circulate all the proposals to representatives of all the groups. Further, the executives ask the representatives to come together, discuss matters with one another, and submit one proposal that integrates the points on which all the groups agree. A likely outcome of such a procedure is that the groups will not be able to agree among themselves, and consequently the executives will never see an integrated proposal.

Tactics such as introducing deadlines can sometimes counter the stalement brought on by the presence of many groups. I was a minor figure in a lawsuit brought by a school principal against a group that desired his removal. My two oldest children were attending the school whose principal was under fire. A number of parties hired lawyers: the principal, the group desirous of his removal, a group of parents who liked the principal, and a group of parents who did not like the principal. There was little chance that all these factions could be represented in court. Protracted court proceedings, of course, could have affected the morale of the teachers and interfered with their teaching effectiveness. The judge was wise enough to call the lawyers together in her chambers and give them a deadline for an agreement that would satisfy all the parties. Since they had to come up with an agreement to collect their fees, the lawyers hammered out a compromise. No one was perfectly happy with the agreement, but all felt that it was an acceptable solution to a difficult problem.

Variants on the tactic of encouraging competing factions to prevent concerted action can be seen in politics. Representatives of minority groups do not always combine their efforts; rather, they devise proposals that meet the needs of their own group, be they Japanese-Americans, Chinese-Americans, Blacks, Chicanos, or Native Americans. Upon entering the political arena, they find themselves competing for resources with other ethnic groups, other factions *within* their group, and groups with other kinds of common identities: gays, the handicapped, welfare recipients, and so forth.

In preparing for elections, each ethnic group may propose and work in behalf of its own candidate instead of combining efforts and supporting one. Consequently, five or six candidates may compete against the incumbent representative of the status quo. The multiple candidates put forward by the minority groups are likely to split the opposition vote;[21] if no one minority is numerous enough to elect its own candidate, the representative of the status quo will win. Sophisticated and wealthy powerholders with the status quo can encourage such outcomes. They can contribute to the campaigns of minority candidates and urge them to participate as full players in the political process. By supporting a number of candidates with their behind-the-scenes contributions, the powerholders try to ensure that the eventual opposition vote will be split, leaving the status quo unscathed.

Bottom Lines and Unarticulated Threats

Before any face-to-face negotiations, people should decide what their "bottom line" will be.[22] This term refers to the point at which people will say no and leave the negotiations. The tactic is seen most clearly in negotiations for the price of a consumer item such as an automobile. Buyers can do their homework and decide upon a fair price for the car they want. For instance, a service provided by *Consumer Reports* will inform people of the price that dealers pay. After adding a reasonable markup and the cost of the options desired (the wholesale price of which can also be obtained), the buyers have determined their bottom line. They will offer a *lower* amount and will dicker with the salespeople, who will suggest a higher amount. But if the salespeople do not agree to the bottom-line figure, buyers should say no and walk out.

Bottom-line figures are admittedly more difficult to determine in other types of negotiations. People selling their services, such as freelance writers, have to take into account such matters as the direct payment, based on the number of hours the job demands and their ability to meet the deadline. But there are other factors: Is a low figure better than doing nothing, given a set of upcoming bills that have to be paid? If the writers do well, will this job lead to other work for people in the employer's network? Will the products be widely disseminated, and will the writers' names be prominently attached? In such cases, the bottom line resembles more a pattern of outcomes than just one monetary figure. People have to decide whether the pattern of outcomes should lead to a yes or no decision.

In the case above in which powerholders widened the arena of discourse in a labor–management negotiation, the final decision will involve a pattern of agreements: salary, expected output, promotions, quality control, and flextime. As the issues are added to the negotiations, breaks are frequently called, during which the negotiators for each side confer among themselves and develop a new bottom line for each issue. Without these figures the negotiations would flounder and the representatives would feel that they had lost control. The issues are later combined into a package at meetings where all groups are present.

One reason negotiators are carefully groomed over a number of years is that they need a great deal of experience before they can recognize favorable patterns of outcomes. Inexperienced negotiators are first allowed to sit in on meetings, then are given minor tasks, later are asked to speak at meetings, and so forth. Only after many years are they allowed to take on tasks involving large amounts of responsibility. The ability to recognize favorable patterns of outcomes can be compared to the skill of a great chess player. Champion chess players do not study the positions of individual pieces; rather, they see the patterns that the pieces form and then develop strategies and tactics based on those patterns.[23] One reason why they offer a draw earlier than novices is that they see their own and their opponents' patterns and recognize what is and is not possible. If they see that there is little chance for any other outcome, they offer to draw. Similarly, the reason why a champion can play 50 games simultaneously with novices is that the champion is working from patterns, not from memories of exactly how each game has progressed. They walk from opponent to opponent and make their moves based on their knowledge of what can be done, given each configuration of pieces at any point during the games. Recognizing favorable patterns across such issues as salaries, hours, health benefits, vacations, unionization, and pensions is a similarly complex skill that separates experts from novices.

When people have done their homework and have developed a bottom line for each important issue, they will inevitably communicate their preparedness and sophistication to the opposition. They will send the message, without articulating it directly, that "if you don't respect my bottom line, I will say no and leave." This is the unarticulated threat in negotiations, and it is often a good tactic to employ. It is especially impactful when people clearly are talking with other parties in separate negotiations. For instance, buyers can quietly let it be known that they are in communication with other automobile dealerships. Representatives of the mining concerns for a government can let the opposition know that they are "talking things over with other multinational organizations."

Of course, the threat must be carried through into actual behavior if the opposition does not respect the bottom line. In such cases, however, the other side is likely to call later and suggest another meeting. This can be of benefit, since the opposition may feel that it has to make additional concessions to get people to come to the newly scheduled meeting. More subtly, the people on the receiving end of the request for another meeting are now being courted. They are seen as having the limited resources that many others want. The other side is likely to increase the attractiveness of its offer, since it is now in the role of the *suitor* seeking a favorable answer. People who play "hard to get" often receive the most attractive offers, since the other party has to work intensely to obtain an agreement. To justify its time and effort, the other side is likely to say to itself, "This deal is worth much more than we first thought." At times the worth of the resource is not in question; rather, it is the *perception* of worth. If many people are perceived as wanting a certain outcome, that outcome increases in value. Skilled manipulators who can increase the perception of worth, for instance by "leaking" information about the number of people who want a certain outcome, can often obtain favorable agreements.

Referring Back to Authority

Whether they consciously use it as a tactic or not, many people influence negotiations by claiming that they have to consult with another authority. Customers in an automobile dealership have to leave to consult with their spouses. Negotiators representing management in contract talks have to refer back to the CEO. Presidents of the United States cannot formulate and sign arms control treaties without approval by the Senate. Besides the overt reasons for these appeals, they have a number of other benefits. The time needed for consultation can provide a break in emotionally charged meetings, can generate time to obtain more information, and can provide opportunities to develop new and favorable patterns of possible outcomes. Just the *perception* that consultation with others is always a necessity can be used to obtain concessions. During negotiations, people can use powerful others as bogeymen. They can say, "I'm in favor of your proposal, but it will never pass with the people I represent. Can you make things easier for me by moving toward the position that they want?"

A constant danger is that the excitement generated upon reaching a tentative agreement will cloud people's judgment. People should not sign anything when excited or emotionally aroused: instead, they should withdraw. In the company of the people they represent, negotiators can calmly consider all aspects of the agreement to determine whether or not they are reasonable. Harvey Mackay[24] tells of the time he was offered a basketball franchise in a new professional league. The executives of the new league announced their plans during an exquisite dinner held at one of a city's best restaurants. As the evening progressed, the executives went from table to table to obtain commitments from wealthy people. A spotlight was literally focused on people as they stood up to announce their statements, into a microphone, concerning the purchase of a team. While it was difficult to avoid the excitement of participating in a new sports venture and to set aside the knowledge that he was in the spotlight, Mackay stood up and "passed" on a decision. He later chose not to become involved and was eventually proven correct, since the basketball league was a total failure. The advice sophisticated powerholders give is never to make decisions when others are trying to make one feel excited, special, or singled out for attention. It is best to leave the setting and deliberate calmly the positive and negative aspects of the proposal.

Sophisticated powerholders also know that the negotiators for the other side have to "sell" the eventual agreement to the people they represent. Assume that Side A and Side B are involved in labor negotiations. Side A might have a set of skilled negotiators who are able to use clever tactics so that its position is represented perfectly in the proposed agreement. They might be able to force this agreement upon the naive negotiators for Side B. But these negotiators are not the people who have to be persuaded. The negotiators for Side B have to report back to the people whom they represent, and these others may recognize that their requests have disappeared and that the proposal is one sided. Given this knowledge, negotiators for Side A may want to include some of Side B's requests so that the proposal will eventually be accepted and implemented.

There are further benefits for long-term relations among members of the two sides. If for some reason the one-sided agreement is accepted by all parties, there may be a short-term victory for Side A but a long-term debacle for both sides. Sooner or later the members of Side B will discover that the agreement is not benefiting them. They are then likely to put their resources into breaking or sabotaging the agreement. Their activities will lead to legal fees, ill will, and distractions from the organization's mission for all concerned.[25] A better procedure is for the most sophisticated negotiators to insure fairness from the start, thus encouraging positive long-term relations among members of the various parties to the agreement.

RECOGNIZING TACTICS DIRECTED AGAINST ONESELF

Given that this chapter deals with tactics that are used to deal with the opposition, people need to recognize when *they* are seen as the opponents. If people learn that they are being targeted as members of the opposition or the enemy camp, they may be able to take steps to assuage the problems that will inevitably arise.

The ability of people to know when others consider them as enemies begins with a fine-tuned sensitivity to problems of all sorts. Consider the example of people who work for a large company. The most general approach to recognizing problems is to determine whether the behavior of coworkers, as well as activities within and outside the organization, are more or less intense than usual. Detecting this means that people have a good idea of the baseline—the normal, everyday level of activities in an organization and the typical day-to-day behaviors of people. There are baselines for such behaviors as the amount of informal conversation around watercoolers, the number of print and television reporters that drop by over the course of a week, and the number of meetings called by power-holders. Deviations from these baselines, either higher or lower, are signs of possible difficulty. In one organization for which I worked there was a *decrease* in the number of requests for employees to submit budget suggestions. This turned out to be the first sign that the incumbent CEO was to leave and a new one hired. Budget commitments, it was thought, would tie the hands of the new CEO, so money was placed in holding accounts to make funds available for the new CEO to put new policies into action.

Individuals known to be good at "reading people" work from baselines. One of my colleagues recently recognized a difficulty in the life of a mutual friend. Our friend has a low-key, mild-mannered personality and does not betray personal difficulties in any obvious manner. I asked my colleague how he knew. He replied, "At a party, she left a conversation with a group of people, and the topic was of special interest to her. She would usually participate actively in the conversation. She went to the kitchen to help prepare and serve food. She is not a 'go-to-the-kitchen-to-serve-food' type. So I knew something was wrong."

If people have developed an ability to interpret implicit and subtle communications, there are a number of signs that should let them know if they have incurred the displeasure of powerholders. One sign is to be assigned an important task but to be given a hopeless budget, an inadequate staff, and little authority. When the task cannot be completed, the powerholders may claim that there is cause for the unsuccessful people to be removed.

Another sign is that powerholders are bringing in old friends to act as their assistants. A naval officer told me, "I was making good career progress and was assigned to a Pentagon position under one of the very successful young admirals on his way to Chief of Naval Operations. But he brought in his old roommate and close friend from his days at Annapolis. I figured this would be an impossible situation for me, since the friend would receive the important assignments and I would just sit around. So I requested a transfer and joined a unit where I could use my skills."

A third sign that things are going badly is that colleagues suddenly begin to request transfers, ask to be assigned to other work groups, or seek out the company of different people during informal work breaks. A more subtle sign is that colleagues begin to show great enthusiasm for their work, put in extra hours, and bring work home with them. The danger here is that all of these people have been put in competition for one promotion. The powerholder calls people in, one by one, and says, "The vice-presidency is open, and I'll be making my choice in about six months. I hope that I can consider you for that promotion. I don't want everybody to know about this, however, because I don't want them working hard just because the vice presidency is open." If the powerholder tells this to large numbers of people, it is difficult for any one individual to determine where he or she stands in the competition. A decision has to be made whether to participate in this possibly manipulative action, change positions within the company, or seek employment elsewhere.

As people gain more and more experience, they should become so knowledgeable about their areas of expertise that they can anticipate difficulties. A good exercise is to sit down with pen and paper and ask, "If I propose a certain policy, what obstacles might be put in the way by opponents? What tactics might they direct against me? How can I best be prepared for these obstacles and tactics?" The answers to such questions can then be incorporated into written proposals or can produce readiness for question-and-answer sessions. For example, politicians who propose tax cuts have to be prepared for questions inquiring about the funding of social programs such as support for AIDS patients or job training for inner-city youth. If they do not have well-formulated answers, the politicians can come across as insensitive to unfortunate people faced with catastrophic illnesses or a lifetime of hopelessness. Businesspeople who propose to manufacture complex machinery in overseas locations cannot take for granted the protection of U.S. patent law, because legal systems in other countries do not look upon patents in the same way. Instead, the value reflected in law is that knowledge should be widely shared and that research-based technologies should quickly be made available to all interested parties. Unprepared businesspeople may find that local companies in these other countries are soon using the patented technology and that the presumed competitive edge stemming from the most advanced manufacturing methods has disappeared.

During a public lecture, I once made a mistake for which I should have been prepared. At the height of the movement for women's rights, I was asked to give a talk at a luncheon for businesspeople. My topic was race relations, and I dealt with ways of reducing prejudice and discrimination when people are separated by barriers of skin color, language/dialect, and cultural practices. The question-answer part of the luncheon talk, however, focused on male-female relations and the passage of the Equal Rights Amendment. Given the heightened sensitivity to sexual discrimination at the time, I should have realized that many people's reactions to my treatment of prejudice would center on male-female relations. But I had not thought through this possibility and consequently did not handle the question-answer session particularly well.

Once people find themselves with a difficulty they cannot handle, they should cut their losses as soon as they can. The ability to cut losses quickly is important for the acquisition and maintenance of power. It is far better to admit to a loss than to justify or pursue it through one's time, energy, money, and other resources. A classic case is the burglary at the Democratic Party offices in the Watergate Buildings, carried out by people who were working for President Nixon's reelection. As soon as the incident became public knowledge, Nixon or a high administration official should have appeared before the press. A statement should have been read saying, "In the enthusiasm surrounding reelection efforts, a number of workers committed a serious offense. While I did not, of course, know about their plans, I take full responsibility for their actions. I apologize to the American people and regret deeply this incident, which has besmirched the values we all hold so dear." Nixon would have cut his losses. There would have been no cover-up for reporters to pursue and no reason for a congressional inquiry. The incident would have faded from memory after a number of weeks, given the competition for people's attention from coverage of other newsworthy events.

In my public presentation on race relations, I should have said, "I prepared for questions on race relations and so cannot handle issues such as the Equal Rights Amendment as well. Does anyone have a question that raises issues involving both race *and* sex?" If there had been such questions, I might have been able to handle the racial aspects and, by extension, have given adequate attention to the gender aspects.

I have been in sessions with powerholders who know how to cut losses. A typical session proceeds as follows. The powerholder is chairing a meeting, and several staff members bring up a problem about which they have extensive documentation. They are prepared to talk for 30 minutes and have good visual aids and well-thought-out arguments. Recognizing immediately that they have a good case, the powerholder says, "You're right. We'll take care of it. What's the next issue to be discussed?" The staff members cannot easily pursue the problem, because its existence has been acknowledged. If they persist, they may come across as whiners and time wasters. But because so little time has been spent on the issue, it may either not enter most people's minds or may not be seen as particularly important. By cutting their losses early and admitting a problem, the powerholders move along on the agenda to issues *they* want to treat in more depth.

A great deal of information has been covered in Chapters 1 through 6 concerning various strategies, tactics, and skills. Chapter 7 will attempt to answer the question, "How can the relevant skills be acquired, and how can the strategies and tactics be learned, in the most efficient manner?" The general answer to this question is that to learn them people should force themselves into social situations where the skills, strategies, and tactics are demanded. By relating verbal descriptions, for instance of tactics aimed at neutralizing an opposition, to *their* experiences, they can make the tactics relevant to the acquisition of their own goals in their own lives. Personal experiences are essential. Admittedly, the call for experience will remind people of the old joke about applying for one's first job—employers want experience, but how can this be obtained if no one will hire inexperienced people? Fortunately there are ways to acquire these skills, tactics, and strategies without jobs that involve salaries or hourly wages. Participation in voluntary activities will serve the purpose. Those who join community service organizations, who participate in amateur sports, and who partake in extracurricular activities during their formal schooling will be exposed to people who use power in the ways discussed throughout this book. They can then draw from their experiences, combine these with conceptual treatments of power acquisition, and develop an understanding of the skills, strategies, and tactics they need for the achievement of their goals.

NOTES

1. The classic treatment concerning the unanticipated consequences of policies can be found in R. Merton, *Social Theory and Social Structure* (Glenview, Ill.: Free Press, 1957).

2. S. Hess, *The Government/Press Connection* (Washington, D.C.: Brookings Institution, 1984); H. Smith, *The Power Game: How Washington Works* (New York: Random House, 1988).

3. S. Ramsey and J. Birk, "Preparation of North Americans for Interaction with Japanese: Considerations of Language and Communication Style," in *Handbook of Intercultural Training*, vol. 3, edited by D. Landis and R. Brislin (Elmsford, N.Y.: Pergamon, 1983), pp. 227–29.

4. T. O'Neill, *Man of the House: The Life and Political Memoirs of Speaker Tip O'Neill* (New York: Random House, 1987). Quote is from p. 26.

5. D. Wrong, *Power: Its Forms, Bases, and Uses* (New York: Harper & Row, 1979); W. Slack, *The Grim Science: The Struggle for Power* (Port Washington, N.Y.: Kennikat, 1981).

6. H. Heclo, *A Government of Strangers* (Washington, D.C.: Brookings Institution, 1977).

7. H. Simon, *Administrative Behavior: a Study of Decision-making Processes in Administrative Organizations* (New York: Macmillan, 1957).

8. D. Stockman, *The Triumph of Politics: Why the Reagan Revolution Failed* (New York: Harper and Row, 1986).

9. I. Janis and L. Mann, *Decision Making* (New York: Free Press, 1977); I. Janis, *Victims of Groupthink* (Boston: Houghton Mifflin, 1972).

10. G. Comstock, "Today's Audiences, Tomorrow's Media," In *Applied Social Psychology Annual*, vol. 8 of *Television as a Social Issue*, edited by S. Oskamp (Newbury Park, Calif.: Sage, 1988), pp. 324–45.

11. J. Williams, *Eyes on the Prize* (New York: Penguin, 1987).

12. R. Cialdini, *Influence: Science and Practice*, 2d ed. (Glenview, Ill.: Scott Foresman, 1988)

13. M. Sherif, *In Common Predicament: Social Psychology of Intergroup Conflict and Cooperation* (New York: Houghton Mifflin, 1966).

14. E. Koch, *Mayor: An Autobiography* (New York: Simon & Schuster, 1984).

15. E. Aronson and N. Osherow, "Cooperation, Social Behavior, and Academic Performance: Experiments in the Desegregated Classroom," in *Applied Social Psychology Annual*, edited by L. Bickman (Beverly Hills, Calif.: Sage, 1980), vol. 1, pp. 163–96.

16. T. Tyler and K. McGraw, "Ideology and the Interpretation of Personal Experience: Procedural Justice and Political Quiescence," *Journal of Social Issues* 42 (1986), no. 2, pp. 115–28; F. Crosby and G. Herek, "Male Sympathy with the

Situation of Women: Does Personal Experience Make a Difference?" *Journal of Social Issues* 42 (1986), no. 2, pp. 55–66.

17. O'Neill, *Man of the House*.

18. M. Schatzki, *Negotiation: The Art of Getting What You Want* (New York: New American Library, 1981); H. Cohen, *You Can Negotiate Anything* (New York: Bantam Books, 1982); C. Karass, *The Negotiating Game* (New York: Thomas Crowell, 1970).

19. U. Pareek and T. Rao, "Cross-Cultural Surveys and Interviewing," in *Handbook of Cross-Cultural Psychology*, edited by H. Triandis and J. Berry, vol. 2 of *Methodology* (Boston: Allyn & Bacon, 1980), pp. 127–79.

20. P. T. Barnum, *Barnum's Own Story: The Autobiography of P. T. Barnum* (New York: Dover, 1961).

21. O'Neill, *Man of the House*.

22. Schatski, *Negotiation*.

23. A. deGroot, *Thought and Choice in Chess* (the Hague: Mouton, 1965); also J. Bransford, R. Sherwood, N. Vye, and J. Eieser, "Teaching Thinking and Problem Solving: Research Foundations," *American Psychologist* 41 (1986): 1078–89.

24. H. Mackay, *Swim with the Sharks Without Being Eaten Alive* (New York: William Morrow, 1988).

25. G. Nierenberg, *The Art of Negotiating* (New York: Cornerstone Library, 1968).

7

DEVELOPING A KNOWLEDGE OF RESOURCE EXCHANGES, STRATEGIES, AND TACTICS

I have argued that some people are socialized into an understanding of how power works. Children of the upper and upper-middle classes observe their lawyer fathers, banker mothers, politician uncles, and physician aunts make firm decisions, develop coalitions of influential people who possess a variety of resources, and command the respect of others in the community. The children are frequently invited to accompany their parents to the work place, where they see the use of power and its effects on others. The children also accompany their parents to social gatherings, where pleasantries are mixed with resource exchange, network development, and key information on deals being developed in the community. This sort of knowledge, passed on in a hands-on rather than book-learning context, is worth thousands of dollars in the children's own eventual career development.

My guess is that while male children have traditionally been given access to their parents' knowledge of how power works, only lately are some upper-middle-class females becoming more exposed to the rules of resource exchange, strategies, and tactics discussed throughout this book. Still, the recent inclusion of *some* upper-middle-class females leaves large numbers of people unsophisticated about the nature and uses of power. The naive include females whose parents do not feel it appropriate to have their daughters exposed to power, people from the middle and working classes, people who hold minority-group status in a country, and recent arrivals in any country, such as immigrants, refugees, and people on temporary sojourns (foreign students, overseas businesspeople) from another country.

How can these individuals catch up with the more privileged members of the upper middle class? The answer is that they must place themselves in community activities where the rules of resource exchange, as well as effective strategies and tactics, can be practiced. From time to time it will be wise for these people to review what they have learned by examining their recent experiences in relation to the concepts (summarized in headings within chapters) introduced throughout this book. Further explicit attention should be given to examining skills that *seem to be specific* to a certain task. Many times, those seemingly specific skills will be examples of more general abilities and resources that people can call upon in a wide variety of settings. These general skills can assist people as they pursue a wide variety of goals.

TEAM SPORTS AS A LEARNING ENVIRONMENT

As an example of what can be learned through selected personal experiences, I would like to review the knowledge and skills that can be acquired through participation in team sports. This list of skills, all reminiscent of previous discussions about power, was first developed during discussions with my sister, Joann Brislin, who is a swim coach at a major U.S. university.[1] I will refer most often to sports at the high school and college levels, but will also occasionally discuss other levels, such as teams for preteens and athletic activities for adults.

Working with Others

While an immediate connotation of "power" may be one individual dictating impactful decisions and ordering people around, the more frequent use of power takes place in coalitions of people who combine their resources. In athletics, teams of talented individuals have to mesh their skills to maintain a competitive record. The individual who works only for private glory is often relegated to the bench.

Combining Skills

In team sports, people have different resources that they contribute to a joint effort. A football team needs quarterbacks with good throwing arms, swift running backs and wide receivers, kickers who can be counted on for three-point field goals, and husky defensive linemen who can not be easily shunted aside by opposing blockers. Not everyone can have the glamour position of quarterback. Talented athletes who served as quarterbacks at the high-school level often switch their positions (to defensive or running back, wide receiver, etc.) upon entering college, trading their skills, such as coordination, quickness, and intelligence on the field, for more playing time. A major weakness in any one type of ability can lead to an ineffective team. The concept that various skills are needed for effective coalitions is an important point that people learn through their participation in team sports. I have observed many lackluster coalitions, sometimes as a member; their ineffectiveness was often caused by insufficient attention to recruiting people with a wide variety of necessary skills. A dangerous tendency is to recruit like-minded people, for instance all intellectuals or all political activists. In doing so, important skills, such as the ability to keep volunteer workers satisfied and feeling needed, may be overlooked.

Working with Disliked Others

Given that power is dependent upon participation in coalitions, potential powerholders have to learn to work effectively with many types of people. There is no possibility that all these other people will be likeable. Many will be irritating, abrasive, and generally unpleasant. But if they have resources and their potential contributions outweigh the liabilities brought on by their unpleasantness, then strong consideration should be given to including them. Several respondents pointed out that it matters more that people can work effectively with each other than that they like each other.

On athletic teams, people have to work together despite the fact that they do not care for each other. The quarterback may not be fond of the wide receiver, but there has to be interaction if they are to develop an effective pass play. The ability to set aside personal animosities and work with others toward common goals is an extraordinarily important aspect of power acquisition.

Accepting People as They Are

In their book *All About Politics*,[2] Theis and Steponkus emphasized that good politicians have to accept people as they are. This means that they cannot put their time and energy into *changing* people to fit some desired image of the perfect personality. Rather, powerholders must accept people as they are and employ their existing talents. Certainly latent talents should be encouraged, such as writing and public-speaking abilities, but deep-seated aspects of personality are highly resistant to change. Highly introverted people, for instance, rarely become vivacious extroverts who enjoy cocktail parties where other guests are unknown to them. Unfortunately, deep-seated aspects of personality are the most inviting targets for would-be agents of change. In accepting what people are and encouraging them to contribute their talents and resources, powerholders often have to diagnose latent talents, since many people are not especially insightful concerning the identification of their own resources and abilities.

While coaches can encourage the development of some abilities, certain talents have to be accepted and used as they are. A high-school running back who weighs 180 pounds can hardly expect to become an interior lineman at a Big 10 school. A 310-pound defensive lineman who runs the 40-yard dash in 5.9 seconds may be a valued team member but should not be turned into a safety. Legends abound concerning coaches who tried to make major changes in their players. O. J. Simpson had a unique stutter step that he used while examining the defense to see what openings had developed through which he could run. He could retain his leg action and readiness to accelerate quickly while stutter-stepping and then move forward when an opportunity developed. This style contributed to his record-breaking performances. One coach tried to change this style, but the coach did not keep his job very long.

Accepting Life's Realities

Politics is the art of the possible. Powerholders are concerned with what *can* be done, not what *might* be done in a perfect world. Coming to grips with life's imperfections is a major aspect of maturity and sophistication. Athletes are exposed to such realities. Competent and dedicated college athletes may be willing to spend six hours a day practicing their skills, giving up their social lives in the process. Nevertheless, they may see less playing time, win fewer medals, and command less media attention than naturally gifted peers who excel with only two hours of practice a day. This seems unfair, but lots of what goes on in life is unfair. When people realize this fact and learn to cope with it gracefully, they are better prepared to compete for the benefits in life that *are* open to them. Often the coping involves looking at issues from various angles. The people who worked six hours a day on their athletic abilities, for instance, may have developed work habits and time management skills that will serve them well in their later careers. Naturally gifted peers who take their talents for granted may have few marketable skills once their youthful athletic careers come to an end.

Developing a Thick Skin

Powerholders have to learn to take criticism gracefully. They cannot become so upset that they lash out at innocent others in their immediate environment. Even the most celebrated superstar makes mistakes that demand the firm commentary of coaches. The ability to understand that the criticism is not always meant to personally injure the target's ego, and is instead aimed at improvement of the group effort, is very important.

In trying to move from junior- to senior-level managerial positions, some people complain that they rarely recieve helpful feedback on their perfor-

mance from company executives. One reason is that the executives recognize thin skins, conclude that giving firm feedback will cause more
stresses than benefits, and consequently keep their own counsel.[3] As a
result the employees receive no constructive criticism and risk being kept
at their current levels within their organizations.

Another way that a thick skin can be developed is by putting up with
the taunts of opponents. When they have the opportunity, members of the
other team will make unpleasant and derogatory comments. This happens
in football as the offense and defense line up just a few feet opposite each
other, in basketball as opponents chat less than amiably after someone is
fouled, and in hockey as the players check one another. The comments
deal with the legitimacy of one's parentage, the size of one's reproductive
organs, one's lack of Phi Beta Kappa level intelligence, and comparisons
of one's general character to the less flattering parts of the body. The goal
of the taunts is to divert attention from a team effort and from winning
the game. A player whose goal is to "get even" with an opponent is
effectively taken out of the game. Ignoring the colorful epithets of others
contributes to the development of grace under pressure, a useful character
trait for many important jobs.

Working with Probabilities

People want certainty in their lives, but the pursuit of many desirable
ends is based on an understanding of probabilities. If there are two promotions open within an organization but ten people desiring them, there
is no guarantee that the two people who follow the career-development
advice of a respected elder will be successful in their quest. But they can
increase their probabilities of success if they take the advice that the elder
offers. If they are unsuccessful, they should not become discouraged but
instead should put their energies into future considerations for promotion.
They should prepare themselves in various ways (perhaps by studying the
resources of people who have recently been promoted) to increase their
probabilities of success within the next competition and should continue
in a thick-skinned manner until they are successful.

Working with probabilities is hard for many people. In Chapter 4 I
described a case in which a person did not accept my recommendation to
enter a future competition for overseas study. She was unsuccessful in her
first competition, but I argued that her probability of success would be
greater in future years. She did not accept my analysis, perhaps because
she had not learned to think in terms of probabilities. In Chapter 6 I
discussed the phenomenon of minority groups becoming satisfied with their
treatment by the dominant group if the *procedures* for making complaints
are open to them. Given this satisfaction, they do not calculate their success/
failure ratio to see if they are making reasonable progress with their griev-

ances. One reason is that the act of comparing successes to failures involves statistics, the formal set of procedures for analyzing probabilities. Many people do not know how to work with statistics, or if they do, they do not enjoy it. For students in many fields, such as the behavioral/social sciences, education, business, and public health, statistics is the least favored and most dreaded course that they have to take.

Athletes are inevitably exposed to thinking in terms of probabilities. After the offense of an opposing football team is scouted, coaches and players decide on certain defensive alignments. These do not guarantee success, but they increase the probability of stopping the most effective offensive threats of the opposition.

In baseball, pitchers and catchers work with probabilities. A pitcher who has a very effective slow curve may not be able to use it frequently if there is a skillful runner at first base, because a slow curve takes too long to reach the plate and may be too difficult for the catcher to handle. This would give the runner extra time to steal second base. The pitcher may have to use other pitches to decrease the chances of a successful steal and still maximize the probability of getting the batter out. Facts known about the batter also help in the choice of pitches: Does he bunt well? Can he handle fast balls pitched inside? Will he chase balls that are high and outside the strike zone? No final decision about the choice of pitches can guarantee eventual success, of course. But certain choices should increase the chances of a positive outcome.

Uses of Information

In baseball, knowledge of the sorts of pitches that another team's batters can and cannot hit is an example of the information essential for success. In any kind of endeavor, people who have the greatest amount of information relevant to their goals have tremendous advantages over their opponents and competition. Often the information can be found in public sources. Legal precedents are found in law textbooks and in transcripts of appellate court decisions. The recent history of the performance of a company's stocks and bonds can be obtained from back issues of the *Wall Street Journal*. But just as important, key information is often unpublished and is shared among friends, colleagues, and members of one's network. Rookies who come up to the major leagues in the spring and bat .380 during their first three months sometimes perform far less effectively during the latter part of the season. One reason is that, through trial and error, one pitcher finds out how to pitch to the batter so that the probability of an "out" is maximized. The pitcher may discover that the batter cannot hit a low-inside breaking ball. Pitchers and their catchers then get on the phone and share this information with members of their network, expecting reciprocity of helpful information on other batters in the near future. The information is passed from pitcher to pitcher very quickly, and it is only much later that sportswriters begin to discuss the batter's weakness in their newspaper columns.

When I was 11 or 12 years old, a friend always used to beat me at card games when we played at his house. When we played at my house, we battled to a draw. Years later I figured out the reason for the discrepancy. At his house, he always arranged the playing area so that I sat with my back to a window. After dark he could see my cards reflected on the glass. While this was unethical, the "cards reflected in the window" is a good metaphor to keep in mind. When competing for scarce resources, it is wise to ask, "What are the legal and ethical ways I can obtain information on my competitors' and opponents' plans? How can I learn as much as if I had a mirror over their playing cards?"

Networks

The best way to obtain unpublished and generally unavailable information is to participate in networks. Key and up-to-date information is shared by word of mouth, and this method is far more quick and efficient than waiting for the widespread availability of information in newspapers and magazines or on television. An example of important information is the availability of good jobs.

My sister pointed out the importance of networks from her experience as a swim coach. The parents of high-school swimmers become very involved as timers, members of transportation committees, fund-raisers, and so forth. In fact, part of the uniform of involved parents seems to be an expensive stopwatch. Parents become aware of who their children swim with and against; even though there may be only the most pro-forma interactions as congratulations are dispersed after a meet, the teammates and competitors become known figures—they become part of a network. Parents remember the names of people on their children's teams and on the opposition teams. If two athletes, A and B, swim against each other when they are 17 years old, important events can happen five years later. For instance, the father of Swimmer A may control the hiring process for good jobs at a company, or he may know of other employment opportunities in the community. Swimmer B, now 22 with a college degree, may want to learn about job possibilities in the community. The father of her previous opponent is in her network. She can request an appointment, and it is likely to be granted. "Oh, yes, you used to swim against my daughter. Those were exciting times!" Person B has an advantage that is not possessed by her age peers. Other 22-year-olds are likely to be blank faces to the employer. The fact that the employer can attach a face and some memories to one applicant's resume is a major point in her favor. My sister's only wonder is why more high school athletes do not think through this process and take more advantage of their networks.

Cordial Communication within Networks

In two important articles written for the *Harvard Business Review,* John Kotter[4] contributed to efforts that have broken the myth about the behavior of effective executives. The myth or stereotype is that executives sequester themselves in offices, study various policy options thoroughly, engage in quiet and thoughtful long-term planning, and then issue crisp directives that subordinates quickly implement. In reality, executives rarely find themselves alone for long periods of time. They engage in many short-term meetings and are constantly interrupted by telephone calls, queries from secretaries, exchanges of information with other executives, and drop-ins from subordinates needing quick okays for their proposals. Many of the resources needed for policy implementation come from managers over whom a given executive has little direct control according to the company organizational chart. To obtain the cooperation of these managers, a given executive must, over time, engage in various activities for mutual advantage. The exchange of resources described in Chapter 3 is a good example of such activities.

Executives do not obtain the information necessary for their work solely from published sources such as books, journals, magazines, and newspapers. Rather, much of their information is received during the short discussions with colleagues that Kotter documented. Certain of their colleagues receive more information than others; these include cordial people who signal to others that they welcome interaction; people who frequent gathering places where others meet (water coolers, photocopy rooms, company lunchrooms); and people who make sure that they distribute information as well as receive it. There may be technically competent and intelligent people who find themselves cut off from information networks and who are thus denied key and current information helpful in their jobs. Examples are sour and sullen people who do not interact graciously with others; overconfident people who signal that they do not welcome suggestions from others; and people who never return favors.

The style that executives frequently use, then, might be called "quick face-to-face information sharing." Athletes engage in such communication. During a time out in a football game, a free safety might mention to a wide receiver, "I don't think their Number 42 can follow your hip fake to the left on a long pass pattern." The wide receiver might use this information during a subsequent play. Such communication is dependent upon informal relations among people, because the free safety (defense) and the wide receiver (offense) are part of different units and are coached by different individuals. On a later play, or even in a later game, the wide receiver may share some observations with the safety. "Number 88 may try to decoy you, but he can't catch worth a damn. Number 86 is the primary receiver to follow." The information would not be shared if one of the players involved was uncommunicative with teammates, made it clear during games and practices that no suggestions from others were desired, or insisted on being only the recipient of important information.

Dealing with the Media

While it may not have been necessary fifty years ago, powerholders today have to deal with many forms of media: television, radio, newspapers, magazines, and so forth. The world has become so complex, and there are so many matters competing for the public's attention, that people have to summarize their ideas in a manner that can be efficiently communicated and readily digested. One respondent said, "Sometimes you have to think of your ideas in terms of a bumper sticker slogan. If your ideas can't fit on a bumper sticker, they may not be communicated to the general public." To communicate their ideas, people have to interact graciously and effectively with the media.

Good athletes command media attention, are sought out for individual interviews, and are retained in the public's admittedly short memory for celebrities. Exceptional athletes command national and international attention, but even competent contributors, perhaps members of the second string who support the local team with limited playing time, will receive attention in their hometown newspapers. Though these newspapers have limited circulation, the basic elements of interaction with the media are the same as for national and international publications. Reporters schedule interviews, are impressed with articulate answers, will use the angles and leads fed to them if they are interesting, appreciate color and/or humor, and are most responsive to a generally cooperative attitude on the part of the person being interviewed. The interviewees will reap the most benefits if they are gracious, distribute praise to teammates when it is due, and abstain from communicating personal bitterness about opponents. Personal attacks may attract immediate attention, but they are likely to contribute to a "spoilsport" or "brat" reputation over the long run. A reputation of this sort can shut off the flow of opportunities that might come a sports figure's way.

Identifying Competitors' Weaknesses

In many professions the chances of success can be increased by identifying what the competition does not do well. If a young lawyer moves to a community and finds that no attorney handles divorce cases particularly well, she may communicate her willingness to take on such cases. If the manager of a local department store observes that residents of the community have to travel 100 miles to buy electronic products for their homes, she may decide to carry televisions, microwave ovens, and personal computers in the local store.

Athletes have to identify the weaknesses of their opponents to compete against them successfully. After they have developed a high level of skill, many athletes are told to "play the other person as well as the ball." I have had a few all-American football, basketball, and volleyball players in my classes and have enjoyed attending games with my sports-oriented son to see them play. One day the superb starting defensive linebacker, whom I knew, was ill and had to be replaced by a person with far less skill. The other team quickly saw the lesser ability of the replacement and ran plays to his side of the field all afternoon. When a good defensive player repositioned himself to help the replacement, this left *that* person's normal position underdefended and consequently provided opportunities for exploitation by the opposition. This identification of a weak individual and attention to his inexperience, incidentally, is not considered unsportsmanlike. The coaches would be considered foolish if they did not exploit the absence of the all-American. Ideally the substitute will learn from his mistakes and work hard to increase his skills for use in future games.

Given that the coaches of other teams will be attentive to weaknesses, athletes should learn to cover up their limitations so that they are not easily communicated. On a given day a major league pitcher may not have good control of his curve ball and may have to "get by" on his fastball and change-up. But rather than communicate his inability to throw a curve, he will occasionally offer a breaking pitch just so the batter continues to look for them. The breaking pitch may not end up in the strike zone, but the batter will continue to have "look for the curve" on his mind. Covering one's weaknesses often means integrating one's skills with those of others. In football, if one person's peripheral vision is limited so that a certain type of pass pattern can't be run, a teammate may have to run that pattern. Rather than advertise one's limitations, it may be best to step aside in favor of a teammate more skilled in a particular area. Whatever one's own shortcomings, athletes should not talk about them publicly. This carefully developed inhibition serves people well in virtually any profession; people should learn when it is best to keep their mouths closed. Given their many opportunities to discuss matters with others, athletes may have more practice with this desideratum than age peers who have not participated in team sports.

Intergroup Interaction

If there is any prediction that can be made with certainty about the twenty-first century, it is that there will be more interaction among people from different cultural backgrounds. Even if people would like to interact only with others who have similar interests, have the same skin color, and speak the same language, they will not be able to act on their preferences. The laws of the United States now protect previously excluded people who want to work at a certain job, attend a selective school, live in a certain neighborhood, take out a bank loan, and so forth. People will be almost certain to have coworkers of both sexes and from different cultural backgrounds. Anglo-Americans will be more likely than not to have coworkers who are of Black, Hispanic, and/or Asian ancestry. The all-white, male-dominated organization is going to be a vestige of the past.

The differences in background with which people must deal also include the experiences peculiar to the social classes of which others have been a part. In years past, the fact of birth into the working class could put a damper on people's opportunities to compete for society's benefits. Working class families might not have enough money to send their children to college (or as many opportunities to think about, as I discussed in Chapter 1). Where the family income is low, the children may have to go to work as soon as possible so they can contribute money to the household income. Currently, low-cost community colleges take away some of the financial burden and provide opportunities for advancement into the higher paying jobs associated with middle-class status.

The fact of increased intergroup interaction means that people are likely to be more successful in their careers if they can get along well with people who have different cultural or social class backgrounds from themselves. "Getting along well" includes tolerance of others, respect for their contributions, efforts to understand enough of their background to know why they behave in certain ways, and demonstrations of appreciation for their work. Athletes have many opportunities to develop this respect for different others. Most college athletics, especially football and basketball, have representatives from different ethnic groups. It is now almost a certainty that football and basketball players will have extensive interaction across the once almost inviolate Black-White race barrier. Since the team effort is better served by cooperation among members than by constant bickering, the value and benefits of positive intergroup relations should be one of the lessons learned from participation in athletic activities. Interestingly, athletic teams provide examples of the five major factors that specialists in intergroup relations recommend for positive interaction across racial barriers.[5]

—Equal-status contact. Blacks and Whites have equal status in the eyes of the coaches. All are competing for playing time, and the competition is based on ability rather than skin color. Coaches who put color over ability lose games and possibly their jobs.

—Superordinate goals. This term refers to goals that are desired by all and demand the efforts of everybody concerned for their attainment. A team's goal is to win games; this goal demands the whole team's harmonious efforts. When people work hard toward common goals that are intensely desired, skin color and class background become petty concerns and are given little attention.

—Intimate contact. When people share their private thoughts and their very personal concerns, rather than reiterate their well-rehearsed description about themselves (name, hometown, area of study), the contact is said to be intimate rather than formal. Athletes travel together, practice together, and room together. The extensive time they spend with each other, especially the hours they have to "kill" when traveling to games in other cities, provides many opportunities for intimate contact.

—Sterotype-breaking contact. The most effective contact challenges the preexisting stereotypes that people have of others. If Blacks have the stereotypes of having a talent only for athletics and of being very different from Whites, the intimate contact already discussed can challenge these oversimplified preconceptions. Blacks can be seen as future lawyers and physicians who have the same problems as White teammates: finding time to combine studies and team sports.

—Administrative support. The most effective support from an organization's power structure communicates the clear message that intergroup tolerance is the only policy that will be accepted. "Come hell or high water, there is not going to be racial or ethnic bickering. We have to put our time and energy into competing against other teams, not fighting among ourselves. If you don't like it, the door is over there!"

People are very quick to realize when the rhetoric coming from powerholders advocates intergroup tolerance, in contrast to settings where the actions behind the verbal commentary communicate a less enthusiastic attitude. When rhetoric is backed up by clear action, such as support for people who go out of their way to interact effectively with very different others, then the goal of intergroup tolerance will be advanced.

Humility

In Chapter 2 an important point about the inhibition of power was discussed. Power is intoxicating, and people who begin to acquire it want more. But if they acquire and use more *without* an ability to inhibit it when appropriate, they endanger themselves in a variety of ways. Once they become intoxicated, they do not want the constructive suggestions of others. They begin to downgrade coworkers and take credit for their work. They irritate coworkers, superiors, and other community powerholders. Eventually they may find that they have angered so many people that they have lost the power they once so confidently possessed. It is important to remember that power is a social phenomenon. Once others decide not to recognize a powerholder, that person is damaged. A key ability, then, is the ability to inhibit one's power need so that it does not become an irritant. One way to develop this inhibition is to acquire some humility about one's talents.

In his preface to Stimson Bullitt's *To Be a Politician*, David Riesman [6] speculated about members of the upper-middle and upper classes who become successful governors, representatives, and senators. The danger for a society's wealthy elite is that they may think too highly of themselves and may be unable to relate to their middle-and working-class constituents. During campaigns this feeling may be communicated to voters, who may therefore be attracted to other candidates.

Riesman notes that some upper-class politicians have learned humility, and learned to respect the contributions of working-class individuals, through participation in sports. For a running back there is nothing quite like getting trampled by a 260-pound defensive end. Experiences like this bring the efforts of others forcefully to one's attention.

Boxing is another example. A concerned and supportive father may have been able to send his son to Phillips Exeter and to Princeton and also may have introduced him to members of various elite networks. However, these advantages do little good when the young man laces up his gloves and steps into the boxing ring. There, the "street smarts" of his working-class opponent are likely to count more than a private school education. If the young man had an exalted view of his own self-worth before the match, the effective left-hand jabs of his opponent may contribute to some modesty. Generalized to all of life's endeavors, this can be a valuable asset. The "common touch," or the ability to interact comfortably with many different others and demonstrate respect for their contributions, is an ability well worth acquiring.

Thinking in Terms of Powerful Concepts

When people have well-developed concepts and categories in their minds, they can then behave in ways that put the concepts into action. But if the concepts do not exist, the actions to support them cannot follow. In Chapter 1 I discussed the concept "life-long advantages are brought about by attendance at elite private schools." Since no one in my family or neighborhood had this concept, no one I knew attended such schools. Some parents know the concept "social skills" and consequently shoo their 12-year-old children off to their classmates' birthday parties. "I realize that you don't want to go. But it will do you good to meet people, be gracious, and be cordial even with those classmates that you don't particularly like." I have long felt that some college graduates have the concept "continue to learn a lot from reading" firmly embedded in their minds. Given this idea, they buy books and check others out of the library. They later bring aspects of their continued learning into their jobs. Other graduates have a concept more like "books are what the professors assigned you to read."

Given this orientation, in college they read exactly what they were formally assigned—no more and no less. They do not search out interesting books on their own initiative.

As has been discussed a number of times, power is a phenomenon that involves a number of people. Assume that one person sets and attains a specific goal solely through his or her own actions. The best word for this process is "achievement." Power involves one or more people influencing the efforts of others so that general goals are accomplished: winning, progress, success, profits, growth, recognized excellence in the community, and so forth. Put another way, an achievement-oriented individual sets goals and works toward them, but a powerful person sees to it that others achieve various goals. The relationship between the powerful person and others can be summarized through the use of various concepts indicative of collectives: teams, groups, leader-member relations, status hierarchies, and so forth.

Athletes have an opportunity to internalize a number of power-related concepts, including those that describe the functions of collectives. They certainly learn the advantage of team effort, the role of a leader (as seen in the efforts of the coach), and the nature of status hierarchies (starters and substitutes). They also learn that attention must be given to developing the talents of all team members. If the coaches give attention only to the three or four natural athletes with superstar potential, they will lose games. I have observed coaches who have internalized this concept as they work with 6- to 8-year-olds in baseball. There is a big difference between the 8-year-olds and 6-year-olds, especially on the first day of practice. There is a temptation for the coaches to give all their attention to the bigger 8-year-olds. But the winning coaches also work closely with the 6-year-olds, all of whom are playing their first year of organized baseball. Since the league rules dictate that all children play at least two innings, those 6-year-olds will make appearances at the plate. If the coach has taught them to make contact with the pitch and run the bases, the youngsters may beat out an infield single. Then the bigger and more skilled 8-year-olds can hit the ball out of the infield and drive in the 6-year-olds.

Developing team skills is important for any powerholder. The executive vice president in charge of a team of architects may be extremely skillful. In fact, she may have called herself to the president's attention as a result of her innovative building designs, and the successful erection of these buildings may have led to her vice presidency. But as a vice president, she can no longer be exclusively concerned with her own designs; she has to see to it that the people in her office develop their own skills. If a certain client comes to town, she may be the best person in the office to come up with a design that will win a contract for the firm, but she should consider giving the assignment to someone else. The other architects will not develop their skills sitting at their drawing boards while their superior meets with all the clients and designs all the buildings. Without the concept of "developing the skills of others" firmly in her mind, however, the vice president may take on too many tasks herself. As a consequence, the office will suffer.

Again, concepts have to be firmly embedded in the minds of the powerholders before serious action can take place. In my consulting work with organizations, diagnoses of problems are often based on this point. For example, my consulting work includes attention to the special issues facing managers who take assignments in countries other than their own. Once executives can be found who are knowledgeable about concepts such as "culture shock" and "the stresses of adjustment to major upheavals," then progress can be made. On the other hand, executives who believe that transferring managers from New York to Tokyo is little different than transferring them from New York to Pittsburgh are hard to work with, since they see little need for special attention to overseas assignments.

NEGATIVE POSSIBILITIES

While athletes benefit from large numbers of positive experiences, they may also be exposed to norms and behaviors that will not serve them well in their careers. Take the example of programs at large colleges and universities. Athletes may receive too much attention from the press, alumni, and student body. The adulation may "go to their heads," and if it does, they may lose any possibility of developing a common touch. Another danger is that they may become one-sided, able to talk about athletics but no other topic. They may internalize an image of themselves as "bought-and-paid-for jocks" and feel unable to participate fully in any other part of society. Put another way, athletes run the risk of not developing themselves in ways besides athletics and may find that they have too few resources for use in career development.

If the administrators of an athletic program constantly try to challenge the gray areas of conference regulations and ethical guidelines, the athletes may develop the idea that there are always ways to get around the spirit and letter of the law. For instance, money may be distributed under the table to star athletes. One way of doing this is to suggest that alumni hire the athletes for "jobs" that demand no actual time or work. Or if the national regulations require that athletes register for a full schedule of courses, easy offerings might be established by university administrators. The courses chosen may fill the demand for semester-to-semester credit hours, but the courses may not be those required for the four-year college degree. Professors may also be pressured to be lenient in their grading. All of these experiences may contribute to the thought, "There will always be exceptions to the rules for me."

The major programs at large universities (football, basketball, and sometimes baseball) attract large amounts of money. Even if the university's athletic department makes every effort to run a clean program, groups of alumni who want a winning team sometimes act independently of the university. They identify talented high-school athletes, aid in recruitment through dispersal of funds to the athletes and their parents, and provide them with amusements after they enroll. To modify only slightly a comment made by the comedian Robin Williams, cocaine is God's way of saying that there is too much money around. The distinction between a clean university department and devious alumni can lead athletes to believe that there is always an alternative way to get things done, and that ethical concerns should matter little to the chosen few.

Other problems may plague even the most ethically-concerned athletes. Stanley Milgram pointed out that when people have many demands on their time and attention, they often develop a rather aloof and cool attitude toward others.[7] Milgram's example was big-city dwellers. There are so many people with whom an individual might become involved (street panhandlers, soap-box lecturers, visitors obviously needing some kind of help) that people tend to develop a demeanor that distances themselves from others. The pattern of behavior becomes predictable: a straight-ahead orientation of the eyes, a blank expression, and a brisk forward movement that communicates an unwillingness to engage in casual conversations.

Good athletes run the risk of developing this demeanor if they become well known figures on their college campuses. All sorts of people may want to stop and chat, but the athlete has to get to class, has to walk to the library to study, and has to be prompt at scheduled team practice sessions. To cope with these demands, the "big-city" facial and body orientation may come into play. This may serve the athletes well as they try to satisfy their multiple time demands, but it will not be of use in the long run. If they are to participate effectively in the informal networks discussed several times in this book, they will have to communicate a willingness to be approached by others.

Even if athletes "turn on" the message that the company of others is welcome, a more subtle problem may arise. If athletes are public figures, *others* will want to approach them. Since others initiate the interaction, the athletes may not develop the skills needed to approach people they have not met before. And yet the ability to approach strangers is a key to developing good networks. Most people, even the athletes, will be relatively unknown to a community's powerholders five or ten years after their college athletic careers end. If they do not develop the ability to approach these powerholders (e.g., at a cocktail party, fundraiser, or art gallery opening), they will remove themselves from career development opportunities.

GENERALIZING FROM ONE SETTING TO ANOTHER

If these difficulties can be avoided, the benefits of participation in team sports can be considerable. Networks can be established; skills for working closely with others can be honed; humility can be encouraged; and complex thinking about probabilities, skill development for subordinates, and intergroup interaction can be introduced. The question immediately arises, Why isn't there a direct application of these team sports benefits to people's later careers? Why don't athletes, as a matter of course, move from the playing field to the highest levels of the boardroom?

The answer is that transfer of learning from one setting to another has always been a difficult task. Most frequently it is a "hit or miss" affair; some people make effective transfers and some do not, and there are not extensive guidelines that might increase the number of successes. Readers will surely be familiar with people, for instance, who were extremely successful in their schoolwork but were unable to transfer the skills that led to academic recognition to jobs in an organization. They were unable to apply such skills as reading, writing, and using time efficiently to their careers.

Psychologists and educators have long bemoaned the fact that they do not have many recommendations concerning the transfer or generalization of learning across settings. As Cathie Jordan and Roland Tharp commented, "Can general, transferable skills be identified at all? It is at this question that current knowledge pauses for breath."[8] Kurt Fisher and Michael Farrar also considered the question, and wrote, "Generalization clearly does not occur easily—in all possible applications of a skill. Nor does it occur rarely—in only the most direct possible skill applications. A major task for cognitive scientists is to predict the vagaries of generalization."[9] Despite the difficulties, Jordan, Tharp, Fisher, and Farrar have identified a number of guidelines that I believe are helpful. I have combined their contributions with those of other researchers. Taken together, these contributions can be adapted and can provide a set of guidelines for efforts aimed at encouraging the transfer from specific experiences to general career development. Following the example of athletics, as discussed throughout this chapter, I will analyze the way people transfer the skills they learned in team sports to their later careers.

While the ideas to be presented might be used by individuals working alone, a better approach is to schedule workshops in which people can work cooperatively toward the goal of skill generalization. The advantage of workshops is that the ideas suggested by one person trigger related ideas for others. Workshop participants are often heard to say, "Does that happen to you, too? I thought I was the only one and was worried. That makes me feel much better." Workshops allow people to encourage each other during the frustrating times when ideas do not flow smoothly. For example, a workshop might bring together people moving from an academic environment to the job market. More specifically, college seniors who have completed their athletic eligibility, but are finishing up their degree studies, might be brought together by concerned faculty members. Workshops would be arranged around the athletes' formal course schedules, and high-status faculty members should be involved to contribute to an atmosphere of serious effort. In such a workshop, faculty members familiar with concepts such as those discussed throughout the book would act as facilitators. I have offered workshops like these, and the following procedural guidelines may be helpful to others.

Knowledge Development

David Kolb[10] has analyzed how people best learn complex skills, and the concepts he has developed are useful in workshops. A good starting point is to review people's concrete experiences and reflect upon them. The first question is, "What skills have I learned that are not directly related to the sport in which I specialized?" This would have to go beyond such activities as running a fly pattern (football), mastering the split-fingered fastball (baseball), or developing a three-point shot (basketball). Instead, the skills would be those that can be used off the playing field. The subheadings in the first part of this chapter may be helpful as a checklist: accepting people as they are, working with disliked others, combining skills, and so forth. Since a workshop involves a number of people, the items on the checklist may remind participants of skills not covered here because of space limitations. These include bouncing back from disappointment and failure, making on-the-spot judgements given the changes that opponents have made, finding satisfaction in a secondary but still valuable role on a team, maintaining one's energy through vigorous exercise, and using athletic activities to get rid of the frustrations of a workday.

The workshop facilitators should not hurry the development of the checklist. While it may be tempting to move quickly beyond list making so that more intellectually exciting tasks can be started, each participant must have time to examine his or her own past experiences at a comfortable, unhurried pace. There will be a good deal of trial and error. One participant will make a suggestion, will find that it generates only a polite comment of "keep trying" from the facilitator, and will try again. Interestingly, while trial and error is often considered an inefficient way to learn, it can lead to effective transfer of knowledge from one setting to another. Put another way, while learning new material by trial and error may take a great deal of time, learning by this method may enhance its transfer to other settings.

Two reasons for this non-commonsense assertion come to mind. One is that during the trial-and-error process, participants will eventually consider idiosyncratic examples that are important only to *themselves*. For instance, a shy athlete may remember that after attracting some newspaper publicity, he or she was able to interact comfortably with members of the opposite sex for the first time. This may not be a good example for anyone else in the workshop, but the lack of relevance for the entire group is of little importance. Something of importance has been generated for this athlete's own life, and consequently the rest of the workshop activities are likely to be seen by the athlete as relevant and potentially helpful.

One interesting experience that the facilitators are likely to have is the degree to which their suggestions are twisted and turned in the minds of the participants. The random actions of the human mind often yield good insights of use to the individual. In one workshop an athlete who was a psychology major commented that his grades had gone up considerably from his freshman to his senior year. I was hoping for a stunning reason, such as an insight into human behavior brought on through interaction with teammates from diverse cultural and social class backgrounds, but his analysis was basic. "I used to have a lousy attention span. Probably too many cartoon shows on TV. But I had to listen to the coach's 'chalk talk' presentations on offensive and defensive formations. If I didn't know that stuff, I sat on the bench. So I learned to pay attention."[11]

Another reason for the *long term* benefits of trial and error is that people are doing the work themselves. While it might be more efficient for workshop participants to respond to the facilitator's insightful probes, this teacher–learner interaction style will cease when the workshop concludes. After the workshop there will be no facilitators to structure the learning environment in the most pedagogically sound manner. Participants who learn to do the work themselves and who learn to generate their own relevant examples, then, are preparing themselves for the manner in which they will have to continue their learning after the workshop.

A few other guidelines may be helpful in the knowledge development stage. Learning seems to be maximized when the educational setting is as similar as possible to a setting with which the participants are already familiar. The facilitators should consider holding the workshops in places where the participants may have been exposed to some of the ideas being discussed. For instance, if team meetings were regularly held in a certain room within the school's athletic complex, that may be a good place to hold the workshop. During this phase of the workshop there should be as little clash as possible between the participants' past experiences and the examination of the experiences. If the difference between the two is too large, the participants find the task of listing their skills overly difficult or artificial and consequently lose interest in the workshop.

Understanding

Once the list of skills has been generated, the participants should examine the skills for their possible application to aspects of life beyond athletics. Since this is not an easy step, the facilitators should be prepared to give the participants a great deal of feedback and encourage them to continue their efforts despite frustrations. The goal implied by the word "understanding" is that participants should develop concepts that become part of their long-term thinking. In moving from knowledge to understanding, the participants begin to see the commonalities underlying the specific athletic experiences with which they are familiar. Given a large number of specific experiences and the identification of underlying commonalities, the participants can then give a label that captures the essence of the commonalities. For instance, football players had "chats" in the huddle to give guidance to the quarterback's play selection. Examination of these chats in the workshop leads to the concept "effective interpersonal communication." This skill is essential for career development in many different occupations. Another example will be familiar to baseball players. Infielders have to work hard to develop various combinations of relays (short to second to first) to perfect double-play opportunities. This knowledge becomes "effective teamwork" in the understanding phase.

The workshop participants should be encouraged to verbalize their thoughts as much as possible. Often, the point that people are trying to make becomes clearest *while* they are struggling with the verbal expression of their incompletely formulated thoughts. The natural tendency of friends and colleagues to suggest words while any one speaker is struggling also can be helpful. The speaker can accept the suggested word or reject it, or can use the associations that come to mind upon consideration of the word. While the participants may develop their own conceptual labels, suggestions can also be made by the facilitators. That is, the participants should examine and write down their own experiences, but the facilitators may suggest conceptual labels to capture the possible generalizability of the experiences. A caveat is that the labels should not be from jargon known only to disciplinary specialists in academia.

An understanding of general concepts is aided when examples are brought in from the different arenas of life to which the participants have had exposure. These arenas, however, must be introduced carefully. The facilitators should make sure that the move to different arenas of life is done one step at a time. For instance, most participants will be familiar with interviews by newspaper and television reporters. A set of step-by-step experiences for consideration might be:

1. Athletes being interviewed about an upcoming game;

2. Athletes giving an interview about the team's prospects for the season;

3. Athletes being interviewed about a matter related to their sport (e.g., keeping up grades to preserve eligibility);

4. Athletes talking with the media about a topic unrelated to their sport (e.g., their hopes for areas of academic development within the university);

5. An athlete who is an honor student, more in the latter role, talking with the media about hopes for the future of the university;

6. A politician talking about the future of the university in the presence of reporters;

7. A politician promoting himself or herself as the spokesperson for a certain cause;

8. A politician running for reelection.

Commonalities to be identified under the general label of "media skills" include confidence, ease of delivery, clear pronunciation, graciousness, cooperativeness, succinctness, and facility in providing quotable remarks and sound bites.

In one of the workshops I organized, an athlete said that he had clearly traded his skills for a college degree. He was from a working-class family that did not have money for college tuition, and he was able to attend college only because of an athletic scholarship. Another said that she had "red-shirted" her freshman year (sat out the year to have four more years of eligibility). During her red-shirt year she had built up her strength through frequent visits to the weight room. Another athlete said that he had sat on the bench his first year but played regularly his junior and senior years. During his time on the bench he had worked hard to learn the details of a very complex offensive system. I then suggested that these were examples of the concept "resource exchange" as discussed in Chapter 2. The working-class athlete exchanged the use of his physical prowess for a college education. The red-shirted player traded the year she spent building her strength for later status as a starter. The participant who spent a year warming the bench, but who learned the system, then exchanged his knowledge for a good deal of playing time in later years. I believe that the general concept was understood. As part of career development in many occupations, people exchange resources with others for the benefit of all involved. Those who do not have the resources necessary for their chosen profession must develop them.

Behavior

Once workshop participants have conceptual labels for their knowledge, they can attempt to put their concepts into action. Again, the facilitators should encourage such progress in slow steps.

Guest Speakers

As a good starting point, former athletes who have been successful in their careers might be asked to be guest speakers. This is not a terribly innovative idea: successful people have long been asked to give "helpful hints" about life after school. The key here is the timing. Since the workshop participants will have had access to concepts rather than to isolated and unexamined experiences, they will be able to query the guest speaker with much more sophistication. They will be able to ask questions about resource exchange, about integrating one's talents with those of others, about network development, and about other concepts discussed in this book. Without a grasp of such concepts, the former athlete's suggestions would almost literally go in one ear and out the other. One way to view concepts is as containers in people's memories that can collect information. The piece of career advice, "It's your job to get along with your bosses, not their job to get along with you," might easily be dismissed as a forgettable piece of drivel. But participants who have worked through such experiences as player-coach relations and placing themselves into the priorities set by assistant coaches are more likely to have a concept that can "catch and retain" the former athlete's good advice.

Role Playing

As a second step, the facilitators can suggest role-play exercises in which the participants apply their new knowledge. Role playing is used in many different training programs: for wage laborers about to take jobs as foremen; for politicians about to debate their opponents; for teachers about to enter newly desegregated schools; for witnesses about to make their first courtroom appearances, and so forth.[12] People take on roles that they will either play or be exposed to in real life. A good example is the job interview after graduation. One participant plays the person wanting a job; another plays the head of the personnel department; another plays the head of the department in which the interviewee would eventually work. The participant playing the interviewee might take on the specific task of communicating his or her skills, which have been developed or encouraged through team sports. Such a task encourages the participants to work with their newly developed concepts in a different but important manner. The participants will make mistakes, but other participants are likely to make suggestions for improvement. One assumption of role playing is that the participants benefit from making their mistakes in a supportive workshop environment. It is far better to err in a workshop, where improvements can be made with the encouragement of others, than to stumble in real-world settings.

If the facilitators are concerned that their first role-plays will not go smoothly, they may consider bringing in models who will demonstrate what happens when the technique is used. The models may be recent graduates, other students known to the facilitators, or young faculty members with whom the participants can identify. Interestingly, the models should *not* perform in a superb manner. If the models are too smooth, skillful, and confident, they can discourage the participants. "I'll never be that good. This workshop has gone beyond what I'll ever be." Instead, the models should be merely competent, no more and no less. They should make their fair share of slip-ups, grammatical mistakes, and false starts when answering the interviewers' questions. If the models are competent rather than superb, the participants are more likely to say, "This is possible for me."[13]

Homework

For a third step, the facilitators can suggest homework assignments. Such assignments would entail engaging in various behaviors so that the participants can try out the practical applications of their conceptual understanding. For instance, some participants may have maintained contacts with the local journalists who used to interview them about upcoming games. A good assignment would be to meet with the journalists for a possible story. Further, the content of the story would be guided more by the participants' interests than by the journalists' immediate needs. The participants would have to practice the important skill of linking *their* story to the issues that the journalists find important and interesting. If the topic is a current community cause or concern, the journalist might say, "I'm just doing the sports beat. But my colleagues on the city desk might be interested. I'll introduce you." The workshop participant would then have to meet and interact with a new person under new ground rules, the door having been opened by a contact made through athletics.

Another homework assignment that comes out of networking is to have the participants interview experts in various career paths. Each participant schedules interviews with recognized community leaders in such areas as business, education, recreation, or medicine, depending upon the participant's future career plans. The facilitator might arrange the first interview with a member of the booster club or with a known sports fan. This assistance is another example of the advice already discussed: to avoid frustration, the participants should proceed one step at a time. The participants might themselves schedule a second interview with another known sports fan, and then schedule a third with someone not particularly interested in athletics. In these interviews the participants will have the opportunity to practice various skills, such as clear and concise communication, cordial acceptance of feedback concerning their plans, discovery of current developments not yet widely known, and following through on suggestions offered by the community leader.

Many of the participants will still have some years of schooling ahead of them, as part of either their first or an advanced degree. I have known quite a few athletes who needed a year to graduate after their athletic eligibility had ended. In such cases the interviews can include this question: "I have a year of school left. What areas of expertise do you recommend that I develop so that I will be more attractive to the job market?" My experience has been that community leaders are happy to answer this question and frequently make suggestions that can be pursued in students' choice of coursework.

In the workshops I have offered, two other homework suggestions are accepted by some and rejected by others. In the first, participants who feel that they have developed a thick skin take advantage of this fact. They see a professor after class, or during office hours, and say something like, "I realize that you read a lot of student papers and cannot give extensive feedback on all of them. But I would appreciate it if you would look at mine especially carefully. I'd like feedback on my ideas, my exposition of them, the organization of my material, my ability to bring in related facts from various sources, and so forth." The professors I know are pleased to respond to this request. As discussed earlier, some people fail to advance in their careers because they do not receive adequate feedback on their work. Since they receive no guidance on how to improve, they continue to work in the same way. If their work has been mediocre, they will remain ignorant of ways of improving their contributions to their organizations. This exercise can give participants practice in the important skill of seeking out feedback. While in an ideal world people's superiors regularly schedule sessions during which improved job performance is discussed, in actuality this happens infrequently. More often, people have to purposely seek out ways to improve their job performance.

Another exercise builds on a point introduced in Chapters 3 and 4. Powerful people should make enemies as infrequently as possible. People may disagree, but negative feelings should not overwhelm their ability to interact in a cordial manner. They should be able to leave a meeting disagreeing on one issue but accepting the strong possibility of later working together on another issue. The participants in the workshop might be asked to make a list of people with whom they have a poor relationship. After completing the list, they should make check marks near the names of people with whom they would like to establish or reestablish cordial relations. They then examine ways to change their wishes to actual behaviors, and they are asked to put their plans into action as a homework assignment. These plans might include scheduling a meeting with the listed person, followed by an identification of the problem. "We had a disagreement about a year ago and we haven't had much contact since. I don't think the disagreement was worth long-term ill feelings. What do you think?"

A More Sophisticated Background

Now that the participants have applied generalizations from athletics to other arenas of life, they will have new and different concrete experiences to discuss with others. The cycle already introduced can be repeated. Reflective observations about their new experiences will also yield knowledge. As concepts are developed that summarize the knowledge, the participants gain a more sophisticated understanding of their place in the world after athletics. Applying this understanding in another round of homework assignments allows the participants to test out and refine their understanding.

After several completions of the cycle, especially with the sophistication gained through the homework assignments, the participants will report back with comments like the following: "It's more complex out there than I thought. You think it's going to be easy and it's not. Lots of people are competing for the best jobs. I definitely have to work more on some things." After a workshop that I administered, one participant wrote about her need to put her understanding into action. "Knowledge of the strategies and tactics of power certainly makes it easier to act effectively within an organization, and I certainly shall have opportunities to apply that! But the application! Ah! Guess I do have trouble *using* my networking opportunities. I'm so reticent to do so. So, I'm trying to change that."

A MORE STRUCTURED EXERCISE

The administration of a multisession workshop as discussed here demands the luxury of time. The participants have to be willing, and have to identify the time in their busy schedules, to commit themselves to several workshop sessions and to the homework assignments. When practical concerns make this time investment impossible, another exercise may prove helpful. I have developed and used the following simulation in a single session lasting two and one-half or three hours. The participants were college students and young professionals, some of whom had a background in athletics and some of whom did not.

During the first 45 minutes the participants are introduced to key concepts either through a lecture or group discussion. These concepts are definitions of power, resources, resource exchange, networking, coalitions of interested people who find each others' resources useful, quick and efficient communication, and the importance of graciousness and approachability. Participants are then asked to think of a project they would like to develop that would be related to their career plans. Examples are given to stimulate their thinking:

Starting a travel agency to send people to exotic places

Manufacturing water sports equipment

Starting a grocery chain specializing in Asian foods

Establishing a local advertising agency

Establishing middle-income housing

Developing a program to prepare teachers to take jobs in inner-city schools

Preparing former athletes for careers in communication and/or public relations

Starting a lobbying effort for government support of Olympic athletes

Starting a business to help others raise funds for various causes

Producing a series of television shows on the contributions of less well known ethnic groups in America (e.g., Armenians)

Providing good speakers to conventions that meet in nearby cities

Integrating foreign students into American universities to better prepare American students for their participation in an international society

Recreation programs for senior citizens in nursing homes

After deciding on a project (one of these or another of their own), the participants then pick one card from a batch that the facilitator has prepared. Each card gives a brief description of a resource they have that they are to use. They will later interact with other participants and will exchange resources, as appropriate, so that their project can be developed. The resources written on individual cards are:

You are a good administrator of complex projects. You can see how the many pieces of complex projects fit together.

You have extraordinary social skills. You are charming and gracious. People have a very difficult time becoming upset with you.

You have written a bestseller (topic of your choice) and consequently are viewed as both a public figure and as an expert.

You can talk and negotiate with opposing factions and be trusted by both.

You have a large network. You have a large number of contacts in your community.

You are an extremely effective public speaker and can address crowds of any size.

You are a great salesperson. You can sell objects and ideas to people, almost without regard for what they are.

You write very well, and write well in a wide variety of styles (e.g., persuasive, diplomatic, scientific, popular appeal).

You have $1,000,000 to invest or to give to worthwhile causes.

You have tax expertise and can set up organizations which can take advantage of all tax laws.

You have very good contacts among newspaper and television reporters.

You have a very good sense of politics—you know who has power and who will be in favor of various projects and who will be against them.

You have very good previous job experiences in the production of consumer goods.

Some resources can be placed on more than one card. For example, I usually have several cards that give people a million dollars, and also several that make people good salespeople or tax experts.

Of course, the facilitators can add other projects and resources to suit the needs of the participants with whom they are interacting in a particular workshop. Last-minute additions to the resource list can also be made. In one workshop where a large number of participants had projects requiring sophisticated use of the mass media, I added the resource "You look very good on television." In another workshop where people had projects demanding the start of new businesses, I added the resources "You have had good previous job experience in marketing" and "You have had good previous job experience in the production of consumer goods."

The participants are also given a list of these resources, so that they can be on the lookout for them as they interact with people. They are told that they can also use any resource that they *actually* have in real life. If one person was a stellar athlete who received a good deal of media attention, then that is a real resource. One participant in a workshop I organized had two brothers who had had professional careers in athletics (football and hockey). She could consider integrating them into her project plans. If a participant has a father who works in an import-export business, that is another potential resource. The participants should be given at least ten minutes to think of and write down their actual resources. In many cases people are not aware of what they have to offer others until they are asked to examine their abilities and experiences in an exercise such as this one.

The participants are then told:

You want to develop your project and see it through to completion. You have the following:

1. One thousand dollars from your own savings;
2. Your resource described on the card (for a few, the card will say $1,000,000, and so these people will have $1,001,000 with which to work);
3. Your actual resources;
4. A list of the resources others have on their cards so that you can look for people whose resources you need;
5. Your name on a nametag—please wear it as it will facilitate interactions.

Imagine that you are at a gathering where large numbers of influential people meet. Perhaps it is a fund-raiser for the local symphony orchestra or a well attended meeting of a major political party. Interact in a cordial manner with people— become part of their network. As part of your communication with them, let them know your resource(s) if you think that you can do business with them. If they feel that they can do business with you, they will let you know their resources. Think creatively about the resources to which you have access and combine them in ways that help your project. Remember that you must give others some of your resources if you accept *their* contributions. If you simply take the resources of others, you will probably develop a reputation as a "taker" who never returns favors. If you only give away resources, you may overextend yourself and never develop your own project. If you have any questions about the "rules" of this simulation, you can make up your own rules, as long as they are legal and are consistent with ethical business practices.

The participants then spend an hour interacting with others, acquiring and investing each other's resources for the development of their own and other people's projects. The facilitators should make themselves available to answer such questions as the following. While others are networking, an individual may come to the facilitator and ask:

Q: Can two or more people develop a joint project?

A: Sure. That's quite consistent with standard business practices.

Q: Can I change my project as I discover what resources are available to me?

A: Yes. That may be a good idea.

Q: I don't like the resource I was given on my card. Can I change it?

A: I'd rather you didn't. A fact of life is that at times you have to "play the hand you are dealt." One of the purposes of the simulation is to encourage people to think through how they can use various resources.

Q: What if all the people with a million dollars go off by themselves? What do the rest of us do for financing?

A: The possibility that millionaires will want to work together can certainly happen in real life, and so it may happen in this simulation. Use other resources as links to financing.

With this advice, the participants may enlist the salespeople and holders of extensive networks in their quests for financing.

After an hour, the participants gather together to share their experiences. The facilitators can start by reviewing the concepts introduced during the first 45 minutes—power, exchange, resources, and so on—and asking people if they have new insights into them. I have started with a question about the millionaires. "People often worry that the millionaires will get together and share resources only with each other. Did this happen?" The answer is often no. Instead, the millionaires enjoyed being sought out by others and enjoyed being centers of attention. This leads to a good question for discussion: "What implications does this have for the concept that power brings pleasure to people?" Participants have made these comments:

(1) I had a tough time asking others for help. Even when they asked if they could do something for me, I couldn't say anything. This is something I am going to have to work on.

(2) I didn't feel comfortable mixing with others. I guess I'm shy. I'm going to have to change this or make sure I choose a career consistent with my shyness.

One participant reinforced my decision to write this book:

(3) I got the card about political sophistication. I don't have a clue about what it means. All I could do in using this resource was to say that I knew a lot of elected politicians. I can see that I should know a lot more.

Another participant wondered about the most effective ways of communicating one's resource:

(4) I got the card about social skills. It was hard for me to disclose my resource without sounding tacky.

The participants make suggestions to help each other's thinking. One pointed out that many disclosures of resources can be linked to hobbies. If somebody wants to make sure that others know about his or her recent receipt of a Ph.D. degree, he or she may say: "I'm interested in dogs, too. Right after I got my Ph.D. my family decided to get a Pekingese." The person with social skills can have the hobby of taking psychology courses or reading magazines with articles written by psychologists. "I took one of those psychology tests—you know, the ones that ask you questions and then you score them. Would you believe the results? It said that I . . . " Resources in salesmanship, tax expertise, negotiation, administration, and others can be linked to the inevitable questions people ask at social gatherings: "What do you do?" or "Where do you work?"

The formal workshop ends after these discussions of people's experiences during, and feelings about, their simulated project development. I have also invited participants to write down any thoughts that they have and give these to me at a later date. When they bring them to me at my office, this often allows one-on-one discussion about individual concerns. A participant who recognized that he does not have a good network asked me about developing one. Since he was a good baseball player, I suggested that he volunteer to be a coach, umpire, or scorekeeper in the local Little League. Many quite influential community leaders are involved in Little League, since their sons and daughters play. A similar recommendation can be made for people with skills in basketball, football, or track and field.

Some people feel that they have a thin skin and agree that this may lead to an ineffective use of feedback offered by supervisors and potential mentors. My advice to them is that they enter situations where others will *surely* disagree with them. If they become umpires or referees for community athletic leagues, they will have to make calls on close plays. Almost by definition, half of the players and spectators will feel that a call of a close play is stupid. Practice in continuing one's best efforts in spite of the colorful epithets that emanate from spectators can encourage the development of "grace under pressure." More complex skills can be practiced: firmly but politely telling the spectators to act in a gentlemanly or ladylike manner, or remaining above the fray and communicating a sense that one is a person of dignity in the presence of common scolds. If people are not athletic, another way to develop a thick skin and an air of imperturbility is to join various community organizations: parent-teacher associations, support groups for the Red Cross, or various clubs devoted to support of the arts. As soon as possible, they should join the finance or budget committee. No matter what recommendations for the use of funds one makes to these committees, I guarantee that there will be disagreements. The ability to deal with these disagreements and work with people on Issue B, despite major differences on Issue A, is an essential requirement for the effective use of power.

I have also guided people into opportunities to develop other skills. Poor public speakers might take formal courses in this area (many colleges offer night courses) or join an organization like Toastmasters. Writing skills can also be addressed in formal courses. Many colleges have writing clinics that students can attend as one of their extracurricular activities. People who are uncomfortable meeting others can write for the student or community newspaper and have access to the role of "reporter" when they approach influential leaders. Some individuals feel a need to develop humility. One way is to join activities in which one is less talented than the others. This can be an informal musical group, a heretofore unfamiliar sport, or an activity involving technical knowledge such as the offerings of the local computer-users club. People who feel naive about politics but recognize its importance might volunteer to work on the campaigns of various professional politicians. Work on political campaigns also allows people to meet others from different backgrounds and occupations.

CONCLUSION

The purpose of this chapter has been to suggest various ways people can gain a first-hand understanding of how power is acquired and used. People can best develop an understanding of generalizable concepts related to power if they start with what is already familiar to them. Various ways of putting this advice into practice were suggested. One is to examine past experiences, summarizing them in conceptual terms, and then attempting applications of the concepts in new settings. Another method is to simulate concepts such as "resources" and "exchange" by encouraging people to interact with others and to develop various projects. Both of these exercises will make clear to many people that there are aspects of power that demand their more careful analysis. These aspects can include concepts that they poorly understand or abilities that they do not possess. Activities, many involving participation in community functions, can be suggested that will address these lacunae. The common thread running through all these analyses is that people learn best if they link their *own* personal experiences, recognitions of shortcomings, and desirable future activities to generalizable concepts.

Concepts summarize knowledge and significant personal experiences. Give the link to personal examples, experience-based concepts bring abstract discussions of power "down to earth" and make them applicable in everyday life. There are a number of concepts, I believe, that are appreciated by sophisticated powerholders but not understood by everyone. In the final chapter, I will discuss the concepts that distinguish the sophisticated from the naive.

NOTES

1. Discussions with Joann Brislin and others led to clarification of points about the importance of team sports. These others include Tamara Buetow, Karen Johnson, Hermine Mahseredjian, Judy Van Patten, and Jack Condon. Others who will see our conversations reflected in various parts of this chapter include John Gibney, Clare Murphy, Dorothy Sermol, D. P. S. Bhawuk, and Paula Brannon.

2. P. Theis and W. Steponkus, *All about Politics* (New York: R. R. Bowker, 1972).

3. M. Korda, *Power: How to Get It, How to Use It* (New York: Random House, 1975).

4. J. Kotter, "Power, Dependence, and Effective Management," *Harvard Business Review* 55 (1977), no. 4, pp. 125–36; J. Kotter, "What Effective General Managers Really Do," *Harvard Business Review* 60 (1982), no. 6, pp. 157–67.

5. G. Allport, *The Nature of Prejudice* (Reading, Mass.: Addison-Wesley, 1954); R. Brislin, *Cross-Cultural Encounters: Face-to-Face Interaction* (Elmsford, N.Y.: Pergamon, 1981).

6. D. Riesman, preface to S. Bullitt, *To Be a Politician* Garden City, NY: Doubleday, 1959.

7. S. Milgram, "The Experience of Living in Cities," *Science* 167 (1970): 1461–68.

8. C. Jordan and R. Tharp, "Culture and Education," in *Perspectives on Cross-Cultural Psychology*, edited by A. Marsella, R. Tharp, and T. Ciborowski (New York: Academic Press, 1979), p. 269.

9. K. Fischer and M. Farrar, "Generalizations about Generalization: How a Theory of Skill Development Explains both Generality and Specificity," *International Journal of Psychology* 22 (1987): 666.

10. D. Kolb, *Learning Style Inventory* (Boston: McBer, 1976); D. Kolb, *Experiential Learning* (Englewood Cliffs, N.J.: Prentice-Hall, 1984).

11. The athlete was also beginning to have insights into the next step of the process, understanding, since he could see use of the same skill in lectures in two settings: from the coach and from professors. There are considerable similarities between a coach and a professor, both talking in front of a blackboard with a piece of chalk in hand. Advances in understanding occur when the settings are different. One participant in a workshop I organized was the daughter of a campaign manager for presidential candidates, a man whose name would be instantly recognizable to readers of the political pages in large newspapers. The daughter and I had conversations about why she had been advanced in her job more quickly than her peers, even though her superiors had no knowledge of her father's influence. We centered on the skill of paying attention. During her adolescence, she had helped her father by acting as a hostess at various social gatherings, where she had to pay

attention and to show interest in what visitors like George McGovern and Edward Kennedy had to say. She later used this skill by paying attention to what her superiors had to say, showing interest in their ideas, and never showing boredom, even though she may have secretly felt this emotion. Who will be more popular with executives: people who pay attention and show interest, or people whose minds obviously wander while the executive is speaking?

12. A good introduction to role playing can be found in A. Elms, *Social Psychology and Social Relevance* (Boston: Little, Brown, 1972).

13. D. Meichenbaum, *Cognitive-Behavior Modification: An Integrative Approach* (New York: Plenum, 1977).

8

SUMMARY: WHAT THE
SOPHISTICATED KNOW

When asking powerful people to explain what they do, I also questioned them about their observations of colleagues and subordinates. I asked them to distinguish between people who "get things done" and people who do not. I tried to narrow the focus of the interviewees' thinking by stipulating that doers and nondoers should be about equal in the key advantages: well educated, hard working, physically attractive, and able to generate good ideas. But one set of people is successful in implementing ideas and plans while the other is not. What were the factors on which the 102 powerholders focused? I believed that the best term to summarize their thinking is "political sophistication."

Sophisticated people have learned to accept power as part of their professional lives. This does not mean that power is the *only* factor that successful people consider, but it does mean that they acknowledge the role power plays in decision making and in the allocation of resources. Further, they learn to think of power in terms of its usefulness and to think of powerholders in terms of their potential "clout" in implementing plans and proposals. They do not lose sight of their plans and do not become bogged down in the more negative connotations that the term "power" suggests, such as "back-room deals" and "manipulation." While recognizing these negative connotations, they have learned to deal with them so that the more positive connotation of "getting things done" remains foremost in their minds.

To get things done and achieve their goals, powerholders use resources, skills, strategies, and tactics as discussed in Chapters 1 through 7. To put this considerable amount of specific material into a helpful perspective, I would like to organize some thoughts about power around several broad themes that were touched upon in the interviews. These themes are:

1. Dealing with the powerful and recognizing the effects of power;
2. Using one's network;
3. Sharing resources, or being useful to people;
4. Developing sophistication in the use of strategies and tactics;
5. Seeing power as only one of many important aspects of life.

I believe that an intuitive (if not explicit) understanding of these themes, and the ability to use them when thinking about the implementation of ideas and plans, separates sophisticated from unsophisticated users of power.

DEALING WITH THE POWERFUL

Multiple Motives

Naive people frequently make the mistake of attributing single motives to behaviors that they observe. An altruistic act is seen as the result of a person's generosity. An aggressive act is seen as the result of a person's violent nature. In actuality, people often decide how they will behave after taking into account several motives. Put another way, people are collections of potentials that can be called upon in various social situations. These potentials include aggressiveness, altruism, use of power, achievement, kindness, the need to affiliate, and so forth. People's decisions about how they will behave concerning important matters are frequently based on several of these potentials. Sophisticated people recognize this and include "power" in their analyses of potentials and motives. Politicians may communicate a "concern for the needs of the poor" when they support affordable housing projects, but they also realize that this support will generate a favorable publicity and an enthusiastic following when reelection is sought. Businesspeople may communicate the quality of "unselfish with their time" when they give free lectures at luncheons sponsored by charitable organizations. They may indeed be altruistic, but their businesses will also benefit from the positive word-of-mouth publicity generated by the free talks. The Peace Corps volunteers in the 1960s had idealistic motives; they wanted to help people in the Third World. But many of the volunteers also benefited from the fact that Peace Corps assignments took them out of the pool for the military draft.

There is no intention here of impugning the positive motives of the people in the three examples. Good deeds were done, but they were generated from more than one motive. A long-term legislative aide in Washington, D.C., told me: "There *is* a substantive review to proposed legislation. Is it a good bill and will it be beneficial for the country? But there is also a political review. How will the congressman be helped and hurt through support of the bill? Lots of people can do the substantive review. Fewer can do the political review, and so the people able to do political analysis achieve more status 'on the Hill.' "

People have many motives, but some are more central to their lives than others, and the strength of the various motives is not the same from person to person. For some, power is a low priority, and they would rather emphasize other aspects of their lives: achievement, affiliation with close friends, nurturing of their young children, and so forth. For others, power is central to their everyday behavior. People who interact with the powerful have to keep this point in mind. "Power is central to their existence. How can I use this knowledge to advance my own plans?" For instance, people with proposals should be prepared for powerholders to ask such questions as the following:

"Who else is for it?" (Translation: "What other powerful people, who might later benefit me, want to see the plans implemented.")

"Where will the funding come from?" (Translation: "Are you asking me to use *my* resources to provide funding?"

"What are the goals of the program?" (Translation: Who will be helped and hurt, and do they have resources such as money and good networks that can be used for or against me?")

"Have you thought about the long-term consequences?" (Translation: "If I help you now, what will you do to assist me in the future?")

"Why do you come to me?" (Translation: "Do your plans advance my own pet concerns?")

People who decide to emphasize power in their lives become accustomed to the pleasure that it brings. Part of the pleasure is receiving deference from others, and powerholders become upset when this expected deference is not forthcoming.

An analogy can be made between powerholders and mildly intoxicated people. When people have a few drinks too many at a party, they sometimes become mildly obnoxious. They are not open to suggestions from others. Concerning matters under discussion, one acceptable opinion exists: their own. To deal with these people, others must "play to" their knowledge of how people act when intoxicated. A conversation might proceed as follows:

Helpful Person: "John, wouldn't it be best if you drive home with Peter?"

Few-too-many Person: "What do you mean! I can drive home by myself. I am perfectly capable of taking care of myself."

Helpful Person: "There's been some construction at the end of the street. Peter knows the best alternative route."

The helpful person is playing to the other's intoxicated state when he refers to the road conditions.

Similarly, people who deal with powerholders must appeal to the deference that is expected. In Nepal there is a maxim, "If you want to live in water, you don't want to quarrel with crocodiles." If a mid-level executive wants to confront a senior vice president on a policy matter, his or her friends may say, "Remember, if you want . . . " When friends use the maxim, they are reminding the mid-level executive that there are risks to be considered when an individual decides to disagree with senior powerholders. Although not as frequently heard in the United States, the advice that "It is your job to get along with your bosses, not your bosses' job to get along with you" contains similar guidance about on-the-job behaviors.

Another helpful image is one person courting another in the hope that marriage will result. Courtship involves special behaviors: dinners at fine restaurants, gifts, and attention to the needs and desires of the other person. Powerholders enjoy a similar kind of attention. Few powerholders go door-to-door asking, "How can I help?" Far more wait in their offices for people to come in, pay court, and ask favors. As long as the cost/benefit ratio is advantageous, powerholders enjoy granting favors. They gain pleasure from acting like Marlon Brando in *The Godfather*, waving his right hand in a gesture that states that a favor will be granted.

People who want favors, then, cannot sit back and hope that benefits will come their way. They have to seek out and court powerholders. They must defer to the status of powerholders, treat them as special individuals, and allow them the pleasure of granting requests. Of course, those who receive these favors must realize that they may someday be asked to return the favors.

A senior senator in Washington, D.C., received a request from a constituent whose husband was on active military duty in another country. Due to a family emergency involving a young child, the woman requested that the husband be assigned to a duty station that would allow him to be close to his family. The senator was on the military appropriations committee. He called up a senior officer at the Pentagon, and the husband was reassigned. The senator pointed out that there is a pleasurable "rush" when he is able to use his power in such cases. The fact that pleasure results from the ability to make impactful decisions, I believe, is a key to understanding the behavior of powerful people. Another important point, however, is that the pleasure derived from making large numbers of eventful decisions can eventually cloud one's judgment.

Inhibitors

Some powerholders recognize the potentially intoxicating effects of power and purposely add inhibitors to their lives. I believe that people who successfully wield power *over a long term* are aware of the importance of inhibitors. They put limits on their use of power so that they do not damage themselves through intoxication and addiction. The long-term danger of addiction is that the powerholders irritate too many colleagues and subordinates. Over time, the colleagues and subordinates become opponents rather than supporters. People cannot hold power for long periods of time unless they have the good will of others.

During World War II, Admiral Louis Mountbatten was supreme commander of the Allied forces in South Asia. Later, he was viceroy of India, with unique powers. He did not have to clear his decisions regarding the future of India with the British government. During his tenure as viceroy and later as governor general of India, however, people who were once his subordinates in the British navy remained on regular duty and were advanced to ranks superior to his. When he returned to the navy, he commanded the First Cruiser Squadron in Malta, where he found himself thirteenth in order of social precedence. Lord Moutbatten reflected upon the positive effects of this assignment:

There is a saying that power corrupts and absolute power corrupts absolutely. Well, very few people had argued with me when I was a Supreme Commander, and when I was Viceroy more and more people kept telling me that I was always right. I had begun to believe it myself. And I recognized that this was a symptom of megalomania. I was disturbed by it. I decided the only thing to do was this precise process of stepping down to a position where I could have my backside kicked again![1]

Other people have recognized the dangers that power brings to their physical and mental health. Upon leaving his position as one of President Reagan's closest advisers, Michael Deaver analyzed his feelings:

The longer you stay in politics, the greater the risk that you will begin to think that you are invincible. The hurdles, the potholes, the traps that snare others can't happen to you.[2]

You fight it every day in Washington, the battle to remain normal, to be decent. . . . It is not an exclusive American trait, but most of us do not exit well . . . It is harder, I think, on those who have led a public life. You miss feeling important, getting close to the power, to the center of the stage.[3]

Inhibitors can include those chosen by Mountbatten and Deaver: accepting a position where there are many superiors who were once one's subordinates, or purposely leaving the center of power. Interestingly, the frequent turnover of high-level, nonelected officials in Washington, D.C., has some positive effects. People admittedly find it frustrating to work out the details of a proposal with one administrator, only to find that they have to begin again when that administrator moves on. But the quick turnover means that people leave their positions before they become abusive with their power.

Other inhibitors include a supportive family; colleagues and subordinates who are willing to disagree on issues; a historical knowledge of successful and unsuccessful powerholders; a sense of humor; self-insight; hobbies that demand different skills from those that have been mastered in one's profession; and the ability to examine and refuse temptations to use one's power in inappropriate ways. Whatever the technique or approach, the result should be the ability to say to oneself, "No, I could use my power but will not. There are too few benefits and too many long-term disadvantages."

Sharing Power

Inhibition can also be added by involving other people and sharing power with them. Given that the egos, priorities, and agendas of others have to be integrated into any plans or programs, the temptation for any one person to abuse power is diminished. Interestingly, sophisticated people realize that sharing with others can increase their power.

This point became clear to me during the time I was doing some consulting work for a professional organization concerned with the delivery of services to the handicapped. One person had developed a good set of educational materials, but he kept them to himself. His goal was to be the sole target of attention whenever the materials were to be used. Whenever people wanted to use the materials, they had to hire him to come into their schools. Eventually he priced his services at a figure higher than the market could bear, exhausted himself trying to find contracts for his services, and lost influence in the professional organization. He quite literally "dropped from sight."

Another person had an equally good set of educational materials but shared them willingly and cheerfully with others. Large number of benefits accrued to her. There were large numbers of people engaging in word-of-mouth compliments: "She's so unselfish in sharing her materials." Consequently, her name became widely known. Given her name recognition, she was invited to various conferences to present her ideas, and this in turn increased her professional visibility even more. Since she shared her materials with others, a certain number of the beneficiaries felt that they should return favors. When they had contracts to offer, especially at the end of their fiscal years when money had to be spent quickly, people would remember her kindnesses and make generous offers to her. Given her positive public image, young professionals wanted to become attached to her. She was able to pick and choose among many potential apprentices who had good qualifications. Her protégés eventually accepted good positions and spread the word about her views on educational matters. Given this support, her ideas were taken seriously whenever she had proposals for action to be taken by the professional organization.

More generally, sharing power with others allows any one person to become more visible, to spread his or her influence more widely, to be on the receiving end of favors, and to become involved in a larger number of important issues. A key to sharing power is to know large numbers of people, *some* of whom can be approached for such activities as coalition formation and resource exchange. The term for the "large number of people" that one can call upon is "network," and the importance of this concept would be hard to overstate.

NETWORKS

The way to initiate and to gain support for new proposals, to maneuver around red tape, to become aware of important current information, and to advertise the benefits of completed projects will always involve one's network. The network provides the "who" that allows people to communicate "what" they have to offer. While I do not care for this unfortunate term, it has achieved a status in the English language that prevents its imminent displacement. "Circle of acquaintances" is preferable, but a seven-syllable phrase competes badly with a two-syllable word already in widespread use. When people need information, favors, variances from standard policy guidelines, invitations to important gatherings, and introductions to powerful others, their desires are much more likely to be satisfied if they are active participants in a large network.

The use of the term "network" often seems cold, calculating, and distasteful. To point out that the members of one's network are not necessarily one's friends, and that people in a network retain membership because of mutual usefulness, also seems to connote selfishness rather than a more positive view of humanity. Yet the distinction between friends and network members may be basic to an understanding of human behavior. Dean Barnlund[4] studied acquaintance patterns in both the United States and Japan. He asked people to list the people "you have felt closest to in the last twelve months." He gave further guidance to his respondents by asking them to consider the "people you like best, who know and understand you best, with whom you feel most comfortable, and with whom you feel closest." Respondents in both the United States and Japan had a difficult time if they were asked to write down more than about fifteen names. Apparently there is a limit to the number of people with whom any one individual can have close friendships.

Closeness involves the sharing of emotions, with the result that the emotionally stimulating events in one person's life became important to one's friends. In a close relationship, people do *not* constantly calculate the relative advantages and disadvantages that accrue to them. Instead, they assist one another because of their emotional commitment. Since people's *own* lives are complex, however, there may be a limit to the number of others whose emotions can be shared. If one person becomes involved in too many close relationships, where direct or empathetic participation is expected, his or her coping skills and mental health can be threatened. But people *know* and are *acquainted with* more than fifteen others. The best single term for this "beyond fifteen" set of people is one's "network."

A distinction between one's close friends and one's network, then, is the amount of attention given to the cost/benefit ratio in deciding whether or not to maintain a relationship. People find it easy to ponder whether or not *others* are contributing favorably to this cost/benefit analysis. They are less skilled at putting themselves in the shoes of others and determining whether *they* are good network members from the viewpoint of these others. Network membership involves mutual usefulness. One person exchanges a resource such as extensive contacts, writing skills, or public speaking ability. The other person receives this benefit and reciprocates immediately or at a later time with a resource such as money, technical information, or administrative skills.[5] Effective coalitions can be formed in the pursuit of common goals when network members have complementary skills. This became clear to me when I was editor of the college literary magazine during my undergraduate years. At one point the printing of an issue had been done, but the machine to collate and bind the pages was broken. Since the magazine had attracted contributions from overseas students, I asked the college's International Friendship Club to come in on a Saturday to collate and staple. In return, the faculty adviser to the magazine would see to it that a long article about the club would be printed in the student newspaper (of which she was also an adviser). So a seemingly effective coalition had been formed. Unfortunately, I failed to think through two important questions:

"What resources are needed for goal attainment?" and

"Who has these resources?"

When lunchtime came, there was no food. I had forgotten that the cafeteria was closed on Saturday and foolishly had made no plans for an alternative. With their blood sugar on the downswing, people began to drift away at about 1:00 P.M. We had to come in again the next Saturday, and the indirect impact of the literary muse was delayed a week.

Besides having the necessary resources, there are other important aspects of successful network maintenance. People must be careful to return favors whenever possible. Many potential network members become excluded if they are always on the "taking" rather than on the "giving" end of a network's resources.

At times, delicate information is learned through network membership, especially information about the perceived or real shortcomings of people. Confidential information should not be carelessly spread. There are various benefits for people who leak information, including self-aggrandizement. "I'm so central to powerful networks that I have this important information, and you don't." But the long-term disadvantages include the reputation of having a loose tongue. Further, well established negative reputations remain with people a long time despite attempts to change through frequent performance of good deeds.

Another delicate matter involves the move from network membership to a close friendships with a powerful person. Occasionally this will happen, but mistakes can be made if the move is made too quickly. People can be seen as too pushy, too eager, and too demanding if they attempt to initiate close relationships before the powerholder is ready. The best strategy is to move slowly and take cues from the powerholder concerning any move from acquaintance to friend. Frequently there will be no such move. People will remain part of each other's valued network but will not become close friends.

Admission to Networks

I believe that powerholders have a set of informal guidelines that they use before admitting people to their networks. One criterion is whether or not the potential members "know the rules." These rules are often unwritten, vary according to type of network and locality, and must be learned through careful observation. For instance, when people communicate with elected political officials there is sometimes but not always a direct trade-off of resources. A handsome contribution to the politician's reelection campaign is not necessarily followed by favorable attention to a certain piece of legislation. By making the contribution, the potential network members show that they know the rules and that they have an understanding of reality. A great deal of money is needed for reelection campaigns, whether anybody likes it or not. Prominent politicians are expected to raise funds not only for themselves but also for junior colleagues. By participating in the election process through their monetary contributions, the network applicants bring themselves to the politicians' attention. In return, they will have greater access to the politicians, should they need help on legislative matters. Often, however, access does not guarantee favorable treatment. The network members have to demonstrate that they know other rules, such as the need to do a "who will be helped and hurt" analysis for the politician's inspection.

Other informal rules are associated with other arenas where power is wielded. In universities, sophisticated young professors who have learned the unwritten rule that benefits follow the ability to bring in contract and grant money find themselves welcome in the office of the president. In the business world, junior-level executives have to learn to communicate their accomplishments to their seniors. Many people feel that if they work hard, their efforts will be automatically rewarded. While true in an ideal world, so many issues compete for the attention of powerholders that the accomplishments of subordinates are often overlooked. Successful young executives find ways (many of which are reviewed in Chapters 4 and 5) to let their bosses know about the benefits they are bringing to the organization. Given the greater name recognition among powerholders that stems from these communication efforts, these juniors are more likely to be asked to participate in ventures initiated by the senior executives. "Who are some go-getters that we can ask to take on this task? Didn't I see in the newspaper that Jenkins and Harrison have been representing us in community organizations recently? Let's get them in here!"

Many times, people will become noticed by powerholders if they *act* in a manner indicative of competence. Guidelines to action follow careful observation. Do the powerholders in an organization prefer short and precise proposals or elaborate and detailed projections? Do they expect a certain standard of dress, or are they relaxed about this matter? Is certain office space associated with high status, or are concerns with "who has what office" trivial in the organization?[6] Do powerholders prefer that people eat lunch quickly and then get back to work, or do they prefer that people use the lunch hour to share information widely across departments within the organization? I once observed striking differences in the behavior of people from two departments within an organization. One group of people was always on time for meetings, and the other group dragged itself in ten to fifteen minutes late. I asked an insider about this. He replied, "The second group has little influence on final decisions around here. In a way, it doesn't matter whether the people are present or not. So they've learned to act in a powerless manner." If people are to change the status quo and acquire more power, they often have to change the behaviors that previously marked them as nonparticipants in important decisions.

Some rules are helpful in many arenas. If people are charming and gracious, they will find more networks open to them. Powerholders do not want to be surrounded by sour and sullen individuals who will irritate and perhaps insult others. The others may become upset at powerholders who are seen as the sponsors of socially unskilled, unpleasant newcomers. People will also benefit from the practice of talking positively about others. Powerholders realize that if a certain person is a constant whiner with nothing good to say, then *they* may eventually be the target of such treatment. It is far better to offer network membership to people who know the wisdom of their mothers' advice: If you can't say something nice, don't say anything at all. Later, after full membership is granted, with its key demand that confidences be honored, powerholders will welcome judgments that involve balanced presentations about the merits and shortcomings of others. By offering membership to people who know the value of positive comments, powerholder-mentors will eventually reap benefits, as the newcomers themselves become more influential in the community.

When approaching powerholders for possible membership in their networks, it is wise to do some homework. Information about most powerholders is available if people take the time to do some digging. Examples are newspaper and magazine articles, descriptions in the annual reports of their companies, stories told by people who work with them, and their own writings. People who study this material before their first meeting with powerholders have a tremendous advantage. The powerholders will be flattered that the visitors have taken the time to study their backgrounds. They will also be impressed that the visitors know the rule (admittedly acknowledged more in the breach than the observance), "Show that you are familiar with the priorities and preferences of powerholders and build your proposals into these."

One participant in a workshop (Chapter 7) wanted to increase the size of his network and asked for my advice. He had some specific people in mind and asked how they might be approached. I gave him the advice reviewed here: "Do your homework so that you can communicate clearly that you know about the powerholders' accomplishments and current interests. Show how you can help these interests. If you do this, you will find a place in the powerholders' memories." The workshop participant countered, "Doesn't everyone do this? If everyone does it, how will I be memorable?" I replied that, in my experience and that of my colleagues, only one out of a hundred people who approach powerholders has done the necessary homework.[7]

Exclusion from Networks

Admission to a network is a privilege that has obligations attached to it. Over time, the powerholders in the network develop a sense of whether or not a given person is a valued member. Sanctions can follow if people commit sins, such as the following:

1. Not returning favors;
2. Not accepting tasks thought important by powerholders but not regarded as such by the people themselves;
3. Talking negatively about others, especially when such action can reflect back badly on the powerholder-sponsor;

4. Developing status in their own eyes, and among peers, by criticizing the perceived shortcomings of the powerholders;
5. Refusing to share resources;
6. Violating confidences;
7. Neglecting activities that would lead to the recruitment of other useful people to the network.

In one example I followed, an influential powerholder in a large city threw his considerable influence behind a project. A project leader was hired, and the unstated assumption was that the leader would lobby various other influential people to obtain their involvement and cooperation. The other figures might then become part of the powerholder's network, increasing his power and visibility in the city. But the project leader had the sort of personality that did not allow easy interactions with large numbers of people. Although he was able to mask this in job interviews, he was not particularly gregarious and did not enjoy large social gatherings. He preferred to define the project narrowly, and he did a creditable job of bringing the project to completion. But the original powerholder felt that too few community leaders knew about the work. As the result, the project leader's contract was not renewed.

While nonrenewal of contracts is one reaction unsuccessful network members might encounter, a more frequent outcome is that there will be no visible response. And herein lies the problem: "no visible response" includes the absence of favors and opportunities. Invitations to important gatherings disappear; advice about job possibilities and investment opportunities ceases; phone calls go unreturned; secretaries suddenly find that their bosses' calendars are full; and helpful advice on career growth is heard no longer. Put another way, silent exclusion from networks is the penalty that powerholders inflict. Powerholders should not be public with their revenge. If they are, they will be seen as bullies, will possibly open themselves to legal retaliation, and will cut themselves off from opportunities because of their hostile reputations. But if they are silent, and simply deny opportunities through lack of communication with formal network members, there is little that the unfavored people can do. If there is a way to sue someone for not issuing an invitation to a private party for influential community leaders, I am unaware of it.

RESOURCE DEVELOPMENT

The key to network maintenance is the mutual usefulness of the members, and the path to usefulness involves possession of a valued resource. Money is the clearest example. People who have this important resource need do little but spread the word that they are looking for investment opportunities or outlets for their charitable motives. The majority of people, strangers to large sums of money, must take advantage of or develop another resource. Some people, without especially planning it, find themselves as young adults in the possession of considerable social skills, public speaking ability, and an attractive appearance. Often these are the result of careful guidance provided by their parents. Some people have to choose whether or not to use one or more of their social resources. For instance, attractive women learn that older and more powerful men enjoy their company. Sexual expression is sometimes but not always involved. Men simply achieve status in their own eyes and in those of their peers if they frequently have lunch with attractive women. The women in question have to decide whether to use this resource, exchanging it for insider information learned during lunchtime, or label the arrangement as sexist and refuse to participate.

Over the long term, most useful resources will be developed out of people's formal and informal education. These include knowledge bases such as tax law and manufacturing methods; negotiation and coalition formation skills learned by apprenticing oneself to experts; and the ability to bring in the contributions of others through possession of extensive contacts in one's community. I have been asked how a person can get started. My recommendation is to (a) develop a knowledge area that powerholders will find useful, and (b) develop public speaking and writing skills. Since the latter recommendation is so unoriginal and so similar to what young people have been told all their lives by various teachers, I then discuss the following cases.

Many publicly funded organizations come into fruition only after extensive discussions among many interest groups. The discussion phase is often fun. Influential people stand up and give speeches; coalition builders meet with differing factions and forge compromises; media coverage is courted; and young up-and-comers hobnob with established community leaders. After the basic decisions are made, a committee is established to write up the policy guidelines for the organizations. This is dull—sitting around a table and writing up guidelines is not as colorful as the discussion phase. There is the temptation to avoid dullness and let others do the writing, but smart people volunteer for the committee. In the long run, it will be the written policy guidelines that executives will consult.

Such consultation will *not* be necessary for the first six months. During this period people will remember the discussions and make decisions based on their memories. But after six months, memories will fade and written guidelines will have to be consulted. Further, some of the leaders will have left for fresher pastures and newcomers will have only the guidelines to consult. The people who were involved in the dull writing phase, then, have the most influence years after their task.

The phrase "God is in the details" is sometimes heard in decision-making arenas. It means that decisions about whether or not an organization can undertake certain projects, and how the projects are to be administered, are often contained in the details of its policy manual. In his biography of Robert Moses, Caro[8] pointed out that Moses wrote a great deal of legislation dealing with highway and building construction in New York City while he was a government aide in Albany. Legislators were too busy or too bored to look at the details of the bills under consideration. Only later was it discovered that Moses had designated a certain administrator as the arbitrator of final decisions, and that he was the person who later filled this administrative position. He then used his legislated authority to plan, approve, and disapprove construction projects and amassed considerable power.

I once participated in an argument about interpretation of a policy matter within a federally funded organization. Members of the committee quoted from a set of general guidelines written 20 years before. I said, "That passage was not written by congressmen. It was undoubtedly written by some 28-year-old legislative aide just out of a master's degree program at some university. Why are we slaves to the passage now? It is absurd to make decisions based on its content." But since there was nothing else in writing to provide direction regarding decisions, the guidelines from the 20-year-old passage were accepted. Accepting the guidance was easier than making an independent decision that might bring criticism.

Another incident occurred in an organization where I worked. In deciding upon ventures that the organization would undertake, a board of governors approved a general plan for the future and then executives made specific decisions. The governing board had a strange mixture of active and passive orientations toward its work. On the one hand, its members belonged to an elite group and flew in for important meetings from their homes in various parts of the world. Because of their distance from the organization, however, the members had little knowledge of its day-to-day activities. On the other hand, the board was comprised of powerholders who took themselves seriously. They wanted to exert their authority and were unhappy when they were underconsulted about the organization's future. People in the organization who were able to satisfy the board's desire to "have its say" were well treated and found themselves on the receiving end of favors.

One ambitious person tried to inform the board more effectively by gathering information about the future plans of individual employees. The goal was to analyze the plans and identify general trends. Each individual, for instance, was asked to predict the number of colleagues who would become attached to the organization *and* who lived in other countries. The projections were to be for one, two, and three years into the future. From the point of view of each employee, this was a nonsensical set of projections. Many factors influenced the availability of potential colleagues from other countries: *their* priorities, visa availability, funding, last-minute political upheavals, and so forth. But the quickest and least stressful way to deal with the request for projections was to write down some numbers, so people did: France, 2; Japan, 3; India, 2; China, 4, and so forth. Summarized over a hundred individual projections, the resulting charts looked impressive. The person collecting the information knew enough about statistics and pictoral presentation of material to develop an impressive report. Bar graphs, with different colors for different countries, allowed presentation of the information in an easily digestible form. The fact that the basic data behind the bar graphs made no sense was lost in the presentation to the board of governors. The board was impressed with what seemed like good planning; members could participate in decision making through their comments ("Can the participation of colleagues from India be increased?"); and the general plans for inviting other-country colleagues were approved. The person who presented the statistical information was seen as a sharp individual with a good future. Given his role, he was able to interact with board members and was able to obtain approval and funding for his individual plans.

In both the case involving interpretation of 20-year-old written guidelines and that involving presentation of statistical information, the importance of communicating one's ideas in written form is clear. People who have this resource can use it to become close to powerholders. In both cases there were also oral presentations to accompany the written work. The person who wrote the guidelines had persuaded the congressmen that their intent had been captured in his or her drafts of the appropriate legislation. The accumulator of statistical information gave an oral presentation during which the implications of the pictoral material could be explained. One of the more poorly kept secrets about powerholders is that many do not read a great deal. Often they simply do not have time, given the multiple matters that compete for their attention. Consequently, they will glance at a written report to determine whether it appears reasonable, but they will also request an oral summary. Someone who can prepare and deliver a well organized, convincing, interesting, and memorable oral presentation possesses an important resource. As a colleague pointed out, "Rarely does one gain a position of power without a gift for articulating ideas clearly and eloquently."[9] Both written and oral presentation skills can be developed through selection of various courses in high school, college, and extension programs attached to universities. Examples I recommend to people include technical writing, creative writing, public speaking, debate, and communication in small groups.

THE DEVELOPMENT OF SOPHISTICATION

As people are developing a more sophisticated understanding of power, there are cues that they can use to inform them about their progress. Since my general recommendation is that people place themselves where power is wielded and resources are developed, the cues are similar to those used by people learning new languages. If immigrants to a country immerse themselves in another language, which they hear, read, and try to speak, they are inevitably frustrated during their early learning period. They can not understand key words, let alone phrases; they can not express their wishes; and they make all sorts of mistakes that make them look silly to native speakers of the language. If they keep trying, however, they begin to understand more and more. Many language learners point to a key day or even a key hour. All of a sudden they begin to understand what is going on around them. They then feel comfortable and can communicate their thoughts with reasonable facility. They realize that on the previous day they were ineffective, but on the day in question they could make sense out of their world. They could predict how conversations would progress, and they could fit themselves into interactions with a status closer to that of an "insider" than that of an "outsider." Some people report other phenomena. The ability to dream in another language is frequently mentioned, as is the absence of the need to keep translating in one's mind between the new language and one's native language. The transformation from feelings of ineffectiveness to feelings of competency is often described in emotional terms much like those used to describe spiritual experiences.

Similarly, immersion into places where power is used and discussed eventually causes people to reach a point where behaviors begin to make sense. In fact, the behaviors that powerholders use seem determined by *common sense*—how could anybody ever think that any other behavior would be appropriate? For instance, it becomes common sense to add issues to negotiation sessions so that people do not become bogged down in the one matter that brought various factions to the bargaining table. With many issues to discuss, a compromise may be reached that develops out of a give-and-take process. One side gives way on issues A, C, and F, and the other relaxes its demands on issues B, D, and E. Both sides try to develop a pattern of results that will be acceptable to the larger groups that they represent. Both sets of negotiators can then go back to their groups and claim victory. This approach to negotiation is common sense only to experienced people.

Another example is the realization at some point in a person's career that hard work is often not enough to earn promotion and recognition, especially in large organizations. While many people would enjoy believing the adage that "if you are willing to work hard, the world will beat a path to your door," the reality is that quiet but effective people are often unnoticed. People must find ways of informing superiors about their contributions, rather than depending upon the superiors to discover what these contributions are on their own. While it is at first painful to engage in self-promotion and self-aggrandizement, at some point the need for such activity becomes part of common sense. "Of course I have to let the top executives know about what I am doing. They are too busy to spend their time ferreting out information about what I do. It's my job to inform them, not their job to follow my day-to-day contributions."

In workshops and discussions with people, I sometimes use the following incident to test their increased understanding of power. Two people are on the opposite sides of a policy matter in their organization. Person A is accustomed to battles, does not give up easily, has a good network, and is generally well liked by colleagues. Person B is younger and is a newcomer to the organization. Person A finds out that Person B will be traveling on company business for a two-week period. Person A schedules a set of key meetings during B's absence and lines up support for a set of policy recommendations. After returning from the trip, B finds that A's recommendations have been accepted by the senior executives. What should Person B do?

There are various temptations: confront A in an angry outburst; snub A whenever possible; complain to A's colleagues; try to get even, and so forth. The correct answer, however, is some variant of "take A out to lunch." If B is gracious, despite A's questionable tactics, then A and B may be able to work together on other issues at a later date. If B makes an enemy of A, then time and energy will be spent maintaining ill feelings rather than on more productive matters. Since A is well liked and has a good network, B may be cutting off access to many other people if A becomes displeased. The best course of action is to develop a cordial relation with A and to integrate A's interests, priorities, and resources into another policy matter on which B will be seen as a winner. It is important to keep in mind that A and B do not have to develop a friendship. While this is an eventual possibility, it is more important that they work together effectively for their mutual benefit and that of their organization.

Dealing with the emotional aspects of power is probably the most difficult step in the development of sophistication. After discussing this incident with me, one woman said, "Yes, I can see it's best to have lunch. Snubbing the person would be easier, and it is certainly the temptation. But I'm beginning to learn: emotions have to be held in check." One reason I recommend coursework or participation in debate activities is that people cannot become too emotionally involved in the issues. Likewise, they cannot become upset with an opposition that clearly disagrees with points being made. One exercise in debate classes and clubs is to change sides at the direction of the judges. The people who were arguing one side of the issue have to switch and argue the other side. If people are unable to control their emotions, they will not do well in this kind of debating.

Still, there is little question that people's emotions and sense of right and wrong will be confronted as they become influential in their communities. When they clearly see decisions made for reasons that include a political component, they will find themselves challenged. Political reasons include the return of past favors, the need to avoid the wrath of powerful people who can inflict damage, choice of people based on their networks, and looking toward the future when those blessed today will return favors. At times political reasons will seem to overwhelm substantive considerations in the decision-making process. Examples of politically loaded decisions are selection of the company that will build a certain government-sponsored housing project, of which young assistant professor will attain tenure, and of which of many volunteer organizations will receive support from a community-wide fund-raising campaign. One congressional staffer told me that he became severely ill after about six months in Washington, D.C. He had left a good academic position to become a legislative aide, and he had a number of liberal social programs that he wanted to see implemented. He literally became ill upon seeing how political considerations determined the outcome of his proposals, and how the purity of his intentions was polluted with the sleaziness of power machinations. He almost left to return to his academic job but he stayed in Washington, D.C. because he was developing a sophisticated knowledge about power that he could attach to his goals of better social programs. With this knowledge, he could be more influential as a congressional staffer than as a professor.[10]

Many people who interact in powerful circles have similar feelings. There are a number of possible outcomes:

1. Consider that participation in the activities of powerholders is distasteful, drop out, and give attention to other aspects of life. This possibility was discussed in Chapter 2.

2. Participate fully in the activities of powerholders and make decisions based on political considerations rather than substance or merit.

3. Remain above the petty concerns of people who participate in the political arena and continue the quest for decisions based on the quality of one's proposals.

4. Develop a knowledge of how power is used and analyze it as one aspect to consider when making decisions.

5. Develop a working knowledge of the strategies and tactics associated with power and use them to press forward with one's substantive proposals.

My recommendation is that people consider developing an awareness of power as summarized in Points 4 and 5. People who embrace point three may not be able to attain their goals. There are many well-educated, attractive, and hard-working people who have good proposals. To catch the attention of busy powerholders, they need some knowledge of the political strategies and tactics that they can use to promote their proposals. Without such political considerations, they are likely to be shunted aside in the competition for resources.

An analogy can be drawn between political sophistication and good manners. People known as experts on questions of etiquette point to the fact that good manners *increase* people's freedom. While on first consideration manners might seem constraining (when to unfold napkins, the necessity of thank-you notes), they free people to pursue their goals. People meet in a cordial manner, make a positive impression on each other, sit down to eat without having to spend time discussing which fork to use, and interact in such a way that they do not insult each other. Good manners allow people to set aside the preliminaries and permit them to "get down to business" so they can pursue their goals. Similarly, a knowledge of political strategies and tactics frees people to move their ideas from a planning state to an implementation stage. Without political sophistication, plans remain on the drawing board and do not become translated into reality. People remain stymied, wondering why colleagues (who sometimes have proposals of lower quality) always seem able to get things done.

POWER IN THE SERVICE OF LEADERSHIP

In applications of power there is always the danger that the use of resources, strategies, and tactics will become an end in itself. Trading resources can be pleasurable, since the people engaged in the exchange are better off after the encounter than before it. The clever use of strategies and tactics can lead to self-satisfaction stemming from the manipulation of colleagues or the defeat of enemies. In these cases, however, power is not necessarily attached to goal accomplishment. The quest for substantive goals becomes lost in the search for pleasure that the use of power can bring.

Power is most wisely used as one tool people use in the attainment of their goals. Power is a phenomenon that leaders must understand, and its use should assist leaders and subordinates in attaining the goals that they set for themselves. Subordinates expect their leaders to possess a certain amount of clout. When leaders say that they will obtain the raw materials necessary for the group's work, they must deliver on their promise. They must persuade their superiors to accept their plans, contact network members to determine the availability of materials, court the people who control the sale and delivery of materials so that they do not favor the competition, and so forth. If the leaders are successful, they can feel a sense of satisfaction; the pleasure, however, is linked to goal attainment rather than to the clever use of power itself. When subordinates say that they want leaders with clout, they are referring to the sophisticated use of power discussed throughout this book. If leaders cannot deliver on their commitments, they lose their status.

As another example, assume that there are three people in an organization who are involved in a decision about promotions. Person A is desirous of the promotion, and his immediate supervisor, Person B, agrees that A is qualified. Person C is the CEO who controls the final decision concerning the distribution of a scarce resource: the number of people who will be promoted given the organization's current financial picture. To maintain *her* position and good reputation among colleagues and subordinates, Person B must make a forceful case when presenting her recommendations to the CEO. Person B might choose from among many strategies and tactics that powerholders know and use:

1. Writing a clear description of A's accomplishments and following it up with an oral presentation;
2. Discovering C's preferences about directions that the organization should take in the future and linking A's accomplishments to those goals;
3. Appealing to colleagues that C is known to respect;
4. Engaging C in first-hand experiences related to A's area of expertise (Chapter 5);
5. Widening the arena of discourse with C, such that the chief executive officer approves the promotion in exchange for a favor from B;
6. If the deliberations concerning promotions take place over a period of time, making sure that A undertakes and completes clear tasks so that he develops the reputation of a "winner" (Chapter 4).

Person A will certainly be concerned with the outcome of the proceedings, but Person B should also follow the deliberations closely. If B's recommendations are not accepted, B will lose influence among subordinates. Person B will also be seen as an ineffective leader and as a person who cannot deliver on commitments. Subordinates will make comments like, "Our so-called leader doesn't have any clout around here!" The well known Peter Principle[11] states that people are promoted until they reach a position where they are no longer competent. One reason a capable person may no longer be competent in a higher position is that the person does not have the political skills necessary for the new position. Just because a sales representative exceeded his or her individual sales projections by a million dollars is no assurance that he or she can lead a team of salespeople. Well published academics and effective teachers are not necessarily able to develop reputable programs for the entire university as a dean or president. In many cases, ineffectiveness in leadership positions is due to a naivete about power and an inability to put its usefulness to work.

The most effective leaders possess a combination of valued resources and wisdom concerning the use of power. I have known people who succeeded for *short time periods* with political skills alone. They could charm powerholders, appeal to their interests and self-importance, and branch out from these powerholders into a wider network. After a few years, however, it dawned on the powerholders that these people had little to offer. They had no goals, no areas of expertise, no substantive proposals, and no resources other than their ability to court powerholders. The people were then dropped from membership in influential circles, and their downfall was painful, since the difference between their former participation and subsequent inactivity was very noticeable.

As has been urged a number of times, there can be an imbalance in the other direction. People can have valued resources, such as the ability to develop workable plans for an organization's betterment, but may not have the political skills to bring the plans to fruition. One of my hopes is that the strategies and tactics discussed throughout this book become so well known that they no longer contribute to the acceptance of one proposal compared to another. That is, so many people will know and practice the useful strategies and tactics that they will *not* differentiate one proposal from another. Once everyone has the same knowledge about power, more time and effort can be invested in the merit and substance of proposals. The quality of ideas, rather than political skills, will play a greater role in decision making within various parts of society: education, religion, social services, government, voluntary organizations, manufacturing, the military, and so forth. While I doubt that this scenario will occur, I do believe that substance and merit have a greater chance of rising to the top if more people become worldly with respect to the role that power plays in decision making.

NOTES

1. J. Terraine, *The Life and Times of Lord Mountbatten* (New York: Holt, Rinehart, & Winston, 1980), pp. 166–67.

2. M. Deaver and M. Herskowitz, *Behind the Scenes* (New York: William Morrow, 1987), p. 200.

3. Ibid., p. 213.

4. D. Barnlund, *Communicative Styles of Japanese and Americans* (Belmont, Calif.: Wadsworth, 1989).

5. An excellent discussion of reciprocity can be found in R. Cialdini, *Influence: Science and Practice,* 2d ed. (Glenview: Ill.: Scott, Foresman, 1988).

6. M. Korda, *Power: How to Get It, How to Use it* (New York: Random House, 1975).

7. A number of friends, colleagues, and students read the entire manuscript and gave me helpful comments. There were three places where at least one person said, "Please don't tell people about this. If everyone starts doing it, then it will lose its effect. I do it, and want to continue to benefit." This is one of those places.

8. R. Caro, *The Power Broker: Robert Moses and the Fall of New York* (New York: Random House, 1974).

9. Barnlund, *Communicative Styles,* p. 38.

10. A friend was involved in high-level negotiations regarding the SALT II Arms Control Treaty. He had a similar reaction. He wanted to see a reduction in nuclear

arsenals, but was outraged when politicians requested modifications to suit their own needs.

11. L. Peter and R. Hull, *The Peter Principle* (New York: William Morrow, 1969).

BIBLIOGRAPHY

Abramson, L., M. Seligman, and J. Teasdale. "Learned Helplessness in Humans: Critique and Reformation." *Journal of Abnormal Psychology* 87 (1978) 49–74.

Allport, G. *The Nature of Prejudice.* Reading, Mass.: Addison-Wesley, 1954.

Argyle, M. "Interaction Skills and Social Competence." In *Psychological Problems: The Social Context,* edited by M. P. Feldman and J. Orford. New York: Wiley, 1980, pp. 123–150.

———, A. Furnham, and J. Graham. *Social Situations.* Cambridge: Cambridge University Press, 1981.

Aronson, E., and N. Osherow. "Cooperation, Social Behavior, and Academic Performance: Experiments in the Desegregated Classroom." In *Applied Social Psychology Annual,* edited by L. Bickman. Beverly Hills, Calif.: Sage, 1980, vol. 1, pp. 163–96.

Atkinson, J., ed. *Motives in Fantasy, Action, and Society.* Princeton, N.J.: Van Nostrand, 1958.

Bailey, F. G. *Stratagems and Spoils: A Social Anthropology of Politics.* Oxford: Basil Blackwell, 1970.

Baker, B. *Wheeling and Dealing: Confessions of a Capitol Hill Operator.* New York: Norton, 1978.

Barnlund, D. *Communicative Styles of Japanese and Americans.* Belmont, Calif.: Wadsworth, 1989.

Barnum, P. T. *Barnum's Own Story: The Autobiography of P. T. Barnum.* New York: Dover, 1961.

Bartley, N. "Politics and Ideology." In *Encyclopedia of Southern Culture,* edited by C. R. Wilson and W. Ferris. Chapel Hill: University of North Carolina Press, 1989, pp. 1151–58.

Batson, C. D. (1987). "Prosocial Motivation: Is It Ever Truly Altruistic?" In *Advances in Experimental Social Psychology,* edited by L. Berkowitz. San Diego: Academic Press, 1987, vol 20; pp. 65–122.

Berscheid, E. "Interpersonal Attraction." In *The Handbook of Social Psychology,* 3rd ed., edited by G. Lindzey and E. Aronson. New York: Random House, 1985, vol. 2, pp. 413–84.

Biddle, B. *Role Theory: Expectations, Identities, and Behaviors.* New York: Academic Press, 1979.

Bransford, J., R. Sherwood, N. Vye, and J. Eieser. "Teaching Thinking and Problem Solving: Research Foundations." *American Psychologist,* 41, (1986): 1078–89.

Brislin, R. "Psychology in Circus Life." *White Tops* 53 (1980), no. 5, pp. 5–8.

———. *Cross-cultural Encounters: Face-to-Face Interaction.* Elmsford, N.Y.: Pergamon, 1981.

———. K. Cushner, C. Cherrie, and M. Yong. *International Interactions: A Practical Guide.* Newbury Park, Calif.: Sage, 1986.

Brownell, K. D. "Obesity: Understanding and Treating a Serious, Prevalent, and Refractory Disorder." *Journal of Consulting and Clinical Psychology* 50, (1982): 820–40.

Bullitt, S. *To Be a Politician.* Garden City, N.Y.: Doubleday; 1959.

Burns, R. "To a Louse." In *The Poetical Works of Robert Burns,* vol. 2, edited by G. Aitkin. London: George Bell & Sons, 1893.

Caro, R. A. *The Power Broker: Robert Moses and the Fall of New York.* New York: Random House, 1974.

———. *The Years of Lyndon Johnson: The Path to Power.* New York: Knopf; 1982.

Chaika, E. *Language: The Social Mirror.* New York: Newbury House, 1989.

Chaplin, W., O. John, and L. Goldberg. "Conceptions of States and Traits: Dimensional Attributes with Ideals as Prototypes." *Journal of Personality and Social Psychology* 54, (1988): 541–557.

Christopher, R. *The Japanese Mind.* New York: Fawcett Columbine; 1983.

Cialdini, R. *Influence: Science and Practice,* 2d ed. Glenview, Ill.: Scott, Foresman, 1988.

Cohen, H. *You Can Negotiate Anything.* New York: Bantam, 1982.

Collier, C., and J. Collier. *Decision in Philadelphia: The Constitutional Convention of 1787.* New York: Random House; 1986.

Comstock, G. "Today's Audiences, Tomorrow's Media." In *Applied Social Psychology Annual,* vol. 8, *Television as a Social Issue,* edited by S. Oscamp. Newbury Park, Calif.: Sage, 1988, pp. 324–45.

Conniff, R. "The So-So Salesman Who Told Millions How To Make It Big." *Smithsonian* 18, no. 9 (October 1987), pp. 82–93.

Cook, T., and W. Shadish. "Program Evaluation: The Worldly Science." *Annual Review of Psychology* 37 (1986): 193–232.

Covey, S. *The Seven Habits of Highly Effective People.* New York: Simon & Schuster; 1989.

Crick, B. *In Defence of Politics,* 2d ed. Middlesex, England, and New York: Penguin; 1982.

Crisp, W., ed. *Winning Strategies for the Woman Manager*. Brooklyn, N.Y.: Omni Litho, 1985.

Crosby, F., and G. Herek. "Male Sympathy with the Situation of Women: Does Personal Experience Make a Difference?" *Journal of Social Issues* 42 (1986), no. 2, pp. 55–66.

Cunningham, M. *Power Play: What Really Happened at Bendix*. New York: Simon & Schuster, 1984.

Deaver, M., and M. Herskowitz. *Behind the Scenes*. New York: William Morrow, 1987.

deGroot, A. *Thought and Choice in Chess*. The Hague: Mouton, 1965.

Diamond, M. and M. Bond. "The Acceptance of "Barnum" Personality Interpretations by Japanese, Japanese-American, and Caucasian-American College Students." *Journal of Cross-Cultural Psychology* 5 (1974): 228–35.

Donaldson, S. *Hold On, Mr. President*. New York: Random House; 1987.

Drucker, P. *Management: Tasks, Responsibilities, Practices*. New York: Harper Row; 1973.

Ehrlich, H. *The Social Psychology of Prejudice*. New York: Wiley; 1973.

Elms, A. *Social Psychology and Social Relevance*. Boston: Little, Brown, 1972.

Endler, N., and D. Magnusson. *Interactional Psychology and Personality*. Washington, D.C.: Hemisphere, 1976.

Felker, C., ed. *The Power Game*. New York: Simon & Schuster, 1969.

Ferguson, E. "Motivation." In *Encyclopedia of Psychology*, edited by R. Corsini. New York: Wiley, 1984, vol. 2, pp. 395–98.

Fischer, K., and M. Farrar. "Generalizations about Generalization: How a Theory of Skill Development Explains Both Generality and Specificity." *International Journal of Psychology* 22 (1987): 643–77.

Fiske, S., and S. Taylor. *Social Cognition*. New York: Random House, 1984.

Foa, U. "Interpersonal and Economic Resources." *Science* 171 (1971): 345–51.

Freedman, J., and S. Fraser. "Compliance without Pressure: The Foot-in-the-Door Technique." *Journal of Personality and Social Psychology* 4 (1966): 195–202.

Gardner, H. *The Mind's New Science: The History of the Cognitive Revolution*. New York: Basic Books, 1985.

Gardner, J. "Leadership and Power." Leadership Papers, no. 4. Washington, D.C.: Independent Sector, 1986.

Gershon, D., and G. Straub. *Empowerment: The Art of Creating Your Life as You Want It*. New York: Delta, 1989.

Gilbert, D., and J. Kahl. *The American Class Structure: A New Synthesis*. Homewood, Ill.: Dorsey, 1982.

Greenfield, M. "Victims of Good Fortune." *Newsweek*, December 28, 1987, p. 68.

Gudykunst, W., ed. *Intergroup Communication*. London: Edward Arnold, 1986.

Hagberg, J. *Real Power: The Stages of Personal Power in Organizations*. Minneapolis, Minn.: Winston, 1984.

Harrison, M. *Diagnosing Organizations: Methods, Models, and Processes*. Newbury Park, Calif.: Sage, 1987.

Heclo, H. *A Government of Strangers*. Washington, D.C.: Brookings Institution, 1977.

Helmstetter, S. *Choices*. New York: Simon & Schuster, Pocket Books, 1989.

Helson, H. *Adaptation Level Theory*. New York: Harper, 1964.

Hess, S. *The Government/Press Connection*. Washington, D.C.: Brookings Institution, 1984.

Hofstede, G. "Cultural Differences in Teaching and Learning." *International Journal of Intercultural Relations* 10, (1986): 301–10.

Hollander, E. "Leadership and Power." In *The Handbook of Social Psychology*, 3d ed., edited by G. Lindzey and E. Aronson. New York: Random House, 1985, vol. 2, pp. 485–537.

Hui, C. H. and H. Triandis. "Individualism-Collectivism: A Study of Cross-Cultural Researchers." *Journal of Cross-Cultural Psychology* 17 (1986): 225–48.

Janis, I. *Victims of Groupthink*. Boston, Mass.: Houghton Mifflin, 1972.

————— and L. Mann. *Decision Making*. New York: Free Press,1977.

Jordan, C., and R. Tharp. "Culture and Education." In *Perspectives on Cross-Cultural Psychology*, edited by A. Marsella, R. Tharp, and T. Ciborowski. New York: Academic Press, 1979, pp. 265–85.

Karass, C. *The Negotiating Game*. New York: Thomas Crowell, 1970.

Kennedy, M. *Powerbase: How to Build It, How to Keep It*. New York: Macmillan, 1984.

Kipnis, D. *The Powerholders*. Chicago: University of Chicago Press, 1976.

Klinberg, F. *Cyclical Trends in American Foreign Policy: The Unfolding of America's World Role*. Boston: University Press of America, 1983.

Klineberg, O., and F. Hull. *At a Foreign University*. New York: Praeger, 1979.

Koch, E. *Mayor: An Autobiography*. New York: Simon & Schuster, 1984.

Kohn, M. L. *Class and Conformity*, 2d ed. Chicago: University of Chicago Press, 1977.

Kolb, D. *Learning Style Inventory*. Boston: McBer, 1976.

—————. *Experiential Learning*. Englewood Cliffs, N.J.: Prentice-Hall, 1984.

Korda, M. *Power: How to Get It, How to Use It*. New York: Random House, 1975.

Kotter, J. "Power, Dependence, and Effective Management." *Harvard Business Review* 55 (1977), no. 4, pp. 125–36.

—————. "What Effective General Managers Really Do." *Harvard Business Review* 60 (1982), no. 6, pp. 157–67.

Larson, C. E., and F. M. La Fasto. *Teamwork*. Newbury Park. Calif.: Sage, 1989.

Lasswell, H., and A. Kaplan. *Power and Society: A Framework for Political Inquiry*. New Haven: Yale University Press, 1950.

Lazarus, R. S. "The Stress and Coping Paradigm." In *Models for Clinical Psychopathology*, edited by C. Eisdorfer, D. Cohen, A. Kleinmen, and P. Maxim. New York: Spectrum, 1981, pp. 177–214.

Lindgren, H. C., and W. N. Suter. *Educational Psychology in the Classroom*, 7th ed. Monterey, Calif.: Brooks/Cole, 1985.

Lindsay, J. "The Rites of Power." In *The Power Game*, edited by C. Felker. New York: Simon & Schuster, 1969.

Machiavelli, N. *The Prince. The Discourses*. New York: Modern Library, 1940.

Mackay, H. *Swim with the Sharks Without Being Eaten Alive*. New York: William Morrow, 1988.

Magnussen, D., and N. Endler, eds. *Personality at the Crossroads: Current Issues in Interactional Psychology*. Hillsdale, N.J.: Erlbaum, 1977.

Mannix, D. *We Who Are Not As Others*. New York: Simon & Schuster, 1976.

McClelland, D. "The Two Faces of Power." *International Affairs* 24 (1970), No.1, pp. 29–47.

———. *Power: The Inner Experience*. New York: Irvington, 1975.

———. "Motive Dispositions: The Merits of Operant and Respondent Measures." In *Review of Personality and Social Psychology*, edited by L. Wheeler. Beverly Hills, Calif.: Sage, 1980, pp. 10–41.

——— and D. Burnham. "Power Is the Great Motivator." *Harvard Business Review* 25 (March–April 1976): pp. 159–66.

——— and D. Winter. *Motivating Economic Achievement*. New York: Macmillan, 1969.

McCormack, M. *What They Still Don't Teach You at Harvard Business School*. New York: Bantam, 1989.

McGhee, P., and J. Goldstein, eds. *Handbook of Humor Research*, 2 vols. New York: Springer-Verlag, 1983.

McWilliams, P., and J. Roger. *You Can't Afford the Luxury of a Negative Thought*. Los Angeles: Prelude, 1989.

Mehrabian, A., and S. Ksionzky. *A Theory of Affiliation*. Lexington, Mass.: Heath, 1974.

Meichenbaum, D. *Cognitive-Behavior Modification: An Integrative Approach*. New York: Plenum, 1977.

Merton, R. *Social Theory and Social Structure*. Glencoe, Ill.: Free Press, 1957.

Milgram, S. "The Experience of Living in Cities." *Science* 167 (1970), 1461–68.

Mills, C. W. *The Power Elite*. New York: Oxford University Press, 1956.

Mintzberg, H. "The Manager's Job: Folklore and Fact." *Harvard Business Review*, 25 (July–August 1975): 49–61.

———. *Power in and around Organizations*. Englewood Cliffs, N.J.: Prentice-Hall, 1983.

Moscovichi, S. "Towards a Theory of Conversion Behavior." In *Advances in Experimental Social Psychology*, vol. 13, edited by L. Berkowitz. New York: Academic Press, 1980, pp. 209–39.

Ng, S. H. *The Social Psychology of Power*. London: Academic Press, 1980.

Nida, E., and C. Taber. *The Theory and Practice of Translation*. Leiden: Brill, 1969.

Nierenberg, G. *The Art of Negotiating*. New York: Cornerstone Library, 1968.

———. *The Complete Negotiator*. New York: Nierenerg & Zief, 1986.

O'Neill, T. *Man of the House: The Life and Political Memoirs of Speaker Tip O'Neill*. New York: Random House, 1987.

Ouchi, W. G. *Theory Z: How American Business Can Meet the Japanese Challenge*. Reading, Mass.: Addison-Wesley, 1981.

Pareek, U., and T. Rao. "Cross-Cultural Surveys and Interviewing." In *Handbook of Cross-Cultural Psychology*, edited by H. Triandis and J. Berry, vol. 2: *Methodology*. Boston: Allyn & Bacon, 1980, pp. 127–79.

Peter, L. J., and R. Hull. *The Peter Principle*. New York: William Morrow, 1969.

Ramsey, S., and J. Birk. "Preparation of North Americans for Interaction with Japanese: Considerations of Language and Communication Style." In *Hand-*

book of Intercultural Training, vol. 3, edited by D. Landis and R. Brislin. Elmsford, N.Y.: Pergamon, 1983, pp. 227–259.

Riesman, D. Preface to S. Bullitt, *To Be A Politician*. Garden City, N.Y.: Doubleday, 1959.

Rodin, J. "Current Status of the Internal-External Hypothesis for Obesity: What Went Wrong?" *American Psychologist* 36 (1981): 361–72.

Ross, M., and G. Fletcher. "Attribution and Social Perception." In *The Handbook of Social Psychology*, 3rd ed., edited by G. Lindzey and E. Aronson. New York: Random House, 1985, vol. 2, pp. 73–122.

Salancik, G., and J. Pfeffer. "The Bases for Use of Power in Organizational Decision Making: The Case of a University." *Administrative Science Quarterly* 19 (1974): 453–73.

Schatzki, M. *Negotiation: The Art of Getting What You Want*. New York: New American Library, 1981.

Schoenberg, R. *The Art of Being a Boss*. New York: Harper & Row, 1978.

Seeger, P. "Appleseeds." *Sing Out!* 33 (1988), no. 2, pp. 53–56.

Sherif, M. *In Common Predicament: Social Psychology of Intergroup Conflict and Cooperation*. New York: Houghton Mifflin, 1966.

Simon, H. *Administrative Behavior: A Study of Decision-making Processes in Administrative Organizations*. New York: Macmillan, 1957.

Slack, W. *The Grim Science: The Struggle for Power*. Port Washington, N.Y.: Kennikat, 1981.

Smith, H. *The Power Game: How Washington Works*. New York: Random House, 1988.

Snyder, M., and W. Ickes. "Personality and Social Behavior." In *The Handbook of Social Psychology*, 3rd ed., edited by G. Lindzey and E. Aronson. New York: Random House, 1985, vol. 2, pp. 883–947.

Sommer, J. "Voluntary Action and Economic Development in Third World Countries." In *Cultural Relations in the Global Community: Problems and Prospects*, edited by V. Bickley and P. Philip. New Delhi: Abhinan, 1981, pp. 135–53.

Sommer, R. *Personal Space*. New York: Prentice-Hall, 1959.

Sternberg, R., and R. Wagner, *Practical Intelligence*. Cambridge: Cambridge University Press, 1986.

Stockman, D. *The Triumph of Politics: Why the Reagan Revolution Failed*. New York: Harper and Row, 1986.

Stryker, S., and A. Statham. "Symbolic Interaction and Role Theory." In *The Handbook of Social Psychology*, 3d ed., edited by G. Lindzey and E. Aronson. New York: Random House, 1985, vol. 1, pp. 311–78.

Terraine, J. *The Life and Times of Lord Mountbatten*. New York: Holt, Rinehart & Winston, 1980.

Theis, P., and W. Steponkus. *All about Politics*. New York: R. R. Bowker, 1972.

Thibaut, J., and H. Kelley. *The Social Psychology of Groups*. New York: Wiley, 1959.

Triandis, H. *Interpersonal Behavior*. Monterey, Calif.: Brooks/Cole, 1977.

———, R. Brislin, and C. H. Hui. "Cross-Cultural Training across the Individualism-Collectivism Divide." *International Journal of Intercultural Relations* 12 (1988): 269–89.

Tyler, T., and K. McGraw. "Ideology and the Interpretation of Personal Experience: Procedural Justice and Political Quiescence." *Journal of Social Issues* 42 (1986), No. 2, 115–28.

Wagner, R., and R. Sternberg. "Tacit Knowledge and Intelligence in the Everyday World." In *Practical Intelligence*, edited by R. Sternberg and R. Wagner. Cambridge: Cambridge University Press, 1986, pp. 51–83.

Wallace, I. *The Fabulous Showman: The Life and Times of P. T. Barnum*. New York: Knopf, 1959.

Walster, E., G. W. Walster, and E. Berscheid. *Equity: Theory and Research*. Boston: Allyn & Bacon, 1978.

Weick, K. "Small Wins: Redefining the Scale of Social Problems." *American Psychologist* 39 (1984): 40–49.

Williams, J. *Eyes on the Prize*. New York: Penguin, 1987.

Williams, T. *My Turn at Bat*. New York: Simon & Schuster, 1969.

Winter, D. *The Power Motive*. New York: Macmillan, 1973.

Woodward, B., and C. Bernstein. *All The President's Men*. New York: Simon & Schuster, 1974.

Wright, J., and W. Mischel. "A Conditional Approach to Dispositional Constructs: The Local Predictability of Social Behavior." *Journal of Personality and Social Psychology* 53 (1987): 1159–77.

Wrightsman, L., and K. Deaux. *Social Psychology in the 80's*, 3rd ed. Monterey, Calif.: Brooks/Cole, 1981.

Wrong, D. *Power: Its Forms, Bases, and Uses*. New York: Harper & Row, 1979.

INDEX

ABOUT THE AUTHOR

RICHARD W. BRISLIN is a psychologist who coordinates research and educational programs at the Institute of Culture and Communication, East-West Center, in Honolulu, Hawaii. He also serves on the graduate faculty of the Department of Psychology, University of Hawaii. His educational programs have involved businesspeople, diplomats, educators, and researchers who are interested in understanding the special issues brought on by extensive intercultural contact in different parts of the world. He became interested in power as he observed the skills, strategies, and tactics that graduates of these programs used as they developed their careers. His other books include *Cross-Cultural Encounters: Face-to-Face Interaction*, and *Intercultural Interactions: A Practical Guide*.